Contents

KU-782-165

Chapter   Page

About this book   iii

1 Starting out
– The 'orange' standards   1

1		Accounting standards - where we are and why?	4
2	IAS 1	Presentation of financial statements	12
3	IAS 2	Inventories	25
4	IAS 7	Cash flow statements	30
5	IAS 8	Accounting policies, changes in accounting estimates and errors	48
6	IAS 10	Events after the Reporting Period*	55
7	IAS 16	Property, plant and equipment	59
8	IAS 18	Revenue	67
9	IAS 37	Provisions, contingent liabilities and contingent assets	72
10	IAS 38	Intangible assets	78

2 For the more advanced student
– The 'green' standards   83

11	IAS 11	Construction contracts	86
12	IAS 12	Income taxes	95
13	IAS 17	Leases	107
14	IAS 20	Accounting for government grants and disclosure of government assistance	118
15	IAS 23	Borrowing costs	122
16	IAS 32	Financial instruments: presentation	125
17	IAS 33	Earnings per share	129
18	IAS 36	Impairment of assets	139
19	IAS 39	Financial instruments: recognition and measurement	144
20	IAS 40	Investment property	154
21	IFRS 5	Non-current assets held for sale and discontinued operations	158
22	IFRS 7	Financial instruments: disclosures	163

* In September 2007 the IASB amended the title of IAS 10 from Events after the balance sheet date to Events after the Reporting Period. The detail in the standard is unaltered.

3 For those interested in group accounts   165
– The 'blue' standards

23	IAS 27	Consolidated and separate financial statements	168
24	IFRS 3	Business combinations	171
25	IAS 28	Investments in associates	199
26	IAS 31	Interests in joint ventures	201

4 For the seriously advanced!   205
– The 'red' standards

27	IAS 19	Employee benefits	208
28	IAS 21	The effects of changes in foreign exchange rates	222
29	IAS 24	Related party disclosures	227
30	IAS 29	Financial reporting in hyper-inflationary economies	231
31	IAS 34	Interim financial reporting	235
32	IAS 41	Agriculture	237
33	IFRS 1	First–time adoption of international financial reporting standards	241
34	IFRS 2	Share-based payment	244
35	IFRS 4	Insurance contracts	248
36	IFRS 6	Exploration for and evaluation of mineral resources	251
37	IFRS 8	Operating segments	257

Appendices

The Key Cards – 'orange' standards	455
The Key Cards – 'green' standards	457
The Key Cards – 'blue' standards	459
The Key Cards – 'red' standards	461

Index

A student's guide to international financial reporting standards

By Clare Finch

KAPLAN

PUBLISHING

British library cataloguing-in-publication data

A catalogue record for this book is available from the British Library.

Published by:

Kaplan Publishing

Unit 2 The Business Centre

Molly Millars Lane

Wokingham

Berkshire

RG41 2QZ

ISBN 978 1 84710 476 2

Printed and bound in Great Britain.

About this book

Why do you need this book?

The most common reason for accountancy students failing exams is that they try to pass without learning their accounting standards. WHY? – they are soooo boring!!...... BUT it doesn't have to be like that.....

This book is essential reading for all students sitting accountancy exams to international financial reporting standards. Yes it's a "techie" subject... but the book is different because:

- it makes IFRS/IAS accessible for you, the student
- it is the first book to 'colour code' and group the standards on a 'need to know' basis
- it tells the story behind the standards – not just where we are but why
- it focuses on what the key 'need to learn' essential points are for exam room success
- it uses memory techniques
- it is written in a chatty, down to earth, understandable, style
- it includes 'key cards' – excellent for testing yourself.

This book is a 'companion guide to the accounting standards', aiming principally to make a technical subject more digestible.

How to use this book

One of the problems with studying accounting standards is the size of the task. There are so many such standards that it can be difficult for a student to know where to begin. This book, uniquely, breaks the standards down, by difficulty of topic. (The standards are then colour coded on a 'need to know' basis).

The 'orange standards'

The first ten chapters are what we will refer to as 'the orange standards'. These are essential reading for a student who is just starting out – they cover the key basic areas that will be met in most exam situations.

The 'green standards'

As you progress through your studies you will meet more complex, less common transactions. These standards will not feature in every exam and we will refer to them as 'the green standards'.

The 'blue standards'

As well as being examined on individual company accounts, many (but not all) exam papers, ask for a consolidated set of accounts (referred to as 'group accounts'). If that is the case you will need 'the blue standards'.

The 'red standards'

Finally we come to 'the red standards'. These are the seriously advanced topics that you will need to get to grips with when you are say doing a final level professional accountancy exam.

Which topics do you need to know?

The first thing you need to know, therefore, is which topics are you expected to know for your exam. You need to ask your tutor for a list, or check your syllabus/guide to examinable documents to find out exactly what is relevant for you. If you are just starting your studies you may find many of the more difficult topics are not examined until later stages – so you can pick up the book again and study these topics when they become relevant.

About the chapters

Books on accounting standards normally start each chapter with the aims, key definitions etc. This book deliberately avoids such an approach. Each chapter starts with the background of what the issue is that gave rise to the need for a standard. In this way the scene is set for a better understanding of what the standard is about. Only then does the chapter introduce the aims and …**'SO…WHAT'S IT TRYING TO ACHIEVE?'** will become a familiar mantra.

Transactional example

To ensure the understanding of a given issue, each chapter includes a transactional example (excluding those couple of standards which are format rather than transactional based), thus allowing the explanation and application of the standard to the issue.

The pitfalls

We all actually learn a lot from making mistakes – getting something wrong is usually a sure way of making sure we get it right the next time. We can shortcut this process, however, by learning from the mistakes of others. There are some errors that are very common – student after student will trip up at the same point. Being forewarned of the issue helps you to learn from students who have gone before you.

The definitions

We can't avoid them for ever, and once the understanding of the issue is 'anchored' with a transaction, the definitions from the standard are given. Note people do have variable learning styles and those of you who already have some comfort with the standard may like to turn first to the definitions box – reaffirm those and then read the chapter.

Key 'need to learn' bit

If you are facing a closed book exam, it will not be enough to be just comfortable with the subject matter and to feel you understand the issue – there are some key 'need to learn' bits for each standard. You will, therefore, have to commit some issues to memory. These are highlighted for you as you go through the topic.

The memory devices

Each chapter contains a suggested 'memory device'. It could be an acronym, mnemonic, 'cloud diagram' or 'image-story technique'. Remember however, many learners will benefit from constructing their own diagrams and creating their own mnemonics.

More about memory devices

The human brain has evolved to code and interpret very complex stimuli, we all do this everyday. Limiting your learning to just reading words is not using your full potential. While language, i.e. words on a page, reflects one of the most important aspects of human evolution, it is only one of the many skills available to the human mind.

Most books, however, present the information to be remembered in only one way – as words. Memory devices seek to use a broader range of these resources. By coding language and using images, many people find the information much easier to recall. The book provides you plenty of examples so you should easily find yourself preparing ones that are personal to you.

Key points when preparing your own devices:

- many people remember a diagram better than a list (this plays to the right hand side of the brain)
- colour enhances memory – invest in coloured pens
- smell is very evocative – it triggers memory. Have you tried using the scented pens that are available?
- try drawing your own 'cloud diagrams' when listening to a lecture
- when doing your own mnemonics, you can use risqué ones – generally the easiest to remember!

Throughout the book illustrations are provided of memory devices including mnemonics and cloud diagrams for remembering key points from accounting standards. Don't forget, however, learner–generated devices are always the most effective.

(I do appreciate some people have no problem with words on a page – a list does it for them – but hey – we are all different.)

Summary guide to the symbols

 Transactional Example

 Pitfalls

 Definitions

 Key 'Need to Learn' Bit

 Memory Device

Key cards

A key card for each standard is included as an appendix. The cards can be cut out from the book on an 'as need' basis (some students even laminate them!!) The cards are written in a question-driven style – so you can take them on the train/take them to work /study in your lunch break. The question based approach use means you can pass them to a friend who can then test you on the information, even if they don't know anything (about the topic) themselves. This is in the style of the classic revision technique of preparing the 'crib card'.

Thank you to everybody who has supported me during this project, my family, friends, work colleagues, students, and publisher.

All errors are my own and come with apologies.

A special thank you for all the work put in by my proof reader Dr David Holland CMath FIMA to whom I will be eternally grateful.

Starting out

'Knowledge is of two kinds. We know a subject ourselves or we know where we can find information on it.'

Samuel Johnson (1709–1784)

Introduction

There are nine accounting standards which form the 'baseline' for anyone who is starting out studying financial accounting, and preparing their financial statements to the standards of the International Accounting Standards Board (IASB).

- IAS 1   Presentation of financial statements
- IAS 2   Inventories
- IAS 7   Cash flow statements
- IAS 8   Accounting policies, changes in accounting estimates and errors
- IAS 10   Events after the Reporting Period*
- IAS 16   Property, plant and equipment
- IAS 18   Revenue
- IAS 37   Provisions, contingent liabilities and contingent assets
- IAS 38   Intangible assets

However, underpinning the accounting standards is the Framework document. This is arguably the most important examinable document for any student of accounting to be familiar with. This is covered in Chapter 1 – **Accounting standards – where are we and why?** Do not be tempted to miss this chapter, as the concepts and 'buzz words' you are introduced, to or reminded of here, are key to success in many financial accounting exam questions. Do not be tempted to skip this one!

"You do not really understand something unless you can explain it to your grandmother."

Albert Einstein (1879-1955)

> ### Note
>
> *Many books on accounting standards start by giving you the aims and definitions from the standard. This book deliberately does not structure the chapters in that style. Instead the issue is generally explained, with the sort of transactions that the standard relates to being introduced. We do get to the aims and definitions and, for those of you who already feel comfortable with the standard, you may like to turn first to the definitions box – re-affirm those and then read the chapter.*

* In September 2007 the IASB amended the title of IAS 10 from Events after the balance sheet date to Events after the Reporting Period. The detail in the standard is unaltered.

Accounting standards – where are we and why?

1

Introduction

ONCE UPON A TIME a student of accounting only had to get to grips with the mechanics of double-entry bookkeeping and they could produce a set of accounts for any organisation. Definitions were simple – **'A balance sheet* is a summary of assets and liabilities'** we were told; **'assets are things we own and liabilities are things we owe'**. This was the staple diet of accounting lecture number 1 for those of us who trained before the late 1980s. Unfortunately we didn't get to 'live happily ever after' and we constantly have to learn new tricks and keep up with change. The modern accountancy student has a huge list of accounting standards to get to grips with as well as the mechanics of double-entry bookkeeping. Definition of an asset? – well it's not as simple as **'something you own'** any more!

The fairy tales or creative accounting

Unfortunately the accountancy profession has shown itself to be very able in the practices of 'earnings management'/'off balance sheet finance'/'window dressing'. Whatever we call it, it involves deliberately structuring a series of transactions, and exploitation of loopholes in rules – creative accounting, thinking about the presentation of what the company wants to show rather than the needs of the reader of the financial statements. Two key 'hotspots' exist: manipulation of profit, and manipulation of liabilities. The first of these showing profit as a steady upward movement can give the impression of 'quality earnings', This makes it easier for the company to present its results to the market. The second financial 'hotspot' is under-reporting of liabilities, i.e. off balance sheet* finance. This is why modern day accountancy students have so many accounting standards to learn – we really should blame ourselves (or other accountants anyway!!).

Needs of users

Accounting standards have always been about the needs of users. The International Accounting Standards Board (IASB) who produce the International Financial Reporting Standards (IFRSs) are actually not interested in what companies want their annual reports to show. Their job is to ensure that accounting standards help produce high quality, transparent and comparable information. In this way financial statements should help users make economic decisions.

* Please note on 6th September 2007 the IASB issued a revised IAS 1. The effective date of the new standard is annual periods beginning on or after 1 January 2009, with earlier application permitted. If, however, you are being examined on a six month from issue rule, this new standard is examinable for summer 2008 exams. The revised IAS 1 removes the traditional term 'balance sheet' and although the format is unchanged it is to be called 'a statement of financial position'. The traditional income statement is to be replaced by the 'statement of comprehensive income'.

Traditional approach to accounting standards – fire-fighting

Traditionally, standard setters in many countries waited for there to be a corporate collapse or other form of bad publicity before issuing an accounting standard to change accounting practice – waiting as it were, for the horse to bolt before closing the stable door. A classic example from the UK was the collapse of the package holiday business, Court Line Ltd. This company collapsed after receiving a clean audit report for a balance sheet* showing shareholders' funds of £18m. The shareholders quite correctly asked what was the value in these financial statements. As modern day accountants we would find this balance sheet* interesting and hopefully would have raised questions.

The Court Line Ltd balance sheet*

As Court Line was generating revenue by transporting people from the UK to the continent (for their package holidays) we would have expected to see the aircraft involved in their transport on the balance sheet*. However the aircraft were not on the balance sheet as Court Line had not bought them, but had entered into a lease agreement: therefore Court Line was not the legal owner. Under Generally Accepted Accounting Practice (GAAP) of the time, the aircraft, and more importantly the obligation to make payments to the leasing company, which stood at £40m, were not required to be on the balance sheet*. Court Line was following the legal form of the transaction, i.e. the leasing company was the owner of the aircraft, not Court Line.

Needs of users?

Neither the shareholders nor the creditors found it believable that accountants could consider that non-disclosure of a liability of £40m (which dwarfed the shareholders' funds figure of £18m) could be classed as giving a 'true and fair view'. Clearly there was a need for an accounting standard. International Accounting Standard 17 (IAS 17) would now require these aircraft and the associated obligation to be brought 'on balance sheet*'. The **'substance'** of the transaction was that the directors had bought aircraft for their exclusive use with the finance being provided by the leasing company – in commercial reality terms no different to buying the asset on credit – a finance deal. These assets would now be dealt with as 'finance leases', which are required to be capitalised, i.e. shown on balance sheet* along with the associated debt.

Rules v principles

The problem with a 'fire-fighting' approach to producing accounting standards is that it tends to close one 'loophole' with some rules as to how a transaction must now be accounted for, but doesn't stop the underlying problem. For example having rules about finance leases did not stop off balance sheet* finance – it just stopped one particular scheme – so companies simply came up with other methods. Modern accounting standards, therefore, are based on principles rather than rules.

The Framework document

The Framework document was issued in 1989. Instead of producing standards in a fire-fighting way, the Framework provides assistance that the IASB will use in the development of accounting standards. It is based on the premise that financial statements are prepared for the purpose of providing information that is useful in making economic decisions.

So ... what's it trying to achieve?

The **Framework** does not have the force of a standard. Instead, its purposes include, firstly, to guide and assist the IASB as it develops new or revised standards and, secondly, to assist preparers of financial statements in applying standards and in dealing with topics that are not addressed by an accounting standard. If, therefore, there is a conflict between the Framework and a specific standard, the standard prevails over the **Framework**.

Aspects of the Framework document are vital for any accountancy student to learn. If you understand the key parts of the Framework document, it acts as a 'get out of jail free' card in many written questions on accounting standards. You will earn good marks by defaulting to the principles contained in the Framework document, especially when asked to 'explain why' in reference to any accounting standard.

Objective of financial statements

You must learn the objective of financial statements, the qualitative characteristics of financial statements and the underlying assumptions. These are a **'need to learn'**.

 At the user

The objective of financial statements is to provide information about the financial position, performance, and changes in financial position of an entity that is useful to a wide range of users in making economic decisions.

The Framework does note that financial statements principally convey the financial effects of historic events, but they should allow users to make economic decisions, such as whether to buy, sell or hold an investment in the entity.

Qualitative characteristics of financial statements

Comparability

Comparability is a key qualitative characteristic of financial statements. Information provided for one period must be comparable with that provided for the previous period.

Consistency

In order to achieve comparability, information must be given consistently from one period to another, and accounting policies must be fully disclosed.

Understandability

Understandability is also a key qualitative characteristic of financial statements. Information should be comprehensible to users equipped with a 'reasonable knowledge of business and economic activities and accounting'. However the Framework notes that information should not be excluded from the statements on the grounds that it may be too complex for some users to understand.

Relevant and reliable

The final two qualitative characteristics are providing information that is relevant to the needs of the user whilst being reliable – as in free from bias and material error. The Framework recognises that there is a trade-off between these two which needs careful management.

Reliability includes the following qualities: faithful representation, substance over form and neutrality. A key concept for students is that of substance over form. For financial statements to be reliable, the economic substance of a transaction must be reflected, not the legal form. By economic substance we mean 'commercial reality'.

Underlying assumptions

Accruals and Going concern

Accruals and going concern are two principal underlying assumptions adopted whenever we are preparing financial statements. You will have learnt about these from your first introduction to double-entry bookkeeping. Although many modern accounting standards focus primarily on the balance sheet, the going concern and accruals concept are still 'bedrock' to the preparation of financial statements.

Transactional example

Jamie Inc was fined for the receipt of 'illegal' state subsidies of $600 million that were used to offset trade losses in previous years. Jamie Inc has to repay the government the $600 million plus interest of $320 million. Jamie Inc has decided to treat the repayment as an intangible asset which is being amortised over 20 years with a 20th being charged in the current year accounts. You need to discuss whether the accounting treatment is acceptable.

Even if you didn't know any accounting standards you could answer this question from the principles of the Framework document. As follows:

The Framework
The Framework describes the elements of financial statements as broad classes of financial effects of transactions and other events.

Definition of an asset
An asset is a 'resource controlled by the entity as a result of past events and from which future economic benefits are expected to flow'.

Payment of a fine
The payment of a fine does not meet this definition. Future economic benefits will not flow to the entity as a result of paying this fine. It is not a resource controlled by the company.

Inappropriate treatment
It is inappropriate to treat this transaction as an asset, as the payment of the fine is actually a cost to the company and needs to be treated as such.

Definition of an expense
Expenses are 'decreases in economic benefits during the accounting period in the form of outflows or depletions in assets or incurrences of liabilities that result in decreases in equity, other than those relating to distributions to equity participants'.

The fine should be charged against profit
Clearly the payment of this fine decreases economic benefit and incurs a liability for the company that will result in a decrease in equity (shareholders' funds) – it is an expense to be charged against current year profit.

Summary
By learning the definitions of the elements of financial statements you can apply the Framework to transactions – even if you don't know the specific standard you will be giving a very good answer.

Sorry but you need to know ... DEFINITIONS

The elements of financial statements

The Framework also gives definitions for the elements of financial statements – clearly all accountancy students need to be able to define an asset and a liability when answering questions.

- **Assets** – an asset is defined as 'a resource controlled by the entity as a result of past events and from which future economic benefits are expected to flow to the entity'.

- **Liabilities** – a liability is defined as 'a present obligation of the entity arising from past events, the settlement of which is expected to result in an outflow from the entity of resources embodying economic benefits'.

- **Equity** – the residual interest in the assets of the entity after deducting all of its liabilities.

- **Income** – increases in economic benefit during the accounting period in the form of inflows or enhancements of assets or decreases of liabilities that result in increases in equity, other than those relating to contributions from equity participants.

- **Expenses** – decreases in economic benefits during the accounting period in the form of outflows or depletions in assets or incurrences of liabilities that result in decreases in equity, other than those relating to distributions to equity participants.

These definitions are **ABSOLUTELY MUST LEARNS** for all accountancy students.

Cloud diagrams

As explained in the 'About this book' section (page iii), different students have different learning needs. When faced with a 'need to learn' area you have to decide what works best for you. For some learners the words on the page are adequate but for others there are better ways to aid recall.

Remember the human brain can code and interpret from a variety of stimuli, just reading the words is only one available way. Some, when faced with the task – 'OK so I need to remember the five elements of financial statements' – will benefit from drawing a diagram (see the following 'cloud diagram' as an example). This plays to the strengths of the right-hand side of the brain, which has been proven to recall colour and diagrams better than black and white writing.

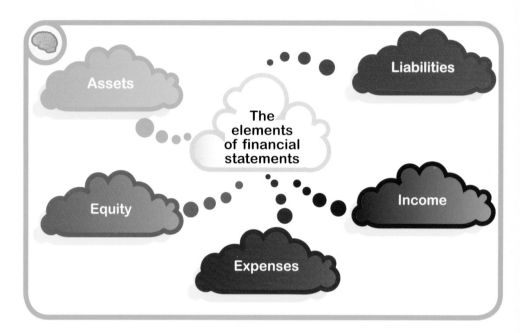

The Framework document does not say financial statements must be **ACCURATE** but students may find it useful as a mnemonic:

At the user
Comparability
Consistency
Understandability
Relevance and reliability
Accruals and going concern
Timely
Elements of financial statements

Key to the success of students is the use of such words when attempting written questions, particularly those asking them to 'Explain why…'.

Pitfalls

When using mnemonics students need to be careful to apply them to the particular question – don't try to get all eight parts of ACCURATE into every 'Explain why'. In our solution to Jamie Inc we have used:

- At the user
- Understandability
- Relevance
- Elements of financial statements (definitions of assets/liabilities).

Remember each answer is different – **apply, apply, apply.**

Conclusion

Key to success is the use of the words triggered by ACCURATE when attempting written questions, particularly ones asking them to 'Explain why…'. The Framework document will be central to the success of accounting students at all levels. It may appear to be painful to learn definitions of the elements, but hey, you have chosen to study accountancy, so it hardly seems unreasonable. The sooner you learn the definitions, the easier it will be to get to grips with the standards as they are based on these definitions.

IAS 1 – Presentation of financial statements

Introduction

Economic models explained – with cows

Socialism
You have two cows, and you give one to your neighbour.

Communism
You have two cows. The State takes both and gives you some milk.

Fascism
You have two cows. The State takes both and sells you some milk.

Bureaucracy
You have two cows. The State takes both, shoots one, milks the other, and then throws the milk away...

Traditional capitalism
You have two cows. You sell one and buy a bull. Your herd multiplies, and the economy grows. You sell them and retire on the income.

Enron venture capitalism
You have 2 cows. You sell three of them to your publicly listed company, using letters of credit opened by your brother-in-law at the bank, then execute a debt/ equity swap with an associated general offer so that you get all four cows back, with a tax exemption for five cows. The milk rights of the six cows are transferred via an intermediary to a Cayman Island company secretly owned by the majority shareholder who sells the rights to all seven cows back to your listed company. The annual report says the company owns eight cows, with an option on one more. Sell one cow to buy a new president of the United States, leaving you with nine cows. No balance sheet provided with the release. The public buys your bull.

The Andersen model
You have 2 cows. You shred them.

Anon by e-mail

Enron

Enron was once the seventh largest public-listed entity in the USA. In 2002 it became the most famous bankruptcy of all time. The accounting malpractices that were uncovered culminated in the demise of Enron's audit firm, Andersen (one of the then 'Big Five' accounting firms), due to its alleged document shredding at Enron. It is important that we always consider the needs of the users when we provide financial information. In October 2001, the market valued Enron's shares at around US$89. Some of the Enron staff so believed in their own company (remember it was a top 'buy tip' throughout this time) that they invested their own pension funds heavily in Enron stock. By February 2002, the share price was under US$1 – investors had lost the lot. Enron prepared its accounts to US GAAP not to IFRS, but whenever we are talking about accounting standards it helps to understand the lessons from history. The fact is that presenting misleading financial statements has ruined lives.

When it comes to IFRS the starting point for any trainee accountant has to be with IAS 1 as this is the standard that gives us the content of the primary accounting statements. Accountancy exams are variable – some students are given formats, some do an 'open book' exam. For many, however, all they get to take into the exam hall is their brain and pen, which means you may have to learn a format.

So … it's a 'meet the formats' standard

Well … yes, although it is actually a 'minimum required content,' rather than a prescriptive 'here is the format' standard. From a student perspective, however, your exams will ask you to prepare financial statements. Therefore you will need to find out what you have signed up for – are you going to be given a format to use or do you need to learn one?

When you first learnt double-entry bookkeeping, you were probably preparing financial statements for 'internal use' only, i.e. revenue less a list of expenses equalling profit. Your workings were probably done on the face of the accounts, i.e. non-current assets at cost less accumulated depreciation = Net Book Value (NBV).

Accounting (as opposed to bookkeeping) exams require us to take the detail off the face of the accounting statements, so we are showing summary rather than detailed figures.

Remember, the best way to get familiar with the formats is to access as many past paper questions as you can and **practise, practise, practise!!**

So ... what's it trying to achieve?

IAS 1 aims to prescribe the basis of presentation of financial statements, and to ensure comparability with previous periods and with the financial statements of other entities. The standard gives the minimum information required in financial statements.

Sorry but you need to know ... DEFINITIONS

Fair presentation – implies that the financial statements 'present fairly' or 'give a true and fair view' of the financial position, financial performance and cash flows of an entity.

Materiality – an item is deemed material if its omission or misstatement would influence the economic decisions of a user taken based on the financial statements. Materiality is based on the item's nature, size, and/or the surrounding circumstances.

Aggregation – each material class of similar items shall be presented separately in the financial statements. Material items that are dissimilar in nature should be separately disclosed.

Offsetting – assets and liabilities, income and expenses cannot be offset against each other unless required or permitted by a standard.

Comparative information – information relating to the previous period.

And the really important stuff ... accounting practice

IAS 1 is to be followed by all enterprises in preparing individual and group financial statements.

The content of a set of financial statements is:

- a statement of financial position as at the end of the period* (a balance sheet*)
- a statement of comprehensive income for the period*
- a statement of changes in equity for the period
- a statement of cash flows for the period (this is covered by IAS 7)
- notes, comprising a summary of significant accounting policies and other explanatory information
- a statement of financial position as at the beginning of the earliest comparative period when an entity applies an accounting policy retrospectively or makes a retrospective restatement of items in its financial statements, or when it reclassifies items in its financial statements.

* Please note on 6th September 2007 the IASB issued a revised IAS 1. The effective date of the new standard is annual periods beginning on or after 1 January 2009, with earlier application permitted. If, however, you are being examined on a six month from issue rule, this new standard is examinable for summer 2008 exams. The revised IAS 1 removes the traditional term 'balance sheet' and although the format is unchanged it is to be called 'a statement of financial position'. The traditional income statement is to be replaced by the 'statement of comprehensive income'.

An entity may use titles for the statements other than those used in the standard and an entity shall present with equal prominence all of the financial statements in a complete set of financial statements.

The overall considerations in the presentation of accounts are:

- fair presentation and compliance with IFRS
- going concern (see Chapter 1)
- accruals (see Chapter 1)
- consistency (see Chapter 1)
- materiality and aggregation (see above)
- offsetting (see above)
- comparatives (see above).

The formats are not specified by IAS 1, however the standard gives the minimum information to be included. The proformas over the next pages are interpretations of that minimum information.

A choice also exists with regard to unusual (exceptional) items, which can be presented either on the face of the income statement, or in the notes to the accounts.

A further choice exists with the 'statement of changes in equity'. The amount of dividends recognised as distributions to owners during the period can be presented either in the statement of changes in equity or in the notes.

Note

For a standard with a key aim of comparability we have just talked an awful lot about choice!!! Looking for a criticism? – yes you've found it!!

Notes to the accounts must always be prepared, i.e.

- Accounting policies note
- Disclose information required by any IAS/ IFRS that is not on the face of the primary statements
- Provide other relevant information.

Format of the financial statements

On the following pages are illustrative examples of the formats of financial statements. (**note these full formats do not have a key next to them, so just scan and move on**).

The Statement of financial position* (balance sheet*) – full format

XYX Group- Statement of financial position* as at 31 December 20X7

	20X7	20X7	20X6	20X6
ASSETS				
Non-current assets				
Property, plant and equipment	X		X	
Goodwill	X		X	
Other intangible assets	X		X	
Investments in associates	X		X	
Available-for-sale investments	X		X	
		X		X
Current assets				
Inventories	X		X	
Trade and other receivables	X		X	
Other current assets	X		X	
Cash and cash equivalents	X		X	
		X		X
Total assets		X		X
EQUITY AND LIABILITIES				
Equity attributable to the holders of the parent				
Share capital	X		X	
Other reserves	X		X	
Retained earnings	X		X	
		X		X
Minority interest		X		X
Non-current liabilities				
Long-term borrowings	X		X	
Deferred tax	X		X	
Long-term provisions	X		X	
		X		X
Current liabilities				
Trade and other payables	X		X	
Short-term borrowings	X		X	
Current portion of long-term borrowings	X		X	
Current tax payable	X		X	
Short-term provisions	X		X	
		X		X
Total equity and liabilities		X		X

* Please note on 6th September 2007 the IASB issued a revised IAS 1. The effective date of the new standard is annual periods beginning on or after 1 January 2009, with earlier application permitted. If, however, you are being examined on a six month from issue rule, this new standard is examinable for summer 2008 exams. The revised IAS 1 removes the traditional term 'balance sheet' and although the format is unchanged it is to be called 'a statement of financial position'. The traditional income statement is to be replaced by the 'statement of comprehensive income'.

...nsive income*– full format

...his as two separate statements:

...r loss and displaying components of other

...rehensive income* for the year

...xpenses by function)

	20X7	20X6
	X	X
	(x)	(x)
	X	X
	X	X
	(x)	(x)
	(x)	(x)
	(x)	(x)
	(x)	(x)
	X	X
	X	X
	(x)	(x)
...rations	X	X
...perations	(x)	(x)
	X	X
	X	X
	X	X
	X	X
	X	X
	(x)	(x)
...e of associates	X	X
Income tax relating to components of other comprehensive income	X	X
Other comprehensive income for the year, net of tax	X	X
TOTAL COMPREHENSIVE INCOME FOR THE YEAR	X	X

For students sitting exams to the original IAS 1, the old income statement stops at PROFIT FOR THE YEAR (see page 24). The add on of 'Other comprehensive income' is as a result of the September 2007 revision to IAS 1.

An error that some students make when they initially study IAS 1 is to try to learn the complete formats. In fact, many of the lines will only be relevant at the more advanced stages, e.g. when you prepare consolidated statements for groups of companies. Many students will not need to learn these formats in full. See over for what will be necessary.

The statement of financial position* (balance sheet) – the key bits

The statement of financial position*

XYX Group- The statement of financial position* as at 31 December 20X7

	20X7	20X7	20X6	20X6
ASSETS				
Non-current assets				
Property, plant and equipment	X		X	
Other intangible assets	X		X	
		X		X
Current assets				
Inventories	X		X	
Trade and other receivables	X		X	
Cash and cash equivalents	X		X	
		X		X
Total assets		X		X
EQUITY AND LIABILITIES				
Equity attributable to the holders of the parent				
Share capital	X		X	
Other reserves	X		X	
Retained earnings	X		X	
		X		X
Non-current liabilities				
Long-term borrowings	X		X	
Long-term provisions	X		X	
		X		X
Current liabilities				
Trade and other payables	X		X	
Short-term borrowings	X		X	
Current tax payable	X		X	
Short-term provisions	X		X	
		X		X
Total equity and liabilities		X		X

* Please note on 6th September 2007 the IASB issued a revised IAS 1. The effective date of the new standard is annual periods beginning on or after 1 January 2009, with earlier application permitted. If, however, you are being examined on a six month from issue rule, this new standard is examinable for summer 2008 exams. The revised IAS 1 removes the traditional term 'balance sheet' and although the format is unchanged it is to be called 'a statement of financial position'. The traditional income statement is to be replaced by the 'statement of comprehensive income'.

The comprehensive income statement*- the key bits

The top half is the key bit, instead of learning the full format use a mneumonic such as:

Really cute guys distract accountants preventing infatuated fools passing the paper!

(Obviously a significant chunk of you would prefer to learn the 'REALLY CUTE GALS' version instead!)

To learn the initial key lines of the format for the top part of the comprehensive income statement*.

Cute guys version

Comprehensive income statement

XYX Group- Comprehensive income statement for the year ended 31 December 20X7

(Illustrating the classification of expenses by function)

	20X2	20X1
Revenue (Really)	X	X
Cost of sales **(Cute)**	(x)	(x)
Gross profit **(Guys)/(Gals)**	X	X
Distribution costs **(Distract)**	(x)	(x)
Administrative expenses **(Accountants)**	(x)	(x)
Profit from operations **(Preventing)**	X	X
Investment income **(Infatuated)**	X	X
Finance cost **(Fools)**	(x)	(x)
Profit before tax (Passing)	X	X
Tax expense **(The)**	(x)	(x)
Profit after tax (Paper)	X	X

The bottom half is even simpler when we first start preparing these accounts. Usually there is either no other items of comprehensive income or perhaps just the one - a revaluation gain.

Other Comprehensive income		
Gains on property revaluation	X	X
Total comprehensive income for the year	**X**	**X**

Another problem is time spent learning format 2. Note it doesn't have a key next to it.

The statement of comprehensive income*

XYX Group - The statement of comprehensive income* for the year ended 31 December 20X2

(Illustrating the classification of expenses by nature)

	20X2	20X1
Revenue	X	X
Other income	X	X
Changes in inventories of finished goods and work-in-progress	(x)	X
Work performed by the enterprise and capitalised	X	X
Raw material and consumables used	(x)	(x)
Employee benefits expense	(x)	(x)
Impairment of property, plant and equipment	(x)	(x)
Other expenses	(x)	(x)
Finance cost	(x)	(x)
Share of profit of associates	X	X
Profit before tax	X	X
Income tax expense	(x)	(x)
Profit for the period	X	X
Attributable to:		
Equity holders of the parent	X	X
Minority interest	X	X
	X	X

Other Comprehensive income		
Gains on property revaluation	X	X
Total comprehensive income for the year	**x**	**x**

This format is not used very frequently and, therefore, whilst you will see it in textbooks the important income statement format is the **REALLY CUTE GUYS one!!**

The statement of changes in equity – full format

 Again the format of the statement of changes in equity taken directly from IAS 1 looks pretty daunting ... However, until you get pretty advanced most of this stuff is irrelevant. See below for full format. (Again, note no key!).

* Please note on 6th September 2007 the IASB issued a revised IAS 1. The effective date of the new standard is annual periods beginning on or after 1 January 2009, with earlier application permitted. If, however, you are being examined on a six month from issue rule, this new standard is examinable for summer 2008 exams. The revised IAS 1 removes the traditional term 'balance sheet' and although the format is unchanged it is to be called 'a statement of financial position'. The traditional income statement is to be replaced by the 'statement of comprehensive income'.

XYX Group – Statement of changes in equity for the year ended 31 December 20X7

	Share capital	Retained earnings	Translation of foreign operations	Available-for-sale financial assets	Cash flow hedges	Revaluation reserve	Total	Minority interest	Total equity
Balance at 1 January 20X6	X	X	(x)	X	X		X	X	X
Changes in accounting policy		X					X	X	X
Restated balance	X	X	(x)	X	X		X	X	X
Changes in equity for 20X6									
Dividends		(x)					(x)		(x)
Total comprehensive income for the year		X	X	(x)	X	X	X	X	X
Balance at 31 December 20X6	X	X	X	X	(x)	X	X	X	X
Changes in equity for 20X7									
Issue of share capital	X						X		X
Dividends		(x)					(x)		(x)
Total comprehensive income for the year		X	(x)	(x)	X	X	X	X	X
Transferred to retained earnings		X				X			
Balance at 31 December 20X7	X	X	X	X	(x)	X	X	X	X

Although this is the format you would see in IAS 1 and textbooks, it is covering everything and for most companies will be a lot simpler – it's just a column for each balance sheet line of equity and reserves showing any changes that took place in the accounting period. SEE the example below for the common bits that need to be learnt!

XYX Group – Statement of changes in equity for the year ended 31 December 20X7

	Share capital	Retained earnings	Revaluation reserve	Total equity
Balance at 31 December 20X6	X	X	X	X
Dividends		(x)		(x)
Issue of share capital	X			X
Total comprehensive income for the year		X	X	X
Balance at 31 December 20X7 carried forward	X	X	X	X

Statement in changes of equity

* Please note on 6th September 2007 the IASB issued a revised IAS 1. The effective date of the new standard is annual periods beginning on or after 1 January 2009, with earlier application permitted. If, however, you are being examined on a six month from issue rule, this new standard is examinable for summer 2008 exams. The revised IAS 1 removes the traditional term 'balance sheet' and although the format is unchanged it is to be called 'a statement of financial position'. The traditional income statement is to be replaced by the 'statement of comprehensive income'.

The original IAS 1 formats.

Students sitting exams to the original IAS 1 will need to present the following formats:

The balance sheet*

XYX Group- The balance sheet* as at 31 December 20X7

	20X7	20X7	20X6	20X6
ASSETS				
Non-current assets				
Property, plant and equipment	X		X	
Other intangible assets	X		X	
		X		X
Current assets				
Inventories	X		X	
Trade and other receivables	X		X	
Cash and cash equivalents	X		X	
		X		X
Total assets		X		X
EQUITY AND LIABILITIES				
Equity attributable to the holders of the parent				
Share capital	X		X	
Other reserves	X		X	
Retained earnings	X		X	
		X		X
Non-current liabilities				
Long-term borrowings	X		X	
Long-term provisions	X		X	
		X		X
Current liabilities				
Trade and other payables	X		X	
Short-term borrowings	X		X	
Current tax payable	X		X	
Short-term provisions	X		X	
		X		X
Total equity and liabilities		X		X

Income statement

XYX Group- Income statement for the year ended 31 December 20X7

(Illustrating the classification of expenses by function)

	20X2	20X1
Revenue (Really)	X	X
Cost of sales **(Cute)**	(x)	(x)
Gross profit **(Guys)/(Gals)**	X	X
Distribution costs **(Distract)**	(x)	(x)
Administrative expenses **(Accountants)**	(x)	(x)
Profit from operations **(Preventing)**	X	X
Investment income **(Infatuated)**	X	X
Finance cost **(Fools)**	(x)	(x)
Profit before tax (Passing)	X	X
Tax expense **(The)**	(x)	(x)
Profit after tax (Paper)	X	X

Conclusion

IAS 1 is a key standard for all accountancy students. When you start out-use the simplified formats-then revisit this chapter as you progress through your studies to look at the full versions.

Revised IAS 1 - Presentation of Financial Statements

On 6th September 2007 the IASB issued a revised version of IAS1.The revisions include changes in the titles of some of the financial statements.

The balance sheet is renamed 'a statement of financial position'

The income statement is renamed 'the comprehensive income statement' and has an amended format.

This will not affect you for exams in 2007 but may effect you in 2008.

Please see **www.astudentsguideto.com** for more information.

IAS 2 – Inventory

Introduction

> "We should all take inventory every morning when we wake up, take a pen and list your blessings."
>
> Anon

Inventory eh? Well it could be a stock of famous artwork-but just as easily something less interesting: a stock of metal pipes, cardboard boxes or plastic sink plugs! Whatever it consists of, it's only an itemised list of a company's goods that haven't been sold at the end of the reporting period. How difficult can that be to account for? Well actually this is an important issue for a number of reasons. Firstly, inventories will be shown as an asset on the company's balance sheet*. The measurement of this is important as assets must not be carried at more than their recoverable amount (can we get our money back?) unless we wish to seriously mislead the user of accounts.

Secondly inventory has a direct impact on the measurement of profit – a key hotspot when it comes to creative accounting.

Are we saying inventory measurement can be used to create an accounting fairy tale?

Yes we are – the accruals/matching concept is considered 'bedrock' when we prepare financial statements, so if we recognise revenue we also need to recognise the cost of the goods we have sold. We do this by taking any opening inventory at the start of the period, adding it to the purchases in the period and deducting the closing inventory. This is then held on the balance sheet* (as an asset to be sold in the future). Cost of goods sold is then part of cost of sales in the income statement (other direct costs are added to cost of goods sold to give us cost of sales).

---

* Balance Sheet = Statement of financial position (see page 18)

So ... what's it trying to achieve?

IAS 2 gives the accounting treatment for inventories. This includes the important issues in the recognition of costs and also gives guidance when assessing net realisable values.

Transactional example

Suzanne Inc imports commemorative spoons from many countries, packages them and exports them to Australia.

At the end of its reporting period it has an itemised list of the spoons in stock. It has, however, incurred a range of expenses in obtaining these spoons.

In addition to the direct cost of their purchase, it has also paid carriage inwards, import duties and other handling costs related to imports and has to employ someone in the accounting department to deal with this paperwork.

Suzanne Inc needs to know which costs it can include as part of the cost of the inventory.

IAS 2 provides this guidance to companies like Suzanne Inc. The cost of inventories comprises all:

- costs of purchase
- 'other costs' incurred in bringing the inventories to their present location and condition
- costs of conversion.

The carriage inwards, import duties and other handling costs can certainly be included, but the salary of the person in the accounting department would not be allowed to be included in the cost of inventory.

The common mistake made by students is to either exclude all costs mentioned or to include all costs mentioned, when the answer is usually a bit of both!! Beware particularly of carriage costs – carriage inwards should be included in valuing the inventories of a manufacturing company, but it would **NOT** be appropriate to include carriage outwards.

---

* Balance Sheet = Statement of financial position (see page 18)

What about costs of conversion in a manufacturing company?

If we are looking at the inventory of a manufacturing company, costs of conversion could include variable and fixed manufacturing overheads incurred in converting raw material into finished goods, e.g.

- fixed costs – depreciation of factory building and factory plant
- variable costs – labour costs.

Remember, general administrative overheads that do not contribute to bringing inventories to their present location and condition are never included in valuing inventory. Also excluded are selling costs, storage costs (unless essential to the production process), abnormal amounts of wasted materials, labour, and other production costs.

Remember – SAGS

Excluded costs from inventory valuation

S Selling costs

A Abnormal amounts of wasted material, labour, and other production costs

G General administrative overheads

S Storage costs.

Sorry but you need to know ... DEFINITIONS

Inventories are assets:

- held for sale in the ordinary course of business; or
- in the process of production for such sale; or
- in the form of materials or supplies to be consumed in the production process or in the rendering of services.

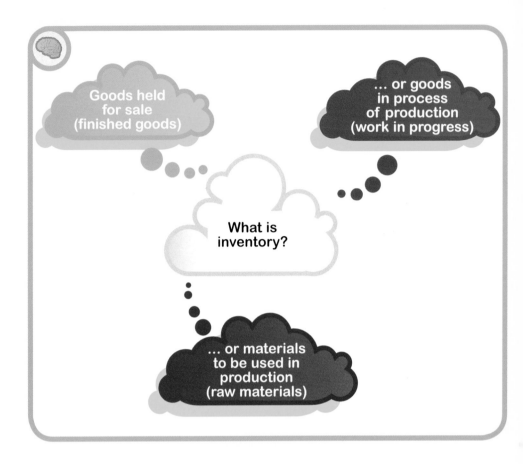

 Net realisable value is the estimated selling price (ordinary course of business) less estimated completion and selling costs.

And the really important stuff ... accounting practice

 Inventories should be valued at total of the lower of cost (all costs incurred in bringing to present location and condition) and net realisable value of separate items of stock, or of groups of similar items.

Inventories can be valued on the first in first out ('FIFO') basis, or using a weighted average method. Other methods would be rarely used.

Inventories should be sub-classified in the notes into main categories (e.g. raw materials, work-in-progress and finished goods).

 Watch the dates in questions – students often end up with opening inventory on the balance sheet* rather than closing inventory!!

* Balance Sheet = Statement of financial position (see page 18)

Disclosures

For a student the key disclosures are:

- accounting policies adopted
- any inventories at fair value less costs to sell
- the write-down of inventories and the reversal of any write-down.

Conclusion

IAS 2 is a vital accounting standard. All questions from the very beginning will include opening and closing inventory – this is very much an 'orange standard', i.e. one you need to know right from the start of your studies.

IAS 7 – Cash flow statements

Introduction

> "Revenue is vanity, profit is sanity and cash is reality."
>
> Anon

During your accountancy studies you will hear the phrase 'cash is reality or cash is king' an awful lot of times. It is certainly true that more companies go bust due to lack of cash rather than lack of profit. We have many of examples of corporate collapse where profit has been seriously manipulated over a long period of time. As mentioned in Chapter 2, the most famous is the US company Enron.

The Enron accounts – a real world fairy tale without a happy ending

Enron were an American company listed on Wall Street. Most Wall Street firms of analysts had Enron as a 'strong buy' right up to them filing for bankruptcy. The figure that the analysts were paying attention to was profit (often referred to by analysts as earnings). Earnings are notoriously easy for companies to manipulate. Enron reported pre-tax earnings for the last two quarters of 2000 at $650 million (accounts prepared to US GAAP). It is now considered that at least 80% were earnings from questionable transactions. It is general opinion that, if analysts had paid more attention to cash flow than earnings, these problems could have been identified as early as 1997.

In the September 1997 accounts Enron reported net operating income of $134 million. However, when converted to operating cash flows we get the following:

---

* Balance Sheet = Statement of financial position (see page 18)

Operating cash flow		$million
Operating income		134
Add back		
Depreciation (not a real cash expense)		110
Adjust for working capital changes	*(i.e. the accruals policy)*	
Inventory increase	*(piling up inventory worsens cash flow)*	(77)
Receivables increase	*(not collecting debts worsens cash flow)*	(969)
Payables/current liabilities increase	*(delaying payment to suppliers improves short-term cash flow but can lead to difficulties with suppliers)*	345
Other current assets decrease	*(selling current asset investments will improve cash flow)*	87
Operating cash flows		(370)

Negative operating cash flows should have rung warning bells. Operating activities are meant, yes, to generate profit, but when those profits are not cash backed there are questions to be asked. Enron continued to expand despite this position by borrowing. (Borrowed cash, of course, has to be repaid with interest).

In fact out of the following 16 quarters all but one reported positive earnings whilst cash flow was only positive three times. Clearly a cash flow statement is important to put the income statement (earnings) in context.

So ... what's it trying to achieve?

IAS 7 is attempting to ensure that companies report their cash generation and absorption in a way which helps provide information to assist users who make economic decisions based on the accounts.

Transactional example

You are required to prepare a cash flow statement for Bear Inc for the year ended 31 March 20X6. The income statement and balance sheet* of Bear Inc are set out below.

Bear Inc – Income statement for the year ended 31 March 20X6

	$000
Continuing operations	
Revenue	14,734
Cost of sales	(8,104)
Gross profit	6,630
Profit on disposal of property, plant and equipment	217
Distribution costs	(2,641)
Administrative expenses	(1,993)
Profit from operations	2,213
Finance costs	(210)
Profit before tax	2,003
Tax	(501)
Profit for the period from continuing operations attributable to equity holders	1,502

Bear Inc – Balance sheet* as at 31 March 20X6

	20X6 $000	20X5 $000
Assets		
Non-current assets		
Property, plant and equipment	22,708	16,797
Current assets		
Inventories	2,701	2,019
Trade and other receivables	2,456	1,009
Cash and cash equivalents	–	392
Total assets	27,865	20,217

---

* Balance Sheet = Statement of financial position (see page 18)

	20X6	20X5
	$000	$000
Equity and Liabilities		
Equity		
Share capital	6,000	4,000
Share premium account	4,000	1,000
Retained earnings	12,540	11,638
Non-current liabilities		
Bank loans	3,000	2,000
Current liabilities		
Trade and other payables	1,140	1,113
Tax liabilities	501	466
Bank overdraft	684	–
Total equity and liabilities	27,865	20,217

Note to the accounts:

Retained earnings	
	$000
Balance at 1 April 20X5	11,638
Dividends paid	(600)
Profit for the year	1,502
Balance at 31 March 20X6	12,540

Further information:

- *The total depreciation charge for the year was $2,952,000.*
- *Property, plant and equipment costing $2,048,000 with accumulated depreciation of $1,011,000 was sold in the year.*
- *All sales and purchases were on credit. Other expenses were paid for in cash.*

You are required to prepare the cash flow statement for Bear Inc for the year ended 31 March 20X6.

A cash flow statement?

IAS 7 believes all entities should prepare a cash flow statement that analyses the actual cash flows of an entity (i.e. cash in less cash out). The starting point is to learn the format (see over for example from IAS 7). It takes the cash flows and divides them into three key sections:

- operating activities
- investing activities
- financing activities.

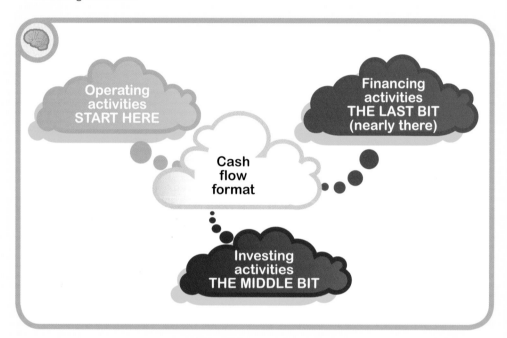

Often when students start this topic it seems very difficult. However, with a bit of practice using the questions from past papers, this can easily become your best topic. Still, it is a problem as to quite where to start, with the size of the format being pretty formidable. When you first begin, therefore, break it down into the three key sections and learn the format chunk by chunk – treat it as three topics not one.

First of all see if you can conquer cash flows from operating activities, using the accounts of Bear Inc.

Lets start with the current year's income statement. Pick up the company's profit from operations. This is the first number that goes into a cash flow statement. As we illustrated with the Enron accounts, just because a company is generating profit does not mean that it is generating cash from operating activities. Accountants, as we know, put non-cash items into an income statement – you will now need to read through the question to find out how much depreciation was expensed in the current year accounts – it is a **notional** expense and therefore to get back to cash flow you need to add it back. Once you've done that you are off!!

* Balance Sheet = Statement of financial position (see page 18)

Cash flows from operating activities	$
Profit from operations	2,213
Adjustments for:	
Depreciation **(always an add back)**	2,952

Other adjustments may be necessary because we are trying to calculate cash flow from operating activities – which means the trading outcome of the company. The income statement however may include non-trading income such as profit on disposal of property, plant and equipment; so read the income statement again and, if this is the case, take it out.

Gain on disposal of property, plant and equipment **(always a deduction)**	(217)

> **Note**
>
> *If it were a loss on disposal of property, plant and equipment it would be an add back.*

Operating cash flows before working capital changes	4,948

Adjustments will be necessary due to movements in the working capital items since the income statement will be prepared on the accruals basis, revenues are sales made in the period whether or not you have received the cash. If the sales are recognised but the cash is not received, you will have put a receivable on your balance sheet*. Look now at the two years, balance sheet*s you have been provided with. You will always need to work out the movement on inventory/trade receivables and trade payables, since these could either have decreased or increased.

Trade and other receivables increase **(failure to collect debt promptly worsens cash flow)**	(1,447)
Inventories increase **(holding increasing stocks of inventory worsens cash flow)**	(682)
Trade payables increase **(paying suppliers more slowly will improve cash flow)**	27
Cash generated from operations	2,846

> **Note**
>
> *If your movement worsens the company's cash flow you need brackets; and if it improves the company's cash flow you won't!!*

Worsens = ( )
Improves = no ( )

Put together – your first section looks like this:

Cash flows from operating activities	$
Profit from operations	2,213
Adjustments for:	
Depreciation	2,952
Gain on disposal of property, plant and equipment	(217)
Operating cash flows before working capital changes	4,948
Inventories increase	(682)
Trade and other receivables increase	(1,447)
Trade payables increase	27
Cash generated from operations	2,846

Again you might find a mnemonic useful here, what about ...

Plainly Dedicated Doctors Inspire Real People

Cash flows from operating activities

Profit from operations **(Plainly)**	x
Adjustments for:	
Depreciation **(Dedicated)**	x
Disposal of property, plant and equipment (gain)/loss **(Doctors)**	(x)/x
Operating profit before working capital changes	x
Inventories increase/decrease **(Inspire)**	(x)/x
Receivables increase/decrease **(Real)**	(x)/x
Payables decrease/increase **(People)**	(x)/x
Cash generated from operations	x

Interest paid and tax paid

The format then recognises that a company needs to be able to cover both its interest payments and its tax payments. These are definitely NOT optional items.

* Balance Sheet = Statement of financial position (see page 18)

Remember, however, that this is a cash flow statement not an income statement. The amounts in the income statement for interest and tax will not necessarily be the same as the interest and tax paid out in cash terms. The accruals concept is being applied, with any outstanding amounts owing being shown on the balance sheet* as accruals/liabilities.

You must therefore make sure you look at the balance sheet*s to see if there are any liabilities for interest or tax at the start of the year and/or at the end of the year. There MAY be one for interest but there is pretty well ALWAYS a tax liability or indeed two!! (including the deferred tax liability).

You will then need to use the following pro forma workings to calculate the actual cash paid out to slot into the cash flow statement.

(Working 1)
Interest paid

	$000
Balance (liability) due on opening balance sheet*	nil
Add: Interest charge (finance costs) for the year from the income statement	210
Less: Balance (liability) still due on closing balance sheet*	(nil)
= Interest paid during year (figure for cash flow)	**210**

Alternatively you might prefer to use 'T' accounts for these workings – it is a personal preference, so decide which you prefer and stick with it.

Interest paid

	$000		$000
		Bal b/fwd	nil
= Interest paid during the year β	**210**	Interest charge on the income statement	210
Bal c/fwd	nil		
	210		210

(Working 2)

Taxation paid

	$000
Current tax liability due on opening balance sheet*	466
Add: Deferred tax liability due on opening balance sheet*	nil
Add: Tax charge for the year from the income statement	501
Less: Current tax liability still due on closing balance sheet*	(501)
Less: Deferred tax liability still due on closing balance sheet*	(nil)
= Tax paid during the year (figure for cash flow)	**466**

or ...

Taxation paid

	$000		$000
		Balance b/fwd – current tax due on opening balance sheet*	466
= Tax paid for the year β	**466**	Bal b/fwd – deferred tax liability on opening balance sheet*	nil
Balance c/fwd – current tax liability on closing balance sheet*	501	Income statement	501
Balance c/fwd – deferred tax liability on closing balance sheet*	nil		
	967		967

* Balance Sheet = Statement of financial position (see page 18)

The format then deducts these two figures from 'cash generated from operations' to give *Net cash from operating activities* (see below)

Bear Inc – Cash flow statement for the year ended 31 March 20X6

	$000	$000
Cash flows from operating activities		
Profit from operations	2,213	
Adjustments for:		
Depreciation	2,952	
Gain on disposal of property, plant and equipment	(217)	
Operating cash flows before working capital changes	4,948	
Increase in inventories	(682)	
Increase in trade receivables	(1,447)	
Increase in trade payables	27	
Cash generated from operations	2,846	
Interest paid **(see Working 1)**	(210)	
Income taxes paid **(see Working 2)**	(466)	
Net cash from operating activities		**2,170**

Cash flows from investing activities

Companies need to invest if they are to keep up with the competition. They may also be following a strategy of growth by acquiring other companies. This is the section which shows the reader what impact these policies have had on the cash flows of the company.

Acquisition of subsidiary net of cash acquired	(x)

(This can be ignored unless you are studying an advanced paper and being asked for a group cash flow)

The format of the investing activities section will commonly look like this:

Purchase of property, plant and equipment **(Purple)**	(x)
Proceeds from sale of equipment **(Pansies)**	X
Interest received **(Interested)**	X
Dividends received **(Dave)**	X
Net cash used in investing activities	(x)

Remember

Purple Pansies Interested Dave!

Remember it is always the cash you are interested in – how much did the company actually pay out to purchase property, plant and equipment and what were the proceeds from selling the old ones?

A common mistake made by students is to put the profit from the disposal of equipment in the cash flow rather than the cash proceeds. Remember the number in the income statement is a calculation of PROFIT – not the cash flow – which can always be worked out.

(Working 3)

	$000
Proceeds from disposal of equipment	
NBV of asset sold (what you expected to get) (2,048 – 1,011)	1,037
Add: Profit made on disposal (taken to income statement),	
i.e. you got more than expected	217
= Proceeds from sale	
(figure for cash flow statement)	**1,254**

or ...

	$000
NBV of asset sold (what you expected to get)	X
Deduct: Loss made on disposal	
(taken to income statement), i.e. you received less than expected	(x)
= Proceeds from sale	
(figure for cash flow statement)	**XX**

You will also need to calculate the amount of cash spent on purchasing property, plant and equipment.

(Working 4)

	$000
Non-current assets/Property, plant and equipment (NBV)	
Bal b/fwd (from opening balance sheet*)	16,797
Less: Depreciation	(2,952)
Less: NBV of asset sold	(1,037)
Less: Bal c/fwd (from closing balance sheet*)	(22,708)
= Additions in period	**9,900**

* Balance Sheet = Statement of financial position (see page 18)

or

Again you may prefer to use a 'T' account – either way we get the same answer.

Non-current assets/Property, plant and equipment @ NBV

	$000		$000
Bal b/fwd (NBV) (from opening balance sheet*)	16,797	Depreciation	2,952
		Disposals at NBV	1,037
= Additions in the period	**9,900**		
		Bal c/fwd (NBV) (from closing balance sheet*)	22,708
	26,697		26,697

Note

Also take to this section any interest and dividends received.

Bear Inc doesn't have any interest or dividend received.
You now have two of the three sections.

Cash flow statement

Bear Inc – Cash flow statement for the year ended 31 March 20X6

Cash flows from operating activities	$000	$000
Profit from operations	2,213	
Adjustments for:		
Depreciation	2,952	
Gain on disposal of property, plant and equipment	(217)	
Operating profit before working capital changes	4,948	
Increase in inventories	(682)	
Increase in trade receivables	(1,447)	
Increase in trade payables	27	
Cash generated from operations	2,846	
Interest paid **(Working 1)**	(210)	
Income taxes paid **(Working 2)**	(466)	
Net cash from operating activities		**2,170**
Cash flows from investing activities		
Acquisition of subsidiary net of cash acquired	nil	
Purchase of property, plant and equipment **(Working 4)**	(9,900)	
Proceeds from sale of equipment **(Working 3)**	1,254	
Interest received	nil	
Dividends received	nil	
Net cash used in investing activities		**(8,646)**

Cash flows from financing activities

Finally you need to look at the two balance sheet*s to see if the company has changed its financing arrangements in the current year. A company can only raise finance from one of two sources: debt (taking out loans) or equity (issuing shares). Any changes in shares or loans giving rise to either a cash inflow or cash outflow in the year are recorded in this section. Also record the actual cash dividend paid in the year (last year's final proposed plus any current year interim dividend).

	$ 000
Proceeds from issuance of share capital **(Purple) (working 5)**	5,000
Proceeds from long-term borrowings **(Pansies) (3,000 – 2,000)**	1,000
Payment of finance lease liabilities **(Poison)**	(nil)
Dividends paid **(Dave)**	(600)
Net cash used in financing activities	**5,400**

* Balance Sheet = Statement of financial position (see page 18)

Remember finally

Purple Pansies Poison Dave!

The proceeds from the issue of share capital can be calculated by looking at the share capital and the share premium accounts. Remember they are 'twin accounts' as far as the cash flow statement goes. It is accounting convention that we post the nominal value of shares issued to the share capital account and post the premium on the issue to the share premium account. For Bear Inc. therefore, the share capital balance has increased by $2,000,000 and the share premium has increased by $3,000,000. You have therefore received total cash of $5,000,000 and this is the figure in the cash flow statement.

(Working 5)	
	$000
Proceeds from issuance of share capital	
Share capital increase (6,000 – 4,000)	2,000
Share premium increase (4,000 – 1,000)	3,000
	————
Total for cash flow statement	5,000

The cash flow relating to loans can be calculated by looking at the movement on the loans line. Bank loans here have increased from $2,000,000 to $3,000,000. A cash injection of $1,000,000 has therefore arisen.

The dividend paid of $600,000 can be picked up from the movement in retained earnings in the notes to the accounts.

This should then reconcile to the movement on the cash and cash equivalents.

Remember, every exam question will vary slightly and there may be other non-standard cash flow items – however, these key elements will allow you to get a very high mark under exam conditions even if you miss something non-standard. Remember, the more past questions you practise the better you get at the standard things – AND – you start to meet and recognise non-standard stuff too.

Again, the key to numeric topics is – practise, practise, practise!!!

The whole thing will now look something like this:

Bear Inc – Cash flow statement for the year ended 31 March 20X6

	$000	$000
Cash flows from operating activities		
Profit from operations	2,213	
Adjustments for:		
Depreciation	2,952	
Gain on disposal of property, plant and equipment	(217)	
Operating profit before working capital changes	4,948	
Increase in inventories	(682)	
Increase in trade receivables	(1,447)	
Increase in trade payables	27	
Cash generated from operations	2,846	
Interest paid	(210)	
Income taxes paid	(466)	
Net cash from operating activities		**2,170**
Cash flows from investing activities		
Acquisition of subsidiary net of cash acquired (note a)	nil	
Purchase of property, plant and equipment	(9,900)	
Proceeds from sale of equipment	1,254	
Interest received	nil	
Dividends received	nil	
Net cash used in investing activities		**(8,646)**
Cash flows from financing activities		
Proceeds from issuance of share capital	5,000	
Proceeds from long-term borrowings	1,000	
Payment of finance lease liabilities	nil	
Dividends paid	(600)	
Net cash used in financing activities		**5,400**
Net increase/(decrease) in cash and cash equivalents		(1,076)
Cash and cash equivalents at the beginning of the period (cash at start of year less bank overdraft at start of year)		392
Cash and cash equivalents at the end of the period (cash at end of year less bank overdraft at end of year)		(684)

Notes to the cash flow statement

Dependent on your examiner you might get asked for the notes to the cash flow statement.

The notes that are normally required for the cash flow statement are:

(1) Acquisition (disposal) of subsidiary (only examined in group cash flows for more advanced students)

This note analyses the net assets acquired and the cash flow on acquisition and disposal. An example (given in IAS 7) is:

	$
Cash	40
Inventories	100
Accounts receivable	100
Property, plant and equipment	650
Trade payables	(100)
Long-term debt	(200)
Total purchase price	590
Less: Cash of subsidiary	(40)
Cash flow on acquisition net of cash acquired	550

(2) Major non-cash transactions

Any major non-cash transactions that require disclosure in order that the financial statements show a true and fair view should be given. Such things as inception of finance leases may meet this category.

(3) Cash and cash equivalents

A disclosure note must be given that analyses cash and cash equivalents and allows the amount to be reconciled into the balance sheet*. This note should also disclose any significant amounts of cash and cash equivalents held by the enterprise that are not available for use by the group.

(4) Segmental cash flow information

IAS 7 encourages the presentation of operating, investing and financing cash flows by segment in a note. This disclosure is also encouraged (but not required) by IFRS 8.

Indirect method

In most circumstances companies should prepare cash flow statements and notes in the formats as shown in chapter 4. The method used to answer Bear Inc is known as 'The indirect method'.

However, there is some choice about the position of some of the items in the cash flow statement:

Interest paid	Operating or financing
Interest received	Operating or investing
Dividends received	Operating or investing
Dividends paid	Operating or financing

Direct method

Companies may, if they wish, use the indirect method which adds the following five lines at the top of the cash flow statement to show the make-up of cash from operating activities:

	$
Cash received from customers	x
Cash paid to suppliers and employees	(x)
Cash generated from operations	x
Interest paid	(x)
Income taxes paid	(x)

Sorry but you need to know ... DEFINITIONS

Cash – cash on hand and demand deposits.

Cash equivalents – short-term, highly-liquid investments that are readily convertible to known amounts of cash and which are subject to an insignificant risk of changes in value.

[The guidance suggests that the investments will be within three months of maturity when acquired.]

* Balance Sheet = Statement of financial position (see page 18)

And the really important stuff ... accounting practice

IAS 7 believes all entities should prepare a cash flow statement that analyses the actual cash flows of an entity (i.e. cash in less cash out). The starting point is to learn the format. It takes the cash flows and divides them into three key sections:

- operating activities
- investing activities
- financing activities.

Conclusion

Cash flow statements are a primary accounting statement, i.e. they are as important as the balance sheet* and the income statement. They are common exam questions. If you hate the topic when you first meet it, it is essential to familiarise yourself with it – with practice you will love this topic – honest!!

IAS 8 – Accounting policies, changes in accounting estimates and errors

Introduction

> "Old accountants never die ... they simply lose their balance!"
>
> Traditional

The use of accounting policy is an important issue because accounting is not actually the science that it can be mistaken for. For example, in the telecoms industry, how should we account for the salary of a cable technician? It may initially seem very clear – if an employee's salary is not a direct cost, to be expensed in the income statement, then what is it? The telecoms industry would argue that it depends on what he is spending his time on – if he is repairing an old network, he is an expense but if he is working on a new one – which will accrue revenues in future periods – it could be argued to capitalise his salary (put it on the balance sheet* as an asset) so it will be 'matched' via a depreciation expense to the future periods that will benefit from the revenue.

Rules v principles

All companies have to decide which accounting policies they are planning to adopt. There is a difference of opinion on how accounting standards should work. One view is that they should be rules-based – this is the US GAAP approach. IAS takes the principles-based approach.

It is a bit like when you were a teenager going out for the first time. Your parents could give you a list of rules – things you must not do, e.g. 'do not be home later than 1.00pm, do not get split up from your friends, do not have more than two drinks' etc. Or maybe your parents took a principles-based approach – 'Be good'!! – a catch all. This is the approach that IAS 8 is trying to take.

---

* Balance Sheet = Statement of financial position (see page 18)

So ... what's it trying to achieve?

IAS 8 prescribes the criteria for selecting and changing accounting policies, together with the accounting treatments for changes in accounting policy and the correction of errors.

Transactional example

D W Swallow Inc noted in 20X6 that in 20X5 it had omitted to record a depreciation expense on an asset amounting to $60,000. Its accounts, before the correction of errors, looked like this:

	20X6	20X5
	$	*$*
Gross profit	*600,000*	*690,000*
Distribution costs	*(60,000)*	*(60,000)*
Administrative expenses	*(180,000)*	*(180,000)*
Depreciation	*(60,000)*	*nil*
Profit from operations	*300,000*	*450,000*
Income tax	*(60,000)*	*(90,000)*
Net profit	*240,000*	*360,000*

Swallow's retained earnings for the two years before the correction of errors are:

	20X6	20X5
	$	$
Retained earnings c/fwd	690,000	450,000
Retained earnings b/fwd	450,000	90,000

IAS 8 (revised) states that the correction of an error that relates to prior periods should be shown as an adjustment to the opening balance of retained earnings.

In the 20X6 accounts (ignoring all tax implications):

Dr Retained earnings b/fwd $60,000
Cr Accumulated depreciation $60,000

i.e. this will have no impact on the current year income statement but is shown as a prior period adjustment in the statement of changes in equity:

	20X6
	$
Retained earnings b/fwd as reported previously	450,000
Prior period adjustment to correct error	(60,000)
Retained earnings, beginning, as restated	390,000
Net profit	240,000
Retained earnings c/fwd	630,000

Comparative information should be restated unless it is 'impracticable' to do so.

The income statement will be presented thus:

	20X6	20X5 (restated)
	$	$
Gross profit	600,000	690,000
Distribution costs	(60,000)	(60,000)
Administrative expenses	(180,000)	(180,000)
Depreciation	(60,000)	(60,000)
Operating profit	300,000	390,000
Income tax	(60,000)	(90,000)
Net profit	240,000	300,000

The statement of changes in equity will also need comparators:

	20X6	20X5 (restated)
	$	$
Retained earnings b/fwd as reported previously	450,000	90,000
Prior period adjustment to correct error	(60,000)	
Retained earnings, beginning, as restated	390,000	90,000
Net profit	240,000	300,000
Retained earnings c/fwd	630,000	390,000

* Balance Sheet = Statement of financial position (see page 18)

Sorry but you need to know ... DEFINITIONS

Accounting policies are the specific principles, bases, conventions, rules and practices applied by an entity in preparing and presenting financial statements.

Prior period errors are omissions from, and misstatements in, the entity's financial statements for one or more periods arising from a failure to use, or misuse of, reliable information. The errors must be ones that were reasonably identifiable when the financial statements were authorised for issue.

And the really important stuff ... accounting practice

Accounting policies selected should be in accordance with International Accounting Standards or interpretations. If no standard is applicable, policies should be selected in accordance with:

- relevance
- reliability
- faithful representation
- substance over form
- neutrality
- prudence
- completeness.

(i.e. be good!!)

Changes and corrections

Right from the start of your studies you will have seen examples where companies have maybe made errors or need to change accounting policies or estimates. You need to be able to handle this.

Changes in accounting policy arise if required by a new standard, or because the new policy is more relevant and reliable. It is not a change in policy if a new policy is applied to a transaction different in substance to those undertaken previously, or a new policy is applied to a new type of transaction.

Changes in **accounting policy** should be applied **retrospectively** unless it is impracticable to do so. This would be very rare. Significant disclosures are required about the change in policy.

Retrospectively – change everything, pretend that the new policy had always been applied.

Changes in **accounting estimates** should be applied **prospectively.** A change in estimate is not a change of policy and occurs if new information becomes available that was not previously known. As a result they also cannot be treated as errors.

Prospectively – apply new policy, but do not restate the financial statements of a prior period.

Correction of **material prior period** errors should be accounted for **retrospectively** unless it is impracticable to do so. Significant disclosures are required if an error occurred.

 Students often get confused between identifying whether a change is a change in an accounting policy, or a change in an accounting estimate. If we are told that a company changes its method of valuation of inventory from weighted average method to 'first – in first out' (FIFO) method, this is a clear example of needing to account for this as a change in accounting policy with the accounting being performed retrospectively. This normally goes well for most students.

However, when we are told that a company changes the useful life of an asset from 10 years to 8 years, then often this is mistaken for a change in accounting policy. In fact the company's accounting policy has NOT changed – the policy was and still is to depreciate the asset over its useful economic life. What we have here is a change in accounting estimate which needs to be accounted for prospectively.

Remember, in accordance with the principle of consistency, an entity should apply the same accounting policy from one period to the next unless:

- the change is required by a standard or interpretation; or
- if the change will result in the financial statements providing reliable and more relevant information about the effects of transactions, other events or conditions on the entity's financial position, financial performance or cash flows.

Common examples of changes in accounting policy

- Changes in legistation.
- A new accounting standard.
- A change from measuring a class of assets at depreciated historical cost to a policy of regular revaluation.
- Changing from writing off to capitalising interest relating to the construction of non-current assets.
- Changing revenue recognition practices regarding the sale of goods and services.
- Changing inventory valuation from weighted average to FIFO.
- Changing the way in which an item is presented in the accounts, i.e. classifying depreciation expenses as cost of sales instead of administrative would also be a change of accounting policy.

---

* Balance Sheet = Statement of financial position (see page 18)

Common examples of accounting estimates

- Bad debts.
- Inventory obsolescence.
- Provision for warranty obligations.
- Useful lives of property, plant and equipment.
- Fair values of financial assets and liabilities.

Changes in accounting policies

Changes in accounting estimates

Apply retrospectively

Apply prospectively

Common examples
A REAL

Common examples
PUB

 A REAL

- **A** Asset measurement changed from depreciated historic cost to revaluation
- **R** Revenue recognition policy is changed
- **E** Expenses reclassified from cost of sales to administrative
- **A** A new accounting standard forces change
- **L** Legislation changes.

 PUB

- **P** Provisions for warranty obligations
- **U** Useful lives of property, plant and equipment
- **B** Bad debts.

Disclosures

When a company has made a material change to an accounting policy in preparing its current financial statements, the following disclosures are required by IAS 8:

- the reasons for the change
- the amount of the adjustment in the current period and in comparative information for prior periods.

Conclusion

IAS 8 is never going to be a 'deal-breaker' when it comes to answering exam questions. It is, however, fundamental to the real world. An understanding of the importance of a company's choice of accounting policies is also key to good performance in ratio analysis/interpretation of accounts questions.

* Balance Sheet = Statement of financial position (see page 18)

6 IAS 10 – Events after the reporting period

Introduction

> "Do not seek to have events happen as you want them to, but instead want them to happen as they do happen, and your life will go well."
>
> Epictetus, Greek Philosopher (ad55–135)

Unfortunately events happen. As you chose to be an accountant rather than a philosopher like Epictetus, you will have to be able to account for such events, not just talk about it! As we know from IAS 1, companies are required to prepare a balance sheet* as at an agreed date. The end of the reporting period is the point at which the financial position of a company is determined and reported. Of course, we will not be able to actually prepare the balance sheet* on the reporting period date as we will not have all the information available. Companies in fact have six months grace on filing their accounts.

Ahh ... stuff happens!

Yes, stuff happens. This means that decisions have to be made with regard to such stuff that we know about due to the time lag – but actually occurred – or at least we found out about them after the reporting period. This guidance is what IAS 10 is all about.

So ... what's it trying to achieve?

IAS 10 explains the duties of companies and directors in looking for and adjusting for events after the reporting period.

When events occur after the reporting period but before the date that the financial statements are authorised, we need to know what we should do about them when we prepare the accounts. The question is should we adjust the accounts, or simply give a disclosure in the notes to the accounts?

In order to make that decision, we need to know whether we have just been made aware of a condition that actually existed at the reporting period (in which case we will be required to adjust the accounts) or have we just been made aware of a condition that arose after the reporting period (in which case we will only be required to give disclosure).

Transactional example

KPB Corp applies IAS 2 and includes its inventory at the end of the reporting period at the lower of cost and net realisable value. It prepares its accounts as at 31 December and as at 31 December 20X5 performed a stock take and itemised and valued its inventory at $20million.

In January 20X6 nothing at all was sold. On 5 February KPB Corp was made an offer by its competitor Mog Corp to take the whole of their inventory for a total price of $12 million. Owing to cash flow pressure, KPB agreed. You are responsible for preparing the accounts which are due to be authorised on 15 February. Do you adjust the inventory down to $12 million as an adjusting event or leave it in the accounts at $20 million and give a disclosure note?

This is a classic example of an **adjusting event** – the sale of inventory at a price substantially lower than its cost after the date of the reporting period confirms its net realisable value at the end of the reporting period.

Transactional example

KPB Corp also acquired a new administration building during 20X5 at a cost of $40 million. At 31 December 20X5 the net book value of the building was $39 million. On 10 February 20X6 (again before the accounts were authorised on 15 February) the building was destroyed by fire due to the negligence of a director who was found drunk by the fire brigade having made a bonfire in a waste paper bin. The insurance company has indicated that this will invalidate any insurance claims.

* Balance Sheet = Statement of financial position (see page 18)

This is a classic **non-adjusting event**, as at the end of the reporting period you had a building. It stays on the balance sheet* and you disclose the details and financial effect of the event in the footnotes ... unless the going concern concept is now undermined – see below.

 A common mistake with IAS 10 issues is to believe that when you are attempting a trial balance question all the supporting information must give rise to an adjustment. This is not true as sometimes if the information provided relates to a non-adjusting event. It needs a disclosure in the notes – not an adjustment in the accounts.

Going concern considerations

IAS 10 requires that an entity should not prepare its financial statements on a going concern basis if management determines after the reporting period that it intends to liquidate the entity or cease trading. In which case the balance sheet* would need to be presented on a non-going concern basis.

 Sorry but you need to know ... DEFINITIONS

 Events after the reporting period are events, both favourable and unfavourable, that occur between the reporting period and the date of approval of the accounts.

 Adjusting events are post-balance sheet* events which provide additional evidence of conditions existing at the end of the reporting period.

 Non-adjusting events are post-balance sheet* events which concern conditions not existing at the end of the reporting period.

And the really important stuff ... accounting practice

The financial statements should be changed to include events after the reporting period if they are adjusting events.

The financial statements should disclose the event in the notes if they are material non-adjusting events after the reporting period.

Dividends declared after the reporting period (and therefore not an obligation at the reporting period) are treated as non-adjusting events.

The going concern basis should not be followed if management determines that, after the reporting period, the company intends to liquidate, or has no realistic alternative but to do so.

Disclosures

The disclosures required from events disclosed in the notes are:

- the nature of the event
- an estimate of the financial effect, or a statement that it is not possible to estimate the financial effect.

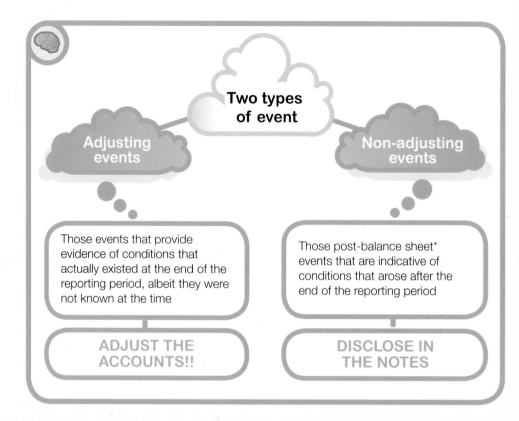

Conclusion

IAS 10 is a commonly examined standard. Once you are familiar with it, you should be pleased to see it featured in any accountancy exam!!

---

* Balance Sheet = Statement of financial position (see page 18)

IAS 16 – Property, plant and equipment

Introduction

> "No man acquires property without acquiring with it a little arithmetic also."
>
> Ralph Waldo Emerson (1803-1882)

Accounting for property, plant and equipment is a very important issue. We have accepted that the accruals concept is 'bedrock' when it comes to preparing financial statements. Clearly if a company purchases a property or any equipment, this will involve a large chunk of cash. It would be wrong to show this as an expense immediately in the income statement of the year they bought it. The equipment is going to be of use for a long period of time; hitting earnings only in the year of purchase will fail to give a correct picture. Earnings would look terrible in the year of purchase, but then particularly good for all the remaining years in which you generate income from the equipment with no expense being reflected.

And so it has passed into legend that the big chunk of cash spent on property, plant and equipment should not be immediately expensed but instead should be capitalised – put on the balance sheet* initially – with depreciation being the accounting mechanism that, in effect, spreads the cost of a capitalised purchase over the useful economic life of the asset. The big chunk of cash appears on the cash flow statement, the asset appears on the balance sheet*, and a depreciation expense appears on the income statement – simple, what's to worry about?

WorldCom – how the books got cooked

"I falsified financial statements of the company … for the purpose of meeting analyst expectations" – quote from Scott Sullivan, former Chief Financial Officer of WorldCom. This was said to the federal court when he testified against his former boss, the WorldCom Chief Executive Officer and President.

One of the scams that WorldCom used was simply a ploy of taking some expenses that should have gone to the income statement but instead putting them as property, plant and equipment on the balance sheet*. Not surprisingly this meant that they were able to deliver earnings at the level expected by the market. WorldCom admitted having used this ploy to the tune of $3.8 billion!!! IAS 16 deals with the issue by being clear that an item of property, plant and equipment should be recognised as an asset *if and only if* it is probable that future economic benefits associated with the asset will flow to the entity and the cost of the item can be measured reliably.

So ... what's it trying to achieve?

IAS 16 prescribes the accounting treatments for property, plant and equipment where the principal issues are the recognition of assets, the determination of their carrying value and the depreciation and impairment charges recognised in relation to them.

Transactional example

Slaney Inc owns equipment with an original cost of $400,000. It was determined on acquisition that the equipment had a useful economic life of 10 years and the residual value was expected to be $40,000. The equipment is now 8 years old.

Each period that benefits from the equipment will be charged with an expense in the form of depreciation. The formula is:

$$\frac{\text{Cost} - \text{Residual value}}{\text{Expected useful life}}$$

($400,000 – $40,000)/10 years = $36,000 each year.

> Dr Income statement – depreciation expense
> Cr Accumulated depreciation

The carrying value of the asset in this year's balance sheet* is:

	$
Original cost	*$400,000*
Less:	
Accumulated depreciation	
(8 x $36,000)	*($288,000)*
Net Book Value	*$112,000*

---

* Balance Sheet = Statement of financial position (see page 18)

A common error made by students is to muddle the accumulated depreciation account with the current year depreciation expense. The accumulated depreciation should NOT appear in the income statement!! – it is the accumulated depreciation to date which is then shown netted against cost in the balance sheet*. The income statement should just show the current year (one year) effect of depreciation.

Sorry but you need to know ... DEFINITIONS

Property, plant and equipment are tangible assets that:

- are held for use in the production or supply of goods and services, for rental to others, or for administrative purposes; and
- are expected to be used during more than one period.

Carrying amount is the amount at which an asset is recognised after deducting any accumulated depreciation and accumulated impairment losses.

Depreciation is the systematic allocation of the depreciable amount (cost or valuation less residual value) of an asset over its useful economic life.

Residual value is the estimated amount that an entity would currently obtain from the disposal of the asset, after deducting the estimated costs of disposal, if the asset were already of the age and in the condition expected at the end of its useful economic life.

Fair value is the amount for which an asset could be exchanged between knowledgeable, willing parties in an arm's length transaction.

And the really important stuff ... accounting practice

Initial recognition and measurement of assets

The cost of an item of property, plant and equipment should only be recognised when its probable future economic benefits will flow to the enterprise, and the cost can be measured reliably. (Remember the definition of an asset from the Framework.)

Assets should initially be measured at cost. Costs include the directly attributable costs incurred in bringing the asset into working condition for its intended use.

Transactional example

Alfie, a sales tax registered trader, purchased a computer for use in his business. The invoice for the computer:

- *Computer*   *$ 890*
- *Additional memory*   *$ 95*
- *Delivery*   *$ 10*
- *Installation*   *$ 20*
- *Maintenance (1 year)*   *$ 25*
- *Sales tax*   *$ 182*

How much should Alfie capitalise as a non-current asset in relation to the purchase?

The cost of the computer is a basic $890. However, Alfie can capitalise the directly attributable costs – the additional memory, the delivery and installation costs. Alfie cannot capitalise the maintenance costs or the sales tax. The non-current asset in relation to the purchase would be $890 + 95 + 10 + 20 = $1,015.

Subsequent expenditure should be capitalised if the expenditure meets the criteria for initial recognition. For example, a replacement of a major part of an asset must be capitalised and the old part being replaced should be derecognised.

Subsequent measurement of assets

Companies can adopt a policy of revaluing assets if they wish. If they revalue assets the carrying amount should approximate to the fair value at the reporting period.

If companies choose to revalue assets they must:

- revalue the full class of asset
- revalue sufficiently often that the asset is retained at an up-to-date value on the balance sheet*.

Note that gains on revaluation should be recognised in the revaluation reserve and losses on revaluation are treated consistently with impairments in value (IAS 36).

---

* Balance Sheet = Statement of financial position (see page 18)

Transactional example

Andrew Inc, which makes up its accounts to 31 December each year, buys an asset on 1 January 20X1 for $10,000. The asset has an estimated useful economic life of ten years with no residual value. Therefore, straight-line depreciation will be $1,000pa and, on 31 December 20X2, the asset will be included in the balance sheet* as follows:

	$
Non-current asset at cost	*10,000*
Accumulated depreciation	*(2,000)*
	8,000

On 1 January 20X3, Andrew revalues the asset to $16,000. The total useful economic life remains at ten years from 1 January 20X1.

Required:

(a) Show the journal to record the revaluation.

(b) Show the journal to record the revised depreciation charge and reserves transfer.

(c) Andrew sells the asset on 1 January 20X4 for $15,000. Show how the disposal is recorded.

It is very important that we can account for all three aspects; the initial revaluation will be as follows:

(a) The revaluation will be recorded by.

1 January 20X3

	$	$
Dr Non-current assets cost/valuation	6,000	
Dr Accumulated depreciation	2,000	
Cr Revaluation reserve		8,000

(b) Equally key is that we can record the annual depreciation as at   31 December 20X3 and in subsequent years

	$	$
Dr Depreciation expense (income statement)	2,000	
Cr Accumulated depreciation		2,000
Dr Revaluation reserve	1,000	
Cr Retained earnings		1,000

Note: A common pitfall is to forget the reserve transfer. The revaluation reserve doesn't sit on the balance sheet* in perpetuity; it gets written out over the useful economic life by a transfer to retained earnings. This way, when the asset is fully depreciated, the revaluation reserve should be written down to zero too.

(c) If we sell a revalued asset we need to be able to deal with that too. The profit on disposal in the profit and loss account for the year will be:

	$
Proceeds	15,000
Less: Net Book Value (16,000 – 2,000)	(14,000)
PROFIT ON DISPOSAL	1,000

The remaining balance on revaluation reserve is transferred to retained earnings as a reserve transfer:

	Revaluation reserve $	Retained earnings $
Transfer of realised profits	(7,000)	7,000

Depreciation of assets

The depreciable amount of a fixed asset (other than freehold land) should be allocated on a systematic basis over its useful economic life in a manner that reflects the consumption of economic benefits.

The residual value of assets should be reviewed each year end and based on year-end price levels.

A change in the method of depreciation is only allowed on the grounds of truth and fairness and does not constitute a change of accounting policy.

The depreciation rate should be reviewed at the end of each reporting period.

---

* Balance Sheet = Statement of financial position (see page 18)

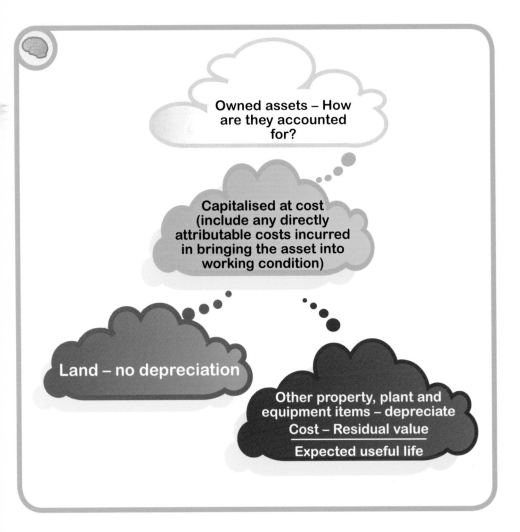

Disclosures

Very extensive disclosures exist for fixed assets.

Revaluations

- The effective date of the revaluation.
- Whether an independent valuer was used.
- The methods and principal assumptions in estimating fair value.
- The extent to which fair value is based on active market prices.
- The historical cost equivalent values of fixed assets.
- The revaluation surplus and change for the period.

Fixed assets and depreciation

- The depreciation methods used.
- The useful economic lives or the depreciation rates used.
- Where material, the effect of a change of depreciation rate or method during the period.
- The cost or revalued amount of the class of tangible fixed assets at the beginning and end of the period.
- The cumulative depreciation at the beginning and end of the reporting period.
- A reconciliation of the movements in fixed assets.
- Restrictions on title to assets.
- Expenditure on assets in the course of construction.
- Capital commitments.
- Impairment losses (if not separated on the face of the income statement).

Conclusion

It is key that we have an accounting standard on property, plant and equipment, because without one we do have a very easy way for profit to be manipulated. IAS 16 provides such a standard.

* Balance Sheet = Statement of financial position (see page 18)

IAS 18 – Revenue

Introduction

> "Corporate accounting does not do violence
> to the truth occasionally and trivially, but
> comprehensively, systematically, and universally,
> annually and perennially."
>
> R J Chambers (1917-1999)

These are harsh words indeed for accountants to read. However revenue manipulation is one of the most common ways of creative accounting ... indeed, if a couple of US cases are anything to go by, some company employees consider faking sales figures a bit of fun. Staff at one software vendor filmed an in-house skit about how they inflated revenue. Employees of a swimwear manufacturer allegedly ran a sweepstake on how long they would have to keep the quarter open to meet sales targets. This was before they were forced into serious reinstatements after their improper accounting practices came to light.

Revenue recognition is an important underlying issue which will be vital at all stages of your studies. We need an accounting standard on revenue recognition because of the tendency for revenue manipulation. All accountancy students need to be completely clear when revenue can be recognised and that 'revenue' is not the same as 'gains'. Revenue arises from a company's ordinary trading activities. Gains will include one-offs such as profit on disposal of property or other non-current assets or on retranslating balances in foreign currencies – these gains are not revenue.

Revenue can take various forms, commonly the sale of goods or provision of a service but also could be other forms such as royalty fees, franchise fees, management fees, subscriptions and so on.

Plenty of hanky panky here!

The two scandals referred to above relate to the 1990s. However it didn't end there. Many of the recent accounting scandals have allegedly been the result of companies recognising revenue based on inappropriate accounting policies. In 2002 a complaint was made by the Securities and Exchange Commission (SEC) in the US alleging that Xerox deceived the public between 1997 and 2000, by using several 'accounting manoeuvres', the most significant involving recording revenue in the period a lease contract was signed, instead of spreading it over the length of the contract. The SEC charged that the accounting irregularities increased fiscal year 1997 pre-tax earnings by $405 million, 1998 pre-tax earnings by $655 million, and 1999 pre-tax earnings by $511 million. Interestingly it happened that in each quarter of the year earnings were inflated just enough to exceed the expectations of the market. (The importance of standards in accounting for revenue has to be recognised by students at all levels).

So ... what's it trying to achieve?

IAS 18 identifies the criteria that need to be met in order to recognise revenue and also the method that should be used to measure the revenue. It addition it provides some practical examples and guidance to help in the application of the standard.

 ### Transactional example

AJF(sg) Inc has a year end of 31 March. It purchased goods costing $5,000 on 8 March 2006. It sells and delivers the items for $8,000 on 14 March. The contract however is one of 'sale or return', with the customer being allowed a 20-day period for approval. At 31 March the delivery has not been formally accepted by the buyer.

IAS 18 states that, if there is uncertainty about the possibility of return, revenue is recognised when the goods have been delivered and the period of time for rejection has expired.

Therefore in this case revenue of $8,000 will not be recognised in the year to 31 March as the conditions for its recognition are not met. The $5,000 spent on goods does qualify to be recognised as an asset as it gives the rights to future economic benefits. The $5,000 is therefore recognised as an asset – inventory.

* Balance Sheet = Statement of financial position (see page 18)

A typical error made by students is just to take the revenue figure from the trial balance to the income statement, without noticing that the supporting information is telling them that some sales included in revenue were made on a sale-or-return basis. Remember to exclude the transaction from both revenue and receivables and instead treat the cost of the goods as inventory.

Sorry but you need to know ... DEFINITIONS

Revenue is the gross inflow of economic benefits during the period arising in the course of the ordinary activities of an enterprise when those inflows result in increases in equity, other than increases relating to contributions from equity participants.

Fair value is the amount for which an asset could be exchanged between knowledgeable, willing parties in an arm's length transaction.

And the really important stuff ... accounting practice

Measurement

Revenue should be measured at the fair value of the consideration received or receivable.

If revenue is deferred it should be measured at present value.

In a barter transaction the revenue should be the fair value of the goods received and, only if unreliable, the fair value of the goods given up.

Recognition

Revenue is recognised for the sale of goods when a number of criteria are met:

(a) the enterprise has transferred to the buyer the significant risks and rewards of ownership of the goods

(b) the enterprise retains neither continuing managerial involvement to the degree normally associated with ownership nor effective control over the goods sold

(c) the amount of revenue can be measured reliably

(d) it is probable that the economic benefits associated with the transaction will flow to the enterprise; and

(e) the costs incurred or to be incurred in respect of the transaction can be measured reliably.

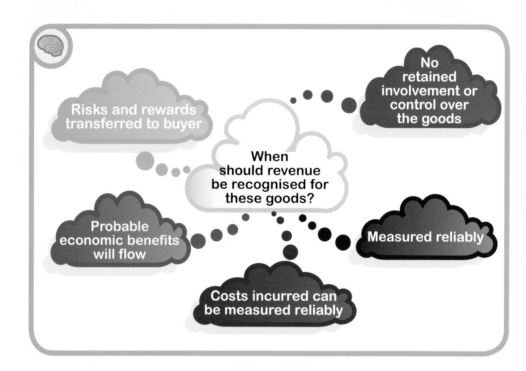

Revenue from services should be recognised over the period of service provided the following criteria are met:

(a) the amount of revenue can be measured reliably

(b) it is probable that the economic benefits associated with the transaction will flow to the enterprise

(c) the stage of completion of the transaction at the reporting period can be measured reliably; and

(d) the costs incurred for the transaction and the costs to complete the transaction can be measured reliably.

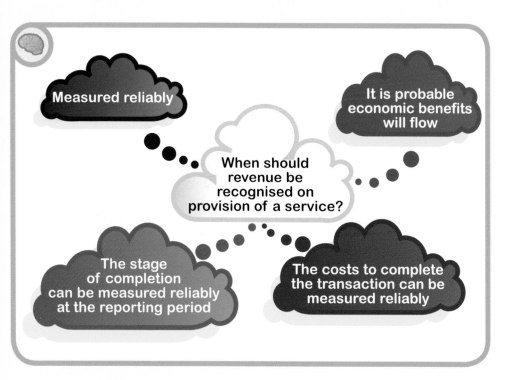

Revenue from interest, dividends and royalties should be recognised as follows:

Interest   Time proportion basis reflecting the effective yield on the asset

Royalties   Accruals basis

Dividends   Right to receive payment is established

Conclusion

It really is vital that the point of recognition of revenue is properly determined. There are multiple possibilities even for a simple transaction such as the sale of an item (sale of goods). Is it revenue when the customer places an order? Is it revenue when you ship the goods to the customer? Is it revenue when the customer receives the goods? Is it revenue when the customer pays? The decision made about when and how revenues are recognised will have a direct impact on the income statement and is therefore a major 'hotspot' in determining a company's 'earnings'. Students will need to understand and recognise the importance of this issue right from the early days of preparation of financial statements.

IAS 37 – Provisions, contingent assets and contingent liabilities

Introduction

> "How many accountants does it take to change a light bulb? … What kind of answer did you have in mind?"
>
> Traditional

An old joke maybe but with a serious undertone. Traditionally there were no rules with regard to accounting for provisions and contingencies. However accountants were taught that, under the prudence concept, revenue and profits are not anticipated but provision is made for all known liabilities and expected losses. This concept on the face of it seems difficult to argue against. However, accountants managed to use this concept as one of the most powerful weapons in the manipulation of profit.

Ideally companies like to present a pattern of 'earnings' showing that in this period the company actually did a little bit better than in the previous period. This gives the impression of 'quality earnings', i.e. that management is doing a great job and deserves a nice bonus. Companies are therefore reluctant to show they have had an exceptionally good period because traditionally the market will then expect them to deliver the same (plus a bit more!!) in the next.

Instead of reporting such profits it became quite normal for companies to start to foresee 'future costs'. Under the guise of 'prudence,' they were able to 'slush' these excess profits on the balance sheet* using a general provision. These non-specific provisions, often referred to as 'big bath' provisions, are now outlawed by IAS 37.

Once these 'big bath' provisions had been created on the balance sheet*, companies would use them to create endless periods of 'good news'. Instead of starting income statements at the top with revenue and deducting costs to calculate profit, it was possible to decide from the bottom, what you wanted profit to be. By releasing some of the provision it was easy to directly manipulate profit.

* Balance Sheet = Statement of financial position (see page 18)

Unfudgeability??

Maybe what the accounting profession needs is the concept of 'unfudgeability'!!! – a reminder that accounts are meant to fairly report profit as it is, rather than a 'fudged' figure. Well, we haven't got a concept of 'unfudgeability' but we have now got an accounting standard covering provision accounting.

So ... what's it trying to achieve?

IAS 37 aims to ensure that appropriate measurement and recognition criteria are applied to provisions, contingent liabilities and contingent assets, and that sufficient disclosure is made in the financial statements to enable users to understand the provisions made.

 ## Transactional example

Hill Corp is a very diverse group. It prepares its accounts to 31 March 20X6. You are responsible for preparing the accounts to 31 March 20X6. Certain events have occurred which need to be considered as possibly giving rise to the need for a provision or a disclosure in the notes:

On 12 February 20X6 the board of Hill Corp decided to close down a large factory in Aylesbury. The board is planning to transfer the production to other factories. A detailed formal plan has been drawn up and it is expected that the closure will occur on 31 August 20X6. Letters were sent out to customers, suppliers and workers soon after 12th February. The employees and any other interested parties have been invited to meetings to discuss the features of the formal plan. The overall costs of this closure are foreseen as $79 million.

In order for Hill to provide for these costs, all of the following conditions must be met:

(a) it has it a present obligation (either legal or constructive) arising as a result of past events

(b) it is probable that a transfer of economic benefits will be required to settle the obligation; and

(c) the obligation can be measured reliably.

Here Hill can provide for the $79 million because, although it does not have a legal obligation to close down this factory, it will have raised a 'constructive obligation'. A constructive obligation arises when a valid expectation is raised in third parties, i.e. the formal plan has been communicated to interested parties. We do have a probable transfer of economic benefit (it is 'more likely than not' that Hill will pay the closure costs) and an estimate of $79 million is made. Provision for these costs should be made on the balance sheet*.

Transactional example

One of Hill Corp's most profitable products is the 'Sophie Beauty' range. However, it has recently come to light that a new brand of face cream was produced with an inappropriately high lead content. Although recalled, one customer has started legal proceedings against the company claiming the product is responsible for a recent skin complaint. The company's lawyers have advised that the chances of this action succeeding are possible with damages being awarded of around $30,000.

This time Hill cannot provide for the $30,000. Again, when we look at the conditions, we can see that we have only a possible, rather than a probable, transfer of economic benefits. This, however, would require disclosure in the notes to the accounts as a possible contingent liability.

It is a common problem with trial balance type questions for students to believe that all additional information gives rise to an adjustment in the accounts. This is not actually the case – some like this give rise only to a disclosure.

* Balance Sheet = Statement of financial position (see page 18)

Sorry but you need to know ... DEFINITIONS

 A **provision** is a liability of uncertain timing or amount.

A **liability** is a present obligation of an entity to transfer economic benefits as a result of past transactions or events.

A **legal obligation** is an obligation that could:

- be contractual or
- arise due to a legislation or
- result from other operation of law.

 A **constructive obligation** is an obligation that results from an entity's actions where:

- by an established pattern of past practice, published policies, or a sufficiently specific current statement, the entity has indicated to other (third) parties that it will accept certain responsibilities; and
- as a result, the entity has created a valid expectation in the minds of those parties that it will discharge those responsibilities.

 A **contingent liability** is a possible obligation that arises from past events whose outcome is based on uncertain future events or, an obligation that is not recognised because it is not probable, or cannot be measured reliably.

 A **contingent asset** is a possible asset that arises from past events and whose existence will only be confirmed by uncertain future events not wholly within the control of the enterprise.

And the really important stuff ... accounting practice

 Provisions should be recognised when:

(a) an entity has a present obligation (either legal or constructive) arising as a result of past events

(b) it is probable that a transfer of economic benefits will be required to settle the obligation; and

(c) the obligation can be measured reliably.

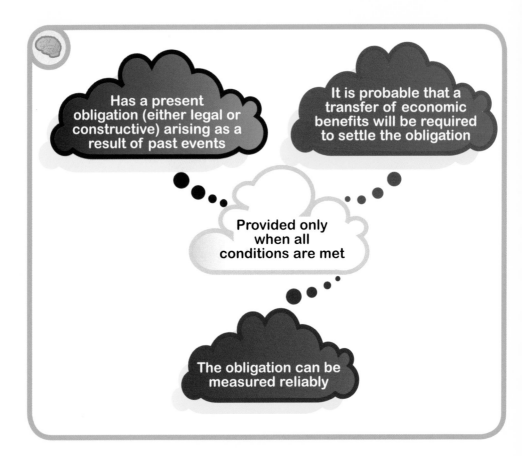

 When deciding if a provision should be recognised, an entity should determine whether the future expenditure can be avoided. If the future expenditure can be avoided no provision should be made.

If material to the amount of the provision, provisions should be discounted.

Contingent liabilities should not be recognised in the financial statements, however disclosure should be made unless the possibility of the transfer of economic benefits is remote.

Contingent assets should not be recognised, and disclosure is only allowed if the possible profit is considered probable. Virtually certain profits could be recognised in the financial statements.

* Balance Sheet = Statement of financial position (see page 18)

The requirements in relation to contingent assets and liabilities are summarised in the following table:

Degree of probability	Liability of uncertain timing or amount	Asset of uncertain timing or amount
Virtually certain (therefore not contingent)	Make provision	Recognise (receivable)
Probable	Make provision	Disclose by note (contingent asset)
Possible	Disclose by note (contingent liability)	No disclosure
Remote	No disclosure	No disclosure

> **Note**
>
> *When there is the possibility of the recovery from a third party of all or part of a contingent liability, this must be treated as a separate matter, and a contingent asset is only recognised if its receipt is virtually certain, as shown in the table.*

Disclosure

Key disclosures include:

- the movements in all classes of provision over the period
- the nature of the provision and any uncertainties and assumptions used in recognising and measuring it
- for contingent liabilities, the nature of the liability, the uncertainties surrounding it and the possible financial effect.

Conclusion

Traditionally it wasn't thought necessary to have a standard on provisions. The reason why you have to learn this one is because of what accountants have done in terms of manipulation of financial statements!

(10) IAS 38 – Intangible assets

Introduction

> "Intangible asset? – Well it's an asset you can't kick isn't it?"
>
> Anon

All successful companies will have assets that we traditionally class as intangible, i.e. without physical substance. The most common one is goodwill – the difference between the value of a business as a whole and the aggregate of the fair value of its separable net assets. When you agree a price for a business you are prepared to pay more than the value of the assets because you are acquiring other stuff:

- an established list of customers
- an experienced workforce
- strategic location
- reputation
- good labour relations, etc.

These items and others can contribute to, or influence, the value of goodwill.

Err ... but purchased goodwill is not covered by IAS 38!! Why are we discussing it?

Exactly – one of the most common mistakes students make when asked about intangibles is to talk about purchased goodwill in their answer. Well yes, purchased goodwill is an intangible asset and yes, the title of IAS 38 is 'intangible assets', but the issue of purchased goodwill is actually covered by IFRS 3 – doh!! Please do not pick it to discuss when you are asked about IAS 38.

---

* Balance Sheet = Statement of financial position (see page 18)

So ... what sort of transactions could you discuss?

You could talk about internally generated goodwill – in essence it's the same as purchased goodwill, the difference between the two being simply that the goodwill is not actually valued, as nobody has bought the company from you. The accounting rule is simple – the standard does not allow you to include internally generated goodwill as an asset on the balance sheet* – period.

Other transactions you could discuss when answering IAS 38 questions would include expenditure incurred on stuff like patents, brands, advertising, training, software, licences, etc. – assets you have purchased without physical substance (things you can't kick!).

So ... what's it trying to achieve?

IAS 38 prescribes the treatment of intangible assets that are not dealt with specifically by other standards. Intangibles can only be recognised if certain criteria are met.

 ## Transactional example

Lockwood Inc, a multinational company, has recently introduced a new razor to its toiletry range. It has decided to hire the services of the famous motorcyclist, turned rock star, Christopher Swallow, to head up its advertising campaign. It is paying $3,000,000 and believes the benefit from this promotion will last for three years. It is planning to spread his fee over the next three years, recognising the rest as an intangible asset.

It will **not** be possible to treat these costs as an asset. The standard is clear – the costs of introducing new products or services such as advertising cannot be included. The costs will have to be expensed immediately.

Sorry but you need to know ... DEFINITIONS

 An **intangible** asset is an identifiable non-monetary asset without physical substance. Assets are identifiable because they are separable, or because they are identifiable through legal or contractual rights.

 Research is original and planned investigation undertaken with the prospect of gaining new scientific knowledge and understanding.

 Development is the application of research findings or other knowledge to a plan or design for the production of new or substantially improved materials, devices, products, processes, systems or services prior to the commencement of commercial production or use.

And the really important stuff ... accounting practice

 Intangibles should be recognised if, and only if, the following criteria are met:

- it is probable that future economic benefits will flow to the enterprise; and
- the cost of the asset can be measured reliably.

It is important to recognise the difference between internally generated intangibles and purchased intangibles.

Internally generated intangible assets

Problems arise with these because of the need as above to identify a probable future economic benefit and to reliably determine its cost. For this reason the standard does not allow internally generated goodwill to go on the balance sheet* as an asset.

The same issue arises if you are being asked about other internally generated intangibles such as internally generated brands, mastheads, publishing titles, customer lists and similar items – you cannot put them on the balance sheet* as an asset.

All internally generated intangibles must be treated as either research or development costs. Costs for assets in the research phase must be charged to the income statement, whilst those in the development phase must be capitalised if certain criteria are met.

* Balance Sheet = Statement of financial position (see page 18)

The criteria for capitalising internally generated intangibles are:

(a) technically feasible (totally)

(b) intention to complete and use or sell the asset (important)

(c) ability to use or sell the asset (always)

(d) existence of a market or demonstration of usefulness of intangible (employ)

(e) availability of technical, financial or other resources to complete the asset (attractive)

(f) measure the cost reliably (men).

Totally important – always employ attractive men!!

Purchased intangible assets

For purchased intangibles the probability criterion is always met and therefore they are recognised on the balance sheet*, albeit subject to an impairment review.

For intangibles acquired in a business combination there is an assumption that the probability criterion is met, and there is always information to measure the cost separately from goodwill. This means the following sorts of intangibles (plus others) must be recognised separately from goodwill:

- customer lists
- in-progress R&D
- employment contracts below market rate
- order or production backlogs.

Intangible assets should be amortised over their useful economic lives. If no amortisation is charged because the life is indefinite, the asset must be subject to an annual impairment review.

Intangibles can be revalued only if an active market exists for the asset (very rare).

Disclosures

The following are key disclosures for intangibles:

- useful lives and amortisation rates
- amortisation methods
- the line items of the income statement where amortisation is included
- reconciliation of the movement in intangibles over the year
- commitments for the purchase of intangibles.

Conclusion

It is necessary to have an accounting standard on intangibles. Without one we had situations such as the 1988 accounts of Rank Hovis McDougall, a UK company. They decided back in 1988 to bring more than 50 of their internally developed brand names such as 'Hovis' (the bread) onto the balance sheet*. The company came up with the figure of £678 million and, hey presto, increased net asset value per share from 83p to 272p. Although other UK companies had purchased brand names and capitalised them on the balance sheet*, this was the start of a new trend – capitalising internally generated brands. There was no accounting standard at the time to prevent such a practice. IAS 38 now provides such a standard.

* Balance Sheet = Statement of financial position (see page 18)

More advanced

"The only thing more expensive than
education is ignorance"

Benjamin Franklin (1706-1790)

Introduction

You mean there's more? – for the more advanced student – yes!! As you get further into your accountancy studies, you find that companies get involved in more complex transactions. Instead of just buying assets they may lease them, instead of building a client a garden wall, they build the new national football stadium. There are twelve 'green' standards that deal with these more advanced but still relatively common transactions:

- IAS 11 Construction contracts
- IAS 12 Income taxes
- IAS 17 Leases
- IAS 20 Accounting for government grants and disclosure of government assistance
- IAS 23 Borrowing costs
- IAS 32 Financial Instruments: presentation
- IAS 33 Earnings per share
- IAS 36 Impairment of assets
- IAS 39 Financial instruments: recognition and measurement
- IAS 40 Investment property
- IFRS 5 Non-current assets held for sale and discontinued operations
- IFRS 7 Financial instruments: disclosures

"Not everything that can be counted counts and not everything that counts can be counted."

Albert Einstein (1879–1955)

> ### Note
>
> *Many books on accounting standards start by giving you the aims and definitions from the standard. This book deliberately does not structure the chapters in that style. Instead the issue is generally explained, with the sort of transactions that the standard relates to being introduced. We do get to the aims and definitions and for those of you who already feel comfortable with the standard, you may like to turn first to the definitions box – re-affirm those and then read the chapter.*

* Balance Sheet = Statement of financial position (see page 18)

IAS 11 – Construction contracts

Introduction

> "The whole difference between construction and creation is this: that a thing constructed can only be loved after it is constructed; but a thing created is loved before it exists."
>
> Charles Dickens (1812-1870)

Accounting for a large construction contract can be problematic. Accounting convention requires that companies prepare accounts on an annual basis. Every year a company has to prepare financial statements that summarise the activity that has taken place. These summaries – the accounting statements – are meant to be useful to the reader of the accounts, who may use them as a basis for an investment decision.

Well that's OK for some companies!!

If the company is one that fits into a normal 'one year's pretty much like another' style of business, then accounts prepared annually should be fairly useful both for establishing a trend of performance, and as a basis for comparison with similar companies. But, and it's a big 'but…' there are many companies whose activities just do not slice up nicely into 12-month chunks. What about companies that undertake large construction contracts?

What's the problem?

If a company is undertaking a large project – say to build a new national football stadium – initially all it will have is costs. The project could take three or four years to complete. Do we think it's helpful to report only costs for years 1, 2 and 3, and only when the project is complete and the first match is played to finally report the company as having made a massive profit? This would not be helpful to the readers of the accounts – all costs in one period and revenues in another. It certainly does not

* Balance Sheet = Statement of financial position (see page 18)

apply our bedrock accruals concept.

The solution?

Companies that are undertaking construction contracts need an accounting standard that deals with their specific circumstances and issues. Sometimes a 'one size fits all' approach is just not going to work, and this is one of those occasions – specific guidance for a specific issue.

So ... what's it trying to achieve?

IAS 11 is trying to provide that guidance by prescribing the accounting treatment for revenue and costs associated with construction contracts. The primary issue is the allocation of revenue and costs into relevant accounting periods.

Transactional example

Michael Inc is part way through a contract to build a new football stadium for Earlswood Town FC at a contracted price of $600 million.

All costs incurred to date are recorded and as Michael Inc invoices Earlswood Town FC for stage payments the progress payments received are also recorded. These are the only records as far as the accounting system is concerned.

The balances are as follows:

Total costs incurred to date $390 million
Total progress payment received $360 million

Michael is preparing accounts for the year ended 31 March 20X7 and has estimated that, at the balance sheet* date, outstanding costs to complete the project will be $90 million. Michael's surveyor has estimated that the sales value of the work completed as at March 20X7 was $440 million.

Michael's accounting policy is to recognise revenue and profits using the work certified to date method – i.e. sales value earned to date compared to the contract price.

How will Michael show this contract in its accounts for the year to 31 March 20X7?

First of all Michael will need to know whether the contract is estimated to make a profit or a loss as expected profits are treated differently to losses. You will need to provide extracts from the accounts and a working paper.

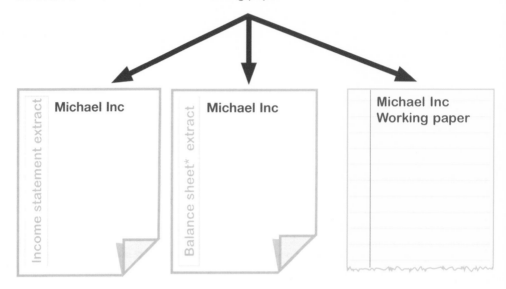

Start with the workings as follows:

(W1) Estimate the outcome

	$m
Contract price	600
Costs to date	(390)
Estimated costs to complete	(90)
Estimated total profit	**120**

Then it needs to estimate the degree of completion, based on its stated policy:

(W2) Estimated stage of completion

	$m
Work certified complete to date/	440/
Contract price	600

As the 440/600 doesn't give us a round percentage but 73.3333%, we are best to use the fraction as the degree of completion in our workings the project is 440/600 complete.

---

* Balance Sheet = Statement of financial position (see page 18)

Therefore profit can be recognised of 120 x 440/600 = $88 million in current year accounts. We will transfer the work certified as complete to revenue. Also we transfer our proportion of total costs (390 + 90) = total costs of $480 x 440/600 = 352 to cost of sales.

Income statement extract

	$m
Sales revenue	440
Cost of sales	(352)
Profit	**88**

We then compare the cash paid out in the form of costs incurred with the amount transferred to cost of sales.

(W3) Cash paid out v cost of sales

	$m
Cash paid out (cost incurred)	390
Cost of sales	(352)
Work in progress (for the balance sheet*)	38

We then compare the sales revenue recognised to the cash received in the form of progress payments.

(W4) Cash received in v sales revenue

	$m
Sales revenue	440
Cash received	(360)
Receivable	80

So the balance sheet* extract will show:

Balance sheet* as at 31 March 20X7 (extract)

	$m
Current assets	
Amounts due re contract work (38 + 80)	118

In the balance sheet* the following balance is recognised:

Costs incurred to date	390
Profit recognised to date (loss) recognised to date	88
Less: Progress billings	(360)
Receivable recoverable on contract, or	
Payable payable on contract	118

 A common mistake is to do the same for a foreseen loss, i.e. only account for proportion. Remember, losses on contracts must be recognised in full as soon as they are foreseen.

 ## Sorry but you need to know ... DEFINITIONS

 A **construction contract** is a contract specifically negotiated for the construction of an asset or a combination of assets that are closely interrelated or interdependent in terms of their design, technology and function or their ultimate purpose or use.

And the really important stuff ... accounting practice

 Revenue and costs on contracts should be recognised over the period of the contract. Profit should also be recognised over the period of the contract as long as it can be assessed with reasonable certainty.

 Losses on contracts must be recognised in full as soon as they are foreseen.

Transactional example-losses

Isaacs is a construction company that prepares its financial statements to 31 March each year. During the year ended 31 March 20X6 the company commenced a contract which it expects to take more than one year to complete. The position on the contract as at 31 March 20X6 is as follows:

	$000
Agreed contract price	1,200
Estimated total cost of contract at commencement	900
Estimated total cost at 31 March 2006	1,250
Agreed value of work completed at 31 March 2006	840
Progress billings invoiced and received at 31 March 2006	880
Contract costs incurred to 31 March 20X6	720

The agreed value of the work completed at 31 March 2006 is considered to be equal to the revenue earned in the year ended 31 March 2006. The percentage of completion is calculated as the agreed value of work completed to the agreed contract price.

What should appear in the income statement and balance sheet* of Isaacs as at 31 March 20X6?

We would need to set up a working paper and estimate the outcome:

(W1) Estimate of the outcome

	$000
Agreed contract price	1,200
Estimated total contract cost	(1,250)
Expected loss	(50)

Note

Because we are expecting a loss instead of bringing in a percentage, we bring in the full loss (remember the Framework document and the need to present 'reliable' information). Losses are therefore easier to account for.

Income statement extract

	$000
Revenue *(value of work completed)*	840
Cost of sales *(balancing figure)*	**(890)**
Loss on contract (W1)	(50)

You have actually spent $720,000 and are also providing for future costs of $170,000 to give you the loss of ($50,000).

For the balance sheet*:

(W2) Cash paid out v cost of sales

	$000
Cash paid out	720
Cost of sales	890
Provision for future costs	(170)

(W3) Cash received in v sales revenue

	$000
Cash received in	880
Sales revenue	(840)
Amount due to customer	(40)

Balance sheet* (extract)

Current liabilities

	$000
Amounts due to customers on construction contract (170 + 40)	210

Estimated stage of completion

Different accounting policies can be used to estimate the percentage completion. The policy used will vary from company to company and therefore exam question to exam question. You will also find variability between a single company with more than one project'

* Balance Sheet = Statement of financial position (see page 18)

If the work certified method is used the percentage completion can be calculated by:

$$\text{Work certified method} = \frac{\text{Work certified to date}}{\text{Contract price}}$$

If the cost method is used the percentage completion can be calculated by:

$$\text{Cost method} = \frac{\text{Cost to date}}{\text{Total contract costs}}$$

The income statement will include:

Turnover	% completion × Contract price
Profit	% completion × Expected profit (or 100% of loss)
Cost of sales	Balancing figure

An image story

Work certified method

An image-story technique works well for remembering these.

Invent a project you have quoted a price to build. Imagine it ¾ built. Now think of the money you are due to get under the contract – that is one way of measuring the degree of completion. The work certified method conjures positive imagery – a building nears completion/loads of money to be earned.

Cost method

The cost method creates more negative imagery – cash going out of your bank whilst you undertake the project.

And under the line even more cash yet to be paid out – a sad face.

If a number of contracts are negotiated together and performed concurrently as a single contract they should be accounted for as a single contract. If an individual contract covers a number of independent assets, each asset should be treated as a single contract.

Fixed cost contract

With respect to a fixed price contract, the outcome can be estimated reliably when:

- total contract revenue can be measured reliably
- it is probable that the economic benefit of the contract will flow to the entity
- both the costs to complete the contract and the stage of completion can be reliably estimated
- the costs attributable to the contract can be clearly identified and measured.

Cost-plus contract

With respect to a cost-plus contract, the outcome can be reliably estimated when:

- it is probable that the economic benefit of the contract will flow to the entity
- the costs attributable to the contract, whether specifically reimbursable or not, can be clearly identified and measured.

Conclusion

IAS 11 is actually a nice easy mark-earning topic if you learn it. Look at your examiner's past questions on construction contracts. Practise a few, learn the approach and hey presto – a favourite topic.

* Balance Sheet = Statement of financial position (see page 18)

(12) IAS 12 – Income taxes

Introduction

> **"In this world nothing can be said to be certain, except death and taxes."**
>
> Benjamin Franklin (1706-1790)

An old quote maybe, but as true today as it was then. Different countries will have different tax rules, and the tax requested may get called by different names such as 'corporation tax' or 'income tax', but at the end of the day if a company makes profit, it will certainly have to pay tax on that profit.

Well, you may ask, companies pay lots of expenses – rent, electricity, telephone. Why is tax so different that it needs an accounting standard? It is true that accounting for the tax of companies could be so easy (maybe it is in a parallel universe!). Imagine a world where the tax rules simply said 'take your calculation of profit from the income statement and multiply it by say 30%' – hey presto, we have a tax expense and the company has a liability to the tax authorities. That however is not our world (and it keeps accountants in work!!).

Why can life never be that simple?

Well it couldn't be could it! For most countries (unfortunately) the way profit is calculated for accounting purposes is not the same as the way profit is calculated for tax purposes. In addition to preparing the income statement down to profit before tax, companies will then need to do a working of their taxable profit. It is this 'taxable profit' that forms the basis of the tax computation commonly known as 'the tax comp'. As accounting profit is different to taxable profit, accounting for tax becomes a subject of two parts: current tax and deferred tax.

Current tax

Current tax is not a problem. Once tax is estimated based on taxable profit (i.e. the tax comp is done) it becomes a current tax liability. It will be debited to the income statement and credited to current liabilities.

Tax rates used to calculate current tax should be those that have been enacted by the balance sheet* date. This will include those 'substantially enacted' by the balance sheet* date.

Deferred tax

This then is the problem child – recognising and dealing with the fact that, because the accounting profit is not the same as taxable profit, there may be future tax consequences based on current period transactions. This is what we call 'deferred tax'.

> ### So ... what's it trying to achieve?
>
> IAS 12 aims to provide guidance on accounting for the current and future tax consequences of the future recovery or settlement of assets and liabilities, and transactions and other events that have occurred in the same period.

Temporary differences

In order to make any sense of IAS 12 we need to look at what happens when we prepare accounts, using the simple approach – only accounting for current tax and ignoring future (deferred) tax consequences.

A company could possibly report an accounting profit of say $200,000 and yet be required to pay no current tax. This is because of temporary differences, which distort the timing of when tax is paid.

The normal effect of temporary differences is to delay when tax is paid (i.e defer) and, as a result there will be a need to provide for a deferred tax liability to ensure that the tax effects of transactions are reported in the same period when they are recognised. This is simply an application of the matching/accruals concept to tax.

---

* Balance Sheet = Statement of financial position (see page 18)

It is possible for temporary differences to accelerate the timing of when tax is paid, in which case, although not as commonly, this will reduce the amount of the deferred tax liability or maybe create a deferred tax asset. It is impossible to understand deferred tax until we understand timing differences. This concept is best understood with the following example.

Transactional example

Let us assume that Tyrrell makes up financial statements to 31 December each year. On 1 January 20X1 the company purchased a piece of equipment for $40,000 that had an anticipated useful economic life of four years but qualified for immediate tax relief of 100% of the cost of the asset. For the year ending 31 December 20X1 the draft accounts of the company showed a profit before tax of $100,000. The directors anticipate that this level of profit will be maintained for the foreseeable future. Tyrrell pays tax at a rate of 30%.

Apart from the differences caused by the purchase of the non-current asset in 20X0 there are no other differences between accounting profit and taxable profit of the tax base and net book value of net assets.

This example illustrates the key issue – the common major difference between accounting profit and taxable profit relates to the difference in treatment of non-current assets. We, as accountants, will spread the cost of the asset over four years' income statements. This is an application of the matching concept – the equipment has a useful economic life of four years and we will depreciate the asset over that period. Most tax jurisdictions, however, do not accept the depreciation expense as part of the calculation of taxable profit. Instead the tax authorities allow companies a tax allowance when they purchase non-current assets.

The tax comp will usually involve taking accounting profit and adding back the depreciation expense. We can then deduct the tax allowance to get taxable profit. This forms the basis of the tax calculation. If we account for current tax based on this calculation but ignore the deferred tax, we will seriously misstate the accounts, particularly in the year we purchase a non-current asset.

Based on the example of Tyrrell above assume you are the accountant preparing the income statement for the year ended 31 December 20X1, and that you have no knowledge or understanding of deferred tax.

Tyrrell – Income statement (extract) for the year ended 31 December 20X1 (ignoring deferred tax)

	20X1
	$000
Profit before tax	100
Current tax at 30% (see tax comp at W1)	(21)
Profit after tax	79

To estimate the current year's tax you would need to have on file a tax computation (as below). This would involve taking current year accounting profit and first of all adding back depreciation. You would then deduct the tax allowance to get taxable profit. This is multiplied by the tax rate (here 30%) to get the current tax liability:

Dr Income Statement - tax expense

Cr Balance sheet* – current tax liability

Workings
(W1) Tax computation

	20X1
	$000
Accounting profit	100
Add back depreciation	
(40/4 years)	10
Less: Capital allowances	(40)
Taxable profits	70
Current tax at 30%	21

The 'can you sleep at night?' test

By ignoring deferred tax you are presenting the accounts of Tyrrell as showing profit after tax of $79,000 (100,000 – 21,000). You prepared them – the test is – 'can you sleep at night?'.

* Balance Sheet = Statement of financial position (see page 18)

Paul Browne now wishes to buy this company and he speaks to the owner who is confident this trading outcome of $100,000 profit before tax can be delivered for the three following years using this one piece of equipment. Paul is delighted, he is not an accountant but buys the company believing next years accounts will show profit after tax of $79,000 – just like the 20X1 accounts.

The director was true to his word, trading profit of $100,000 was indeed delivered – you again do the accounts.

Tyrrell – Income statement (extract) for the year ended 31 December 20X2 with comparators (still ignoring deferred tax)

	20X1	20X2
	$000	$000
Profit before tax	100	100
Current tax at 30% (W1)	(21)	(33)
Profit after tax	79	67

Oh dear! – Paul, the new owner is now grumpy!

You now have to break the news that this year the tax estimate for current tax is not the $21,000 it was last year but an unpleasant $33,000!! – see the tax comp working below, Paul not surprisingly is not happy with you!

(W1) Tax computation

	20X1	20X2
	$000	$000
Accounting profit	100	100
Add back depreciation	10	10
Less: Capital allowances	(40)	–
Taxable profits	70	110
Current tax at 30%	21	33

In the year equipment was bought a temporary difference artificially reduced the tax bill. This was not a permanent reduction in tax but simply a postponement – a deferral. In fact, if you look at the X1/X2/X3 and X4 accounts, you will find that if Tyrrell does make a constant trading profit of $100,000 a year for the four years, i.e. $400,000 total, it will pay $400,000 x 30% tax = $120,000.

	Year ended 31 December				**Total**
	20X1	**20X2**	**20X3**	**20X4**	
	$000	$000	$000	$000	$000
Accounting profit	100	100	100	100	400
Add back depreciation	10	10	10	10	40
Less: Capital allowances	(40)	–	–	–	(40)
Taxable profits	70	110	110	110	400
Current tax at 30%	21	33	33	33	120

The differences between the accounting profit and the taxable profit that occur from one year to another, cancel out over the four years as a whole.

If we ignore deferred tax we get the following income statements for each period and for the four years as a whole:

	Year ended 31 December				**Total**
	20X1	**20X2**	**20X3**	**20X4**	
	$000	$000	$000	$000	$000
Profit before tax	100	100	100	100	400
Current tax at 30%	(21)	(33)	(33)	(33)	(120)
Profit after tax	79	67	67	67	280

Ignoring deferred tax produces a performance profile that appears to suggest a declining performance between 20X1 and 20X2. In fact the decline in profits is caused by the timing of the current tax charge on them. Yes, in the year the asset was bought the tax bill was pushed down to $21,000 but in the next three years it has gone up to $33,000. This is not a surprise; we know that these temporary differences arise, we know they cause a temporary deferment of tax and we should have accounted for the deferred tax if the accounts are to present fairly.

* Balance Sheet = Statement of financial position (see page 18)

The original income statement we prepared did not present fairly because we have ignored the deferred tax. We have misled Paul Browne, he is right to be cross … and, no, we shouldn't have slept that night.

What should we have done to sleep soundly? Well, recognised the deferred tax of course

If we have a temporary difference we should have had a working 2 on our file. It is not enough just to calculate the current tax, we have also to calculate the amount of tax we have deferred and to make a provision on the balance sheet*. To get the provision on the balance sheet* we charge the income statement.

So what does this Working 2 look like?

We calculate a deferred tax provision based on a 'temporary difference'. We have a 'temporary difference' if the figure on the balance sheet* – the Net Book Value (NBV) – is different to its 'tax base', i.e its tax written down value (WDV) – the amount that can be set against future tax bills.

This is the key working for all deferred tax questions – learn it

Working 2 Deferred tax provision required for balance sheet*

	20X1 $000
Cost – Depreciation (NBV) (40 – 10) (Carrying value)	30
Tax value (WDV) (40 – 40) (Tax base)	Nil
Temporary difference at year end	30
Closing deferred tax liability [30%]	9

If you want a memory device for remembering this working an image-story method might work for you.

Imagine a CD on top of a TV with a teddy (TD) under the TV.

Decode it

C – D (Cost less Depreciation)

TV (Tax Value)

TD (Temporary Difference)

Where we have a temporary difference, i.e. when the cost less depreciation (carrying value of the asset) is different to the cost less tax allowances taken (tax base or tax written down value), we have a deferred tax issue. Here the temporary difference is $30, and we multiply it by the current rate of tax. This tells us the amount to provide on the balance sheet* – $30 x 30% = $9 provision for deferred tax is required.

To achieve this we:

Dr Income statement – tax charge
    – transfer to deferred tax

    Cr Balance sheet*
      – provision for deferred tax

If we had done this our income statement in the year we purchased the equipment would have looked like this:

Tyrrell – Income statement for the year ended 31st December 20X1 (after accounting for deferred tax)

	20X1
	$000
Profit before tax	100
Current tax (W1)	(21)
Deferred tax (W2)	(9)
Profit after tax	70

So, we have effectively accounted for all tax on current year transactions, whether current or deferred. This what we mean by 'provide in full for all temporary differences', or 'use full provision method for deferred tax'. The accruals concept is being applied to tax and the tax charge is shown as 30% of accounting profit – we can once again sleep at night!!

Every accounting period would require us to revisit and recalculate any temporary differences. We calculate the required provision on the balance sheet* and use the income statement entry to either increase or reduce the balance. We can illustrate this with Tyrrell's 20X2 accounts.

We need to recalculate the temporary difference, noting the asset will now have been depreciated by two years not one. This will reduce the temporary difference to 20:

(W2) Tax deferred

	20X2 $000
Cost – depreciation (40 – 10 – 10) (carrying value)	20
Tax value (40 – 40) (tax base)	Nil
Temporary difference at year end	20
Closing deferred tax liability [30%]	6
Opening deferred tax liability	(9)
So charge/(credit) to income	(3)

As the temporary difference has reduced then so does our calculation of the deferred tax provision. We already have a provision of $9,000, and we now need to reduce it to $6,000. The entries required would be:

Dr Balance sheet* $3,000 (9,000 – 6,000)

  – Provision for deferred tax

 Cr Income statement $3,000

   – Transfer from deferred tax

For the 20X2 accounts the income statement would look like this:

Tyrrell – Income statement for the year ended 31 December 20X2 (including deferred tax)

	20X1 $000	20X2 $000
Profit before tax	100	100
Current tax	(21)	(33)
Deferred tax	(9)	3
Profit after tax	70	70

* Balance Sheet = Statement of financial position (see page 18)

No shocks here for Paul Browne!!

At 31 December 20X4 the temporary difference is gone and no deferred tax provision is required – see the four-year effect below:

(W2) Tax deferred

| | Year ended 31 December | | | |
	20X1	20X2	20X3	20X4
	$000	$000	$000	$000
Cost – Depreciation (carrying value)	30	20	10	Nil
Tax value	Nil	Nil	Nil	Nil
Temporary difference at year end	30	20	10	Nil
Closing deferred tax liability [30%]	9	6	3	Nil
Opening deferred tax liability	Nil	(9)	(6)	(3)
So charge/(credit) to income	9	(3)	(3)	(3)

The income statement (extracts) for the four year period including deferred tax are shown below:

| | Year ended 31 December | | | | Total |
	20X1	20X2	20X3	20X4	
	$000	$000	$000	$000	$000
Profit before tax	100	100	100	100	400
Current tax	(21)	(33)	(33)	(33)	(120)
Deferred tax	(9)	3	3	3	Nil
Profit after tax	30	30	30	30	280

By accounting for deferred tax we are showing profits of $30,000 each year for the four trading periods. Total tax remains as $120,000, but the way it is being presented reflects the accounting concept of accruals.

---

* Balance Sheet = Statement of financial position (see page 18)

Deferred tax assets

Most companies have deferred tax liabilities not deferred tax assets. This is because they experience temporary differences like we have just seen in Tyrrell. This means that they have an asset on the balance sheet* whose tax base (amount that can be charged against future tax) is lower than the Net Book Value of the asset. Therefore they have postponed tax and need a deferred tax liability on the balance sheet*.

It is possible that the company will have a deferred tax asset, however. The most common example of a temporary difference which gives a potential asset is a company with unused tax losses. This is not shown anywhere on the company's balance sheet* – it has a nil carrying value, but it does have a 'tax base' – it may be utilised to offset a future tax bill. But we don't just automatically put a deferred tax asset on a balance sheet*. We would have to be convinced that the asset will be recoverable. This would mean it was probable that the company will return to profit and only then will it be able to take the benefit.

Sorry but you need to know ... DEFINITIONS

Current tax is the amount of income taxes payable (recoverable) in respect of the taxable profit (tax loss) for a period.

Temporary differences are differences between the carrying amount of an asset or liability in the balance sheet* and its tax base. Temporary differences may be either taxable (giving rise to deferred tax liabilities) or deductible (giving rise to deferred tax assets).

The **tax base** of an asset or liability is the amount attributed to that asset or liability for tax purposes.

And the really important stuff ... accounting practice

Recognition

Current tax should be recognised as a current asset or liability.

Deferred tax is provided in full on all temporary differences (a balance sheet* calculation approach), except for any relating to non-deductible goodwill and assets purchased that are ineligible for capital allowances.

Deferred tax assets can be created (mainly for tax losses) as long as it is probable that the asset will be recovered.

Measurement

Deferred tax must not be discounted to present value.

The tax rate used should be the one when the differences reverse, however based on legislation enacted or substantially enacted by the balance sheet* date.

Presentation

Deferred tax is always presented as a non-current item on the balance sheet*.

If the item giving rise to the deferred tax is in reserves (for example, a revaluation of an asset), then the deferred tax should be recognised in reserves.

The tax line in the income statement is shown as one number including both the estimate for current tax and the transfer to or from deferred tax. The detail is then disclosed in the notes.

Disclosure

There are extensive disclosure requirements for tax including a reconciliation of the accounting profit to the total tax charge.

Conclusion

There are many different circumstances that could give rise to deferred tax, and as you progress with your studies it will become an increasingly important topic. What is important is that you are clear on your understanding of what a temporary difference is. If you understand this, you can apply it to any situation, with a bit of practice.

IAS 17 – Leases

Introduction

> **"The basic drives of man are few: to get enough food, to find shelter and to keep debt off the balance sheet*."**
>
> Anon

Back in Chapter 1 we talked about the concept of substance over form. Accounting statements are not about reflecting the legal form of a transaction but only about reflecting the commercial reality – economic substance. One of the 'hotspots' in financial statements is the attempt that companies sometimes make to understate the company's liabilities. Before we had an accounting standard, we had companies deliberately using leases as a means of 'off balance sheet* finance'. Instead of purchasing assets using loan finance, they leased them. Without IAS 17, because they were not the legal owner of the asset, neither the asset nor the obligation to make repayments under the lease terms were on the balance sheet*.

So do we have to learn IAS 17 because of accountants coming up with ways of manipulating the level of liabilities?

Absolutely! Because of this creative accounting, some lease contracts do now give rise to an asset and an associated liability on a company's balance sheet* even though it is not the legal owner of the asset.

> ### So ... what's it trying to achieve?
>
> IAS 17 gives guidance on the accounting treatments for operating and finance leases for both lessors and lessees.

All lease contracts under IAS 17 have to be categorised. If they are categorised as a finance lease, the assets are brought on balance sheet*. If they are categorised as an operating lease, they are kept off balance sheet* – two radically different treatments.

 Transactional example

Noonan has an accounting year end of 31 December.

Noonan acquired the use of a piece of machinery for the next five years by entering into a lease contract on 1 January 20X1. To buy the machine outright would have cost Noonan $10,000.

Under the terms of the lease contract, however, Noonan has agreed to pay $2,500 in advance (i.e. on 1 January each year). The rate of interest implicit in the lease is 12.6%. The equipment has a useful economic life of five years. Noonan is required to insure the plant and cannot return it to the lessor without severe penalties.

The sort of question you may be asked would include deciding whether the above lease should be classified as an operating or a finance lease. The key to the classification is who bears substantially all the risks and rewards associated with ownership of an asset – the lessee (the user of the asset) or the lessor (the legal owner of the asset).

If the risks and rewards of ownership of the machine are with Noonan (the lessee), this would be classified as a finance lease. If the risks and rewards associated with ownership are with the lessor it will be classified as an operating lease.

Primary indicators of a finance lease

- **The lessee/the user (Noonan) has the use of the asset for the substantial majority of its economic life.**
- **The present value of guaranteed minimum lease payments is substantially all of the fair value of the asset at the start of the lease.**

The lease in the above example would classify as a finance lease.

The contract is for five years and the equipment would normally be expected to last three years – this indicates a finance lease.

---

* Balance Sheet = Statement of financial position (see page 18)

If Noonan had bought the asset outright it would have cost $10,000 – the fair value. We need to compare that to the present value of the minimum lease payments (this just means taking the cash flows to which we are committed and applying a discount factor to take account of the time value of money).

We will need a working paper therefore:

Workings
(W1) Cash flow commitment at present value

Lease payments	Date	Amount	@ PV	Present value
1.	1.1.20X1	$2,500	–	$2,500
2.	1.1.20X2	$2,500	x $1/1.126$	$2,220
3.	1.1.20X3	$2,500	x $1/1.126^2$	$1,972
4.	1.1.20X4	$2,500	x $1/1.126^3$	$1,751
5.	1.1 20X5	$2,500	x $1/1.126^4$	$1,555
				$9,998

As the present value of the lease payments is substantially all of the fair value (cash price), again this indicates a finance lease.

$$\frac{\$9,998}{\$10,000} = \text{virtually } 100\%$$

The substance of the transaction is that, although Noonan is not the legal owner of the asset, it has – in commercial reality terms – acquired the asset, using a finance deal.

You may also be asked to show the impact of this transaction in the balance sheet* and income statement for the year ended 31 December 20X1.

Initial recognition – what we do first

Finance leased assets are capitalised (brought on balance sheet*) at their fair value, or the present value of the guaranteed minimum lease payments if lower than fair value, and a lease creditor is set up for the same amount.

The ledger entry would be:

Dr Non-current assets $9,998

    Cr Obligations under a finance lease $9,998

The non-current asset should be depreciated over the shorter of the useful economic life of the asset and the lease term. This means that thereafter the entries for the leased asset and its associated depreciation will be exactly the same as for a purchased asset.

The annual depreciation charge is $9,998/5 years = $1999.6 per annum.

What about when we pay the leasing company?

The initial payment in advance on the 1 January 20X1 is entirely a repayment of capital – it's like a deposit and means we have only effectively borrowed $7,498 ($9,998 – $2,500).

Dr Obligation under a finance lease $2,500

   Cr Cash $2,500

The balance on the obligations under a finance lease is now showing the initial $9,998 – $2,500 = $7,498. This is a loan from the leasing company on which you are going to pay 12.6% interest.

What about at the year end?

Well at the year end this interest will need to be accrued, $7,498 x 12.6% = $943. This will need to be expensed via the income statement.

Dr Income statement: interest expense under a finance lease

   Cr Balance sheet*: obligations under a finance lease – interest accrual.

You may be asked to extract from the accounts as follows:

Balance sheet* (extract)	$
Non-current assets	
Property, plant and equipment	
(9,998 – 1,999.6)	7,998.4
Liabilities	
Obligations under a finance lease	
– principal outstanding	7,498
– accrued interest	945

* Balance Sheet = Statement of financial position (see page 18)

Income statement (extract)	$
Operating expense	
Depreciation	1,999.6
Finance cost	
Interest	944

Note

To be strictly accurate you really need to show the principal outstanding liability split between current and non-current. The use of the leasing table will be the best way to do this.

(W2) Leasing table

In advance payments

Balance b/fwd	Cash paid	Capital outstanding	Interest at 12.6%	Balance c/fwd
$9,998	(2,500)	$7,498	945	$8,443 (b/s date)
$8,443	(2,500)	$5,943 *(this is still outstanding in 12 months time and is therefore a non-current liability)*		

To be strictly accurate therefore the balance sheet* should show:

Balance sheet* (extract)	$
Non-current assets	
Property, plant and equipment (9,998 – 1,999.6)	7,998.4
Non-current liabilities	
Obligations under a finance lease – principal only	5,943
Current liabilities	
Obligations under a finance lease – principal outstanding (7,498 – 5,943)	1,555
– accrued interest	945

Note

The total liability is $8,443 – made up of the $5,943 + $1,555 + $945

Other potential requirements

Some questions ask for an extract, others could ask you to show the impact over the whole life of the lease. Again the leasing table will give you the numbers you need to answer this sort of question:

In advance payments

Balance b/fwd	Cash paid	Capital outstanding	Interest at 12.6%	Balance c/fwd
$9,998	(2,500)	$7,498	945	$8,443
$8,443	(2,500)	$5,943	749	$6,692
$6,692	(2,500)	$4,192	528	$4,720
$4,720	(2,500)	$2,220	280	$2,500
$2,500	(2,500)	nil	nil	nil

Balance sheet*s (extracts)

Year	1 $	2 $	3 $	4 $	5 $

The asset part is pretty straightforward

Non current assets

Leased plant					
Cost	9,998	9,998	9,998	9,998	9,998
Accumulated dep'n	(1,999.6)	(3,999.2)	(5,998.8)	(7,998.4)	(9,998)
Net Book Value	7,998.4	5,998.8	3,999.2	1,999.6	nil

Balance Sheet* = Statement of financial position (see page 18)

Use the leasing table opposite for the liabilities

Balance sheet*

Balance sheet* (extract)

Non-current liabilities
Obligations under

finance lease	1	2	3	4	5
– principal	5,943	4,192	2,220	nil	nil

Current liabilities

– interest	945	749	528	280	nil
– principal	1,555	1,751	1,972	2,220	nil
		(5,943 – 4,192)	(4,192 – 2,220)	(2,220 – nil)	

Income Statement

Income Statement (extracts)

Year	1	2	3	4	5
Operating expense	$	$	$	$	$
Depreciation	1,999.6	1,999.6	1,999.6	1,999.6	1,999.6
Finance costs					
Interest	945	749	528	280	nil

Sorry but you need to know ... DEFINITIONS

A **lease** is an arrangement whereby a lessor conveys to the lessee in return for a series of payments the right to use an asset for an agreed period of time.

A **finance lease** is a lease that substantially transfers the risks and rewards of ownership to the lessee.

An **operating lease** is a lease other than a finance lease.

And the really important stuff ... accounting practice

Leases must first be classified between operating and finance leases. Examples of the factors that indicate whether the risks and rewards of ownership have passed to the lessee are:

(a) the lessee has the use of the asset for the substantial majority of its economic life

(b) the lease transfers legal title at the end or there is a bargain purchase option for the lessee

(c) the present value of guaranteed minimum lease payments is substantially all of the fair value of the asset at the start of the lease

(d) due to criteria (i) above (which can never be met) land leases are operating leases unless legal title passes at the end of the lease term. Leases of land and buildings must be treated as two leases.

* Balance Sheet = Statement of financial position (see page 18)

Lessee accounting

Finance leases

Finance leased assets are capitalised (brought on balance sheet*) at their fair value, or the present value of the guaranteed minimum lease payments if lower than fair value, and a lease creditor is set up for the same amount.

The fixed asset should be depreciated over the shorter of the useful economic life of the asset and the lease term.

Interest is allocated to the lease creditor and charged to the income statement using either the interest rate implicit in the lease, or occasionally the sum-of-digits method. As the rental payments are made the lease creditor falls.

In numerical questions we use a leasing table to sort the numbers for us. You will need to first of all ascertain whether the lease payments are made in advance or in arrears. This is vital as it will change the calculations.

 It is a common mistake for students to not notice an in-advance payment and to treat it as a payment in arrears.

Leasing tables

 In arrears payments

Period	Balance b/fwd	Interest	Cash paid	Balance c/fwd
	X	X	(X)	X

 In advance payments

Period	Balance b/fwd	Cash paid	Capital outstanding	Interest	Balance c/fwd
	X	(X)	X	X	X

Operating leases

The rentals are charged to the income statement on a straight-line basis over the lease term (unless another systematic basis is more appropriate).

Lessor accounting

Finance leases

The lessor will record a receivable at the amount of the net investment in the lease (total future income less future finance costs).

The gross earnings under the lease should be allocated to give a constant rate of return using the net investment method.

Operating leases

The asset should be recorded in the balance sheet* according to the nature of the asset.

Rental income should be recognised in the income statement on a straight-line basis over the lease term (unless another systematic basis is more appropriate).

Sale and leaseback transactions

If the sale and leaseback results in a finance leaseback, any profit or loss on the sale is deferred and amortised over the shorter of the lease term and the useful economic life of the asset.

If the leaseback is an operating lease:

- if the sale is at fair value, the profit/loss should be recognised immediately
- if the sale is below fair value, any loss can be deferred and recognised over the lease term (as long as the loss is compensated by rentals at less than market value)
- if the sale is above fair value, the excess profit (above a sale at fair value) should be deferred and amortised over the lease term.

Disclosures

Some main disclosures for lessees are:

- the gross amounts for assets held under finance leases and the accumulated depreciation on those assets.
- the obligations under finance leases analysed between amounts due within one year, within two to five years, and over five years
- for operating leases the gross future payments analysed between leases finishing within one year, from two to five years, and over five years.

---

* Balance Sheet = Statement of financial position (see page 18)

Conclusion

IAS 17 is actually very controversial and therefore the topic of leasing is a very current issue. It is not the treatment of finance leases that is causing concern, but the treatment of operating leases which continue to be a form of off balance sheet* finance. It is likely that IAS 17 will be replaced by a standard that requires all non-cancellable leases to be brought on balance sheet*. For now, however, the need to classify remains.

IAS 20 – Accounting for government grants and disclosure of government assistance

Introduction

> **"Never spend your money before you have it."**
>
> Thomas Jefferson (1743-1826)

Without an accounting standard on government grants, we saw some very inconsistent treatments. Remember that often a company receiving a government grant is receiving it to help pay for an item of capital – plant or machinery maybe. Well, if we receive a government grant for such an item, we have a cash injection to account for (let us say $5,000,000).

We definitely:

Dr Cash $5,000,000.

But what to do with the credit!

 Without a standard we saw companies crediting the whole amount to the income statement in the year they received the grant.

– Cr Income statement $5,000,000

Suddenly this company has made massive profits – some would argue this is seriously misleading to a reader who may believe the same will be shown in next year's accounts. If this item of plant and machinery has a useful economic life of say, five years, the accruals concept would clearly require that we spread the benefit of the five periods. A credit of $5,000,000 is unacceptable but $1,000,000 each year for the next five years? Yes, that we can live with.

IAS 20 therefore is not rocket science; it is applying basic principles to a specific area of transactions.

So ... what's it trying to achieve?

IAS 20 is explaining the accounting treatment for government assistance received by companies, and the disclosure required for the government assistance.

 ## Transactional example

Alexandra Inc acquired an item of plant at a gross cost of $800,000 on 1 January 20X6. The plant has an estimated life of ten years with a residual value equal to 15% of its gross cost. Alexandra uses straight-line depreciation and prepares accounts as at 31 December. The company received a government grant of 30% of the plant's cost price at the time of the plant's purchase. Alexandra Inc is unsure of how to account for the government grant.

As the grant relates to a capital item it would be inappropriate to take the whole $800,000 x 30% = $240,000 to the income statement. Instead Alexandra Inc has two options.

Option 1

Treat the cash receipt as a deferred credit, i.e.

Dr Cash $240,000

   Cr Deferred income $240,000

This will then be released to the income statement over the ten-year life of the plant, i.e. each income statement for the next ten years will receive a credit of $240,000/10 = $24,000 and the deferred income account is written down:

Dr Deferred income $24,000

   Cr Income statement $24,000

Option 2

The grant would be deducted from the asset account. i.e.

Dr Cash $240,000

    Cr Asset account $240,000

Note

The effect on the operating results is the same with either option, since with option 1 the grant is being directly taken to ten years' income statements, but with option two, the same effect is achieved indirectly via a reduced depreciation charge for the next ten years.

Sorry but you need to know ... DEFINITIONS

Government refers to government, governmental agencies and similar bodies whether local, national or international.

Government grants are assistance by government given to the enterprise in return for past or future compliance with conditions.

And the really important stuff ... accounting practice

Government grants should be recognised in the income statement to match them against the expenditure to which they contribute.

Non-current asset grants – over the useful economic life of the asset.

For past costs incurred – immediately in the profit and loss account.

For current/future costs – in the period that the costs are recognised.

For non-current asset grants the standard would allow the grant to be deducted from the cost of the asset, or treated as deferred income (a liability) in the balance sheet* and released to income statement over the useful economic life.

---

* Balance Sheet = Statement of financial position (see page 18)

Grants towards future expenditure will be treated as deferred income when they are received and credited to the income statement to match against the expenditure.

 Grants can only be recognised when the conditions for their receipt have been complied with.

 Provision must be made for the repayment of grants if this is likely to happen.

Disclosure

The following should be disclosed:

- the accounting policy for grants
- the nature and extent of government grants recognised in the financial statements
- unfulfilled conditions and other contingencies attached to government assistance that have been recognised.

Conclusion

A full question on government grants is unlikely, but it can crop up as part of a bigger question. It is however an excellent example, if asked, of a conflict between the Framework (Chapter 1) and a standard. The IASB Framework defines liabilities as 'obligations to transfer economic benefit'. The IAS 20 treatment of allowing a government grant to be treated as a deferred credit does not meet this definition. IAS 20 is a simple application of the matching concept. Remember, if there is a conflict between the 'Framework' and a standard – then the standard prevails.

(15) IAS 23 – Borrowing costs

Introduction

> **"Neither a borrower nor a lender be; for loan oft loses both itself and friend; And borrowing dulls the edge of husbandry (economy)."**
>
> **William Shakespeare (1564-1616), Hamlet Act I Scene iii**

Well borrowing does have a cost – if not the loss of a friend, at a minimum we are talking about 'interest payable'. You will have prepared many income statements which have included the line, 'interest payable', without feeling the need to consult IAS 23. The standard treatment for interest payable has always been and continues to be … it's a 'period expense', no harder than dealing with rent payable or telephone costs. Period expenses are charged to the income statement … well almost always!

What's the deal then? Why do we have an accounting standard?

There is a problem with the standard treatment if for example, a company chooses to, construct its new headquarters rather than buy them ready built. If you buy a building, the price you pay will include not just the costs of the bricks, mortar and labour. The seller will have built in a cost of capital (an interest cost) to the selling price. This will end up on your balance sheet* as part of the cost of the asset.

It would seem reasonable, therefore, that if you choose to build the asset yourself, you should be able to include the cost of your own capital, i.e. the interest you are paying, in the asset account.

---

* Balance Sheet = Statement of financial position (see page 18)

So ... what's it trying to achieve?

IAS 23 prescribes the accounting treatment for borrowing costs. Generally it requires recognition as an expense, however if the borrowing cost relates to an asset that takes a substantial period of time to get ready for use or sale, the borrowing costs should be capitalised.

Transactional example

George Inc has raised a long-term loan from a bank for the purpose of constructing a major city centre complex, incorporating an art gallery, restaurants and a variety of shops. The construction is planned to take two years from the date the project is launched.

This sort of transaction would usually involve IAS 23, as the asset will take a substantial period of time to get ready for its intended use. As the borrowing costs that relate to the asset are readily identifiable they should be capitalised.

A common misunderstanding is to believe that, if an asset is expensive to purchase, it is appropriate to capitalise the borrowing costs. If the asset does not take a substantial period of time to get ready for its intended use, it would not qualify for capitalisation.

Sorry but you need to know ... DEFINITIONS

Borrowing costs are interest and other costs incurred by an enterprise in connection with the borrowing of funds. They include:

(a) interest

(b) amortisation of discounts or premiums related to borrowings

(c) amortisation of ancillary costs

(d) finance charges on finance leases

(e) exchange differences on foreign currency borrowings.

A **qualifying asset** is an asset that necessarily takes a substantial period of time to get ready for its intended use or sale.

And the really important stuff ... accounting practice

The benchmark treatment is that borrowing costs should be recognised as an expense in the period they are incurred.

Borrowing costs directly attributable to the purchase, construction or production of a qualifying asset are to capitalised:

If general borrowings are used to finance the construction of the asset, a weighted average borrowing rate should be used to calculate the finance cost to capitalise.

Finance costs can only be capitalised for the period of construction, and must cease when all activities necessary to get the asset to its intended use have been completed. Capitalisation must also cease during periods when construction is suspended.

Disclosures

Key disclosures include:

- the accounting policy adopted
- the amount of borrowing costs capitalised during the period
- the capitalisation rate used to determine the amount of finance costs during the period.

Conclusion

IAS 23 is intended to improve consistency of treatment of borrowing costs and to bring some 'fairness' to the treatment of interest relating to the cost of self-constructing
an asset.

---

* Balance Sheet = Statement of financial position (see page 18)

IAS 32 – Financial instruments: presentation and disclosure

Introduction

> "Comprehensive standards addressing financial instruments are essential if an accounting standards regime is to be credible".
>
> Mary Keegan – in Chair of UK ASB

IAS 32 is a companion standard to IAS 39: They both deal with financial instruments. Whenever a company raises finance, it issues a financial instrument. Sometimes they raise finance by issuing shares – equity finance; sometimes they issue loan notes or debentures or the like – debt finance.

The fundamental principle of IAS 32 is that a financial instrument should be classified as either a financial liability or an equity instrument according to the substance of the contract, not its legal form. The enterprise must make the decision at the time the instrument is initially recognised. The classification is not subsequently changed based on changed circumstances.

So ... when a company raises finance, we have to classify as debt or equity – is that it?

Well, it's actually a very big area and it covers the accounting from the other side also, i.e. for every company that raises finance some other company has to provide it. Every time somebody issues debentures, somebody purchases an investment. Financial instruments are assets as well as equity/liabilities. The definition of financial instruments is:

Any contract that gives rise to both a financial asset of one enterprise and a financial liability or equity instrument of another enterprise.

However a good starting point for a student is with the raising of finance, and the need to classify as debt or equity.

Illustration – preference shares

If an enterprise issues preference (preferred) shares that pay a fixed rate of dividend and have redemption feature at a future date, the substance is that they are a contractual obligation to deliver cash and, therefore, should be recognised as a liability. In contrast, normal preference shares do not have a fixed maturity, and the issuer does not have a contractual obligation to make any payment. Therefore, they are equity.

So ... what's it trying to achieve?

IAS 32 has the aim of defining the presentation requirements for financial assets, financial liabilities and equity instruments and also for ensuring that sufficient disclosures are made in the financial statements to enhance the user's understanding of the significance of financial instruments.

Transactional example

Let us assume that MJF Inc issues preference (preferred) shares that pay a fixed rate of dividend and have a mandatory redemption feature at a future date.

In some GAAP regimes, these would have been treated by their legal form as 'shares', although commonly disclosed separately as 'non-equity' shares.

Under IAS 32, the substance, not legal form, is reflected. In substance, there is a contractual obligation to deliver cash and, therefore, they should be recognised as a liability. The payment of this fixed rate dividend is not in fact dividend, but should be treated as interest.

---

* Balance Sheet = Statement of financial position (see page 18)

Sorry but you need to know ... DEFINITIONS

Financial instrument

Any contract that gives rise to both a financial asset of one enterprise and a financial liability or equity instrument of another enterprise.

Financial asset

Any asset that is:

- cash
- a contractual right to receive cash or another financial asset from another enterprise
- a contractual right to exchange financial instruments with another enterprise under conditions that are potentially favourable; or
- an equity instrument of another enterprise.

Financial liability

A liability that is a contractual obligation:

- to deliver cash or another financial asset to another enterprise; or
- to exchange financial instruments with another enterprise under conditions that are potentially unfavourable.

Equity instrument

Any contract that evidences a residual interest in the assets of an enterprise after deducting all of its liabilities.

And the really important stuff ... accounting practice

Presentation

Equity and liabilities should be presented on the balance sheet* following the substance of the instruments. If an instrument contains an obligation to pay out cash it is a financial liability. Preference shares are therefore often financial liabilities.

Compound instruments (those with both debt and equity elements) issued such as convertible debentures are 'split' accounted. This means the proceeds are recognised as debt and a separate equity option. The debt is measured by discounted cash flows and the equity is the residual of the proceeds.

Interest, dividends, gains and losses treatment follow the presentation on the balance sheet*. If a preference share is treated as a debt instrument, any dividends paid on that share are treated as interest charges.

Financial assets and liabilities should be offset on the balance sheet* if:

(a) there is a legal right of offset; and

(b) there is an intention to settle on a net basis (evidenced by cash flows being offset).

Disclosure

There are extensive disclosure requirements for financial instruments, both narrative and numerical. The principal areas of disclosure are:

- terms, conditions and accounting policies
- price risk (currency, interest rate and market risk)
- credit risk
- cash flow risk
- fair values
- hedges.

Conclusion

As mentioned, IAS 32 is really a companion standard to IAS 39. You really need to study them both as a single topic. IAS 32 covers presentation issues, but in order to know about measurement we need to look at IAS 39. Studying IAS 32 in isolation is therefore liable to give incomplete answers.

---

* Balance Sheet = Statement of financial position (see page 18)

IAS 33 – Earnings per share

Introduction

> "I never knew an early rising, hard-working, prudent man, careful of his earnings and strictly honest who complained of bad luck."
>
> Henry Ward Beecher (1813-1887)

We have to have a standard on earnings per share (EPS) because it is the most important accounting ratio. It forms part of the price/earnings ratio (P/E ratio) and, rightly or wrongly, the stock market places great emphasis on a company's P/E ratio and therefore a standard form of measurement of EPS is required.

The basic EPS calculation is simply $\dfrac{\text{Earnings}}{\text{Shares}}$

This should be presented as cents per share to one decimal place.

We have to have a standard that governs both calculation and disclosure, because companies will follow the calculation rules but will then sometimes do their 'own' calculations of EPS and present them with equal prominence.

It's just a ratio then?

Yes it is just a ratio – 'earnings' means group profit after tax, less minority interests and preference dividends; and 'shares' means the weighted average number of ordinary shares outstanding during the period.

The figure 'earnings per share' (EPS) is used to assess the ongoing financial performance of a company from year to year, and to compute the major stock market indicator of performance, the price/earnings ratio (P/E ratio). The calculation for the P/E ratio is:

$$P/E = \frac{\text{Market value of share}}{\text{EPS}}$$

So ... what's it trying to achieve?

The aim of IAS 33 is to improve the comparison of the performance of different periods and between entities in the same period by prescribing the way EPS is to be calculated and how it is to be disclosed.

Transactional example

Here is some information relating to a listed company, Gerard Inc.

Calculate Gerard Inc's earnings per share (EPS) in respect of the year ended 31 December 20X4 on the basis that there was no change in the issued share capital of the company during the year ended 31 December 20X4.

Gerard Inc

Draft income statement for the year ended 31 December 20X4

	$000	$000
Profit before tax		4,508
Taxation		(2,300)
Profit after tax		2,208

On 1 January 20X4 the issued share capital of Gerard was 9,200,000 6% preference shares of $1 each and 8,280,000 ordinary shares of $1 each.

Calculate the earnings per share (EPS) in respect of the year ended 31 December 20X4 on the basis that there was no change in the issued share capital of the company during the year ended 31 December 20X4.

Basic earnings per share *is calculated by dividing the profit available to ordinary shareholders (profit after tax, minority interest and preference dividends) by the weighted average number of ordinary shares in the period.*

---

* Balance Sheet = Statement of financial position (see page 18)

Basic EPS for Gerard

The amount of earnings generated by the ordinary shares (i.e. exclude the preference dividend) is divided by the number of ordinary shares:

$$\frac{\$2,208,000}{8,280,000} = 26.7c$$

IAS 33 requires public companies to disclose the EPS figure on the face of the income statement, so Gerard would disclose 26.7c as its EPS figure (called the basic EPS).

What if the company issues shares in the year?

Well, if the number of shares has changed during the period, a weighted average number of shares has to be used under the line.

Transactional example

In the example of Gerard, suppose that the company had issued 3,312,000 shares at full market value on 30 June 20X4.

This is the basic weighted average table – you must learn this.

Date	Actual number of shares	Fraction of year	Total
1 January 20X4	8,280,000	$\frac{6}{12}$	4,140,000
30 June 20X4	11,592,000 (W1)	$\frac{6}{12}$	5,796,000
Number of shares in EPS calculation			9,936,000

(W1) New number of shares

Original number	8,280,000
New issue	3,312,000
New number	11,592,000

The earnings per share for 20X4 would now be calculated as:

$$\frac{\$2,208,000}{9,936,000} = 22.2c$$

What if it was a bonus (cash free) issue?

Assume that the bonus shares have always been in issue (and therefore alter the comparative EPS amount).

Transactional example

Suppose now that Gerard Inc made no issue of shares at full price but instead made a bonus issue on 1 October 20X4 of one ordinary share for every four shares in issue at 30 September 20X4.

A bonus issue causes no impact on earnings; but the new extra shares will cause a dilution to EPS. This will need to be reflected. EPS calculated whilst ignoring the bonus issue will need to be restated taking into account the dilutory impact.

Ignoring the bonus issue

$$\frac{2,208,000}{8,280,000} = 26.6c$$

Restated for the dilutive effect

26.6c x $\dfrac{\text{8,280,000 (number of shares before the bonus issue)}}{\text{10,350,000 (number of shares after the bonus issue W1)}}$ = 21.3 c

(W1) 8,280,000 × ¼ =	2,070,000	extra shares
Original number of shares	8,280,000	
New number of shares	10,350,000	

Ahh – but it could be a rights issue – what then?

Assume that the shares issued are a mix of bonus and full price shares. For the bonus element assume that they have always been in issue and therefore adjust the comparative.

Assume that the shares issued are a mix of bonus and full price shares. For the bonus element assume that they have always been in issue and therefore adjust the comparative.

Transactional example

Suppose now that Gerard's only share issue in 20X4 was a rights issue of $1 ordinary shares on 1 October 20X4 in the proportion of one for every five shares held at a price of $1.20. The middle market price for the shares on the last day of quotation cum rights was $1.80 per share.

When a rights issue takes place shares are issued at less than full market price. We treat this as a combination of a bonus issue and an issue at full market price. We will therefore need to calculate the rights issue bonus fraction by using share prices:

Rights issue bonus fraction $= \dfrac{\text{Actual cum rights price}}{\text{Theoretical ex rights price}}$

Actual cum rights price $=$ Price of share with rights attached immediately before rights issue.

Theoretical ex rights price $=$ Expected share price immediately after rights issue (weighted average of actual cum rights price and exercise price of rights issue shares)

In the present case, we have a rights issue made in the proportion of one for every five shares held, (i.e. for every five shares previously owned you now own six).

Rights issue bonus fraction

	$	$	
5 shares at	1.80	9.00	$\dfrac{\$10.20}{6} = \$1.7$
1 share at	1.20	1.20	
6 shares		10.20	

Therefore rights issue bonus fraction $= \dfrac{\$1.80}{\$1.70}$

Use a table for full computation of the number of shares, as follows:

Date	Actual number of shares	Fraction of year	Rights issue bonus fraction	Total
1 January 20X4	8,280,000	$\dfrac{9}{12}$	$\dfrac{1.80}{1.70}$	6,575,294
30 June 20X4	9,936,000 (W1)	$\dfrac{3}{12}$		2,484,000
Number of shares in EPS calculation				9,059,294

 This is the basic weighted average table with an additional column – you must learn this too!

 A common mistake made by students is to apply the rights issue bonus fraction a second time in the second line of the table. This is wrong – apply it once at the point the rights issue takes place as that is when the dilution occurs.

$\text{EPS} = \dfrac{\$2,208,000}{9,059,294} = 24.4c$

(W1) New number of shares

$8,280,000 \times 1 \div 5 \quad = \quad 1,656,000$ extra shares

New number of shares $= \quad 8,280,000 + 1,656,000 = 9,936,000$

* Please note on 6th September 2007 the IASB issued a revised IAS 1. The effective date of the new standard is annual periods beginning on or after 1 January 2009, with earlier application permitted. If, however, you are being examined on a six month from issue rule, this new standard is examinable for summer 2008 exams. The revised IAS 1 removes the traditional term 'balance sheet*' and although the format is unchanged it is to be called 'a statement of financial position'. The traditional income statement is to be replaced by the 'statement of comprehensive income'.

Diluted earnings per share

This is calculated where potential ordinary shares have been outstanding during the period which would cause EPS to fall if exercised (dilutive instruments). It is calculated in addition to basic EPS.

Equity share capital may change in future owing to circumstances which exist now. Diluted EPS (DEPS) attempts to alert shareholders to the potential impact on EPS.

Potential changes may arise for any of the following reasons:

- shares not yet ranking for dividend
- convertible debt or preference shares in issue
- options granted to subscribe for new shares.

To deal with this, adjust basic earnings and number of shares assuming convertibles, options, etc had converted to equity shares on the first day of the accounting period, or on the date of issue of convertibles, options, etc if later.

Diluted earnings per share is calculated as follows:

$$\frac{\text{Earnings} + \text{Notional extra earnings}}{\text{Number of shares} + \text{Notional extra shares}}$$

The earnings should be adjusted by adding back any costs that will not be incurred once the dilutive instruments have been exercised. This will include, for example, interest on convertible debt.

The number of shares will be adjusted to take account of the exercise of the dilutive instrument. This means that adjustment is made:

For convertible instruments By adding the maximum number of shares to be issued in the future.

For options By adding the number of effectively 'free' shares to be issued when the options are exercised.

Some companies have more than one dilutive instrument in issue, such as both convertibles and share options. In this case diluted EPS is calculated by adding each dilutive instrument in turn, with the most dilutive first. If any instrument causes the diluted EPS figure to increase, this instrument, and any subsequent instruments, are ignored.

---

* Balance Sheet = Statement of financial position (see page 18)

Transactional example

Continuing with the example of Gerard we can calculate diluted EPS on the basis that the company made no new issue of shares during the year ended 31 December 20X4, but on that date it had in issue $2,300,000 10% convertible loan stock 20X6 to 20X9. Assume a corporation tax rate of 50%.

This loan stock will be convertible into ordinary $1 shares as follows.

20X6   90 $1 shares for $100 nominal value loan stock

20X7   85 $1 shares for $100 nominal value loan stock

20X8   80 $1 shares for $100 nominal value loan stock

20X9   75 $1 shares for $100 nominal value loan stock

The earnings should be adjusted by adding back any costs that will not be incurred once the dilutive instruments have been exercised. This will include, for example, interest on convertible debt.

The number of shares will be adjusted to take account of the exercise of the dilutive instrument. This means that adjustment is made:

For convertible instruments   By adding the maximum number of shares to be issued in the future.

If this loan stock was converted to shares, the impact on earnings would be as follows:

	$	$
Basic earnings		2,208,000
Add: Notional interest saved ($2,300,000 × 10%)	230,000	
Less: Tax relief $230,000 × 50%	(115,000)	
		115,000
Revised earnings		2,323,000
Number of shares if loan converted		
Basic number of shares		8,280,000
Notional extra shares under the most dilution possible		

$$2,300,000 \times \frac{90}{100} \qquad\qquad 2,070,000$$

Revised number of shares	10,350,000

$$DEPS = \frac{\$2,323,000}{10,350,000} = 22.4c$$

But it could be options outstanding?

Yes, it could, and in that case we need to add the number of effectively 'free' shares to be issued when the options are exercised.

Transactional example

Now assume that Gerard made no issue of shares during the year ended 31 December 20X4, but on that date there were outstanding options to purchase 920,000 ordinary $1 shares at $1.70 per share. The average fair value for the year of ordinary shares was $1.80.

Options or warrants

	$
Earnings	2,208,000
Number of shares	
Basic	8,280,000
Options (W1)	51,111
	8,331,111

The DEPS is therefore $\dfrac{\$2,208,000}{8,331,111} = 26.5c$

---

* Balance Sheet = Statement of financial position (see page 18)

(W1) Number of shares at option price

Options $= 920,000 \times \$1.70$

$\qquad\qquad = \$1,564,000$

At fair value: $\dfrac{\$1,564,000}{\$1.80} = 868,889$

Number issued free $= 920,000 - 868,889 = 51,111$

Where there are several categories of dilutive potential ordinary shares, the IAS requires that they should be taken into account in the calculation of DEPS in their order of dilution (i.e. greatest dilution first). This ensures that the worst possible DEPS figure emerges.

Sorry but you need to know ... DEFINITIONS

An **ordinary share** is an equity instrument that is subordinate to all other classes of equity instrument.

A **potential ordinary share** is a financial instrument or contract that may entitle its holder to ordinary shares.

Examples of potential ordinary shares are:

- convertible instruments
- options.

And the really important stuff ... accounting practice

Basic earnings per share

As we have seen, this is calculated by dividing the profit available to ordinary shareholders (profit after tax, minority interest and preference dividends) by the weighted average number of ordinary shares in the period.

However, a number of complications can arise

If the number of shares has changed during the period the following assumptions are made regarding the weighted average number of shares.

Full price issue   Normal weighted average calculation.

Bonus issues   Assume that the bonus shares have always been in issue (and therefore alter the comparative EPS amount).

Rights issue   Assume that the shares issued are a mix of bonus and full price shares. For the bonus element assume that they have always been in issue and therefore adjust the comparative.

If bonus issues or rights issues occur after the balance sheet* date, but before the date of approval of the accounts, the EPS should be calculated based on the number of shares after the event.

Diluted earnings per share

Equity share capital may change in future owing to circumstances which exist now. Potential changes may arise for any of the following reasons:

- shares not yet ranking for dividend
- convertible debt or preference shares in issue
- options granted to subscribe for new shares.

Diluted earnings per share is calculated as follows:

$$\frac{\text{Earnings} + \text{Notional extra earnings}}{\text{Number of shares} + \text{Notional extra shares}}$$

Disclosure

The disclosures are required are:

- basic and diluted EPS are presented on the face of the profit and loss account
- the numerators for each calculation should be disclosed and reconciled to the net profit or loss for the period
- the denominators should be disclosed and reconciled to each other
- any alternative measures of EPS (other than basic or diluted) must only be disclosed in the notes to the financial statements.

Conclusion

IAS 33 requires that public companies disclose both the basic EPS and the DEPS (where relevant) on the face of the income statement with equal prominence.

You must be able to calculate the basic EPS when the share capital in issue changes during the period, and also the diluted EPS when there are dilutive potential ordinary shares in issue.

* Balance Sheet = Statement of financial position (see page 18)

IAS 36 – Impairment of assets

Introduction

> **"Old accountants never die ... they simply lose their assets."**
>
> Traditional

It would be incorrect if balance sheets* were put together and assets were carried at a figure which could not be recovered, i.e. retrieved, by the shareholders. It has always been the case that accountants believe that assets must not be carried on the balance sheet* at more than their recoverable amount – this is nothing new.

'Recoverable amount ... hmmm ... what exactly does it mean?

Well a company can recover the amount it has invested in its assets in one of two ways:

- it can opt to sell the asset to someone else, generating a net selling price; or
- it can trade with the asset, making stuff, selling stuff, providing some form of service and generating cash flow. If we predict cash will be generated from the asset, the asset has what we call a 'value in use'.

If the asset is on the balance sheet* and carried at a figure bigger than the amount that we can recover from it, it is clearly 'impaired,' i.e. we need to write off some of the value. An impairment loss is therefore like an extra depreciation expense.

So ... what's it trying to achieve?

IAS 36 prescribes the procedures that should be followed by a company to ensure that its assets are not held at more than their recoverable amount. The standard gives the rules to write down assets for impairment and also the circumstances when impairment can and should be reversed.

Transactional example

Mary Inc is a manufacturer of cardboard boxes. However a change in the market means that the inventory produced by the machine that makes small gift boxes is being sold below its cost. Due to this impairment circumstance an impairment test needs to be carried out.

The following information is relevant:

The carrying value of the productive machinery at depreciated historical cost is $290,000 and its net selling price is estimated at $120,000. The anticipated net cash inflows from the machines are now $100,000 per annum for the next three years. A market discount rate is 10% per annum.

An impairment test does need to be carried out due to the impairment circumstance – the change in the market. The machine's carrying value will need to be compared to its recoverable amount. An impairment test needs to be set up.

Impairment test

Carrying amount	$290,000
Recoverable amount (W1)	$248,685
IMPAIRMENT LOSS	$41,315

You will need a supporting working paper to calculate recoverable amount – remember:

Recoverable amount

- they can opt to sell the asset to someone else, generating a net selling price; or
- they can trade with the asset, making stuff, selling stuff, providing some form of service and generating cash flow. If we predict cash will be generated from the asset, the asset has what we call a 'value in use'.

---

* Balance Sheet = Statement of financial position (see page 18)

Note

Recoverable amount is the greater of these two. *A common error made by students is to use the smaller – Doh!!*

Recoverable Amount

(W1) Recoverable amount is the greater of:

Net selling price		Value in use			$
$120,000	Year 1	$100,000 × 1/1.1		=	90,909
	Year 2	$100,000 × 1/1.1^2		=	82,645
	Year 3	$100,000 × 1/1.1^3		=	75,131
	Value in use			=	248,685

Value in use is greater than net selling price so, this becomes the **recoverable amount.**

This is then like additional depreciation. The carrying value needs reducing from $290,000 down to $248,685. An impairment loss of $41,315 has arisen.

Dr Income statement $41,315

Cr Machinery account $41,315

 ## Sorry but you need to know ... DEFINITIONS

An **impairment loss** is the amount by which the carrying value of an asset exceeds its recoverable amount.

 Recoverable amount is the higher of an asset's net selling price and value in use. **(Learn this!)**

Net selling price is the amount obtainable from the sale of an asset in an arm's length transaction between knowledgeable, willing parties, less the costs of disposal.

Value in use is the present value of estimated future cash flows expected to arise from the continuing use of an asset and from its disposal at the end of its useful life.

And the really important stuff ... accounting practice

Fixed assets and goodwill should be reviewed for possible impairment where there are indications that the asset could be impaired. These indications would include both internal and external factors to the business (e.g. damage of asset, future plans, new competitors, etc).

Goodwill and intangibles with indefinite lives should be tested annually for impairment.

Where possible the review should be carried out on individual assets; however, if this is impractical, a group of assets should be considered. The group of assets should be the smallest group on which cash flows can be identified and is called a **cash-generating unit (CGU).**

If an asset has impaired in value the asset should be written down to its recoverable amount. If a group of assets is impaired they should be written down to recoverable amount but charging the impairment in the order:

1st   goodwill allocated to the group

2nd other assets pro-rated according to their carrying value (or on some more reasonable basis).

Goodwill should be allocated into CGUs on a reasonable basis if possible. If not, all goodwill is allocated to 'small' CGUs, then a larger CGU made up of small CGUs plus unallocated goodwill is tested. For example, a subsidiary with branches should be initially tested at a branch level, but for goodwill all the branches (at the lower of carrying value or recoverable amount) plus the goodwill in the subsidiary is treated as a large CGU.

The impairment losses should be charged to the income statement, unless the asset had previously been revalued upwards, in which case the impairment losses can be charged against the revaluation reserve to reduce the asset to depreciated historical cost, with any additional losses going to the income statement.

Reversals of impairment losses can be recognised in the income statement to the extent that the original impairment was charged there, with the exception of impairments of goodwill. It is not acceptable to reverse an impairment of goodwill.

* Balance Sheet = Statement of financial position (see page 18)

Disclosures

Extensive disclosures are required for impaired assets including:

- the amounts of impairment losses recognised
- segmental information
- how the recoverable amounts have been calculated
- information on the reversal of impairment losses.

Conclusion

IAS 36 is an important standard. It is frequently examined and often carries lots of marks. Learn the basics, and apply to past questions set by your examiner.

IAS 39 – Financial instruments: recognition and measurement

Introduction

> "Annual income twenty pounds, annual expenditure nineteen nineteen and six, result happiness.
>
> Annual income twenty pounds, annual expenditure twenty pounds ought and six, result misery."
>
> Charles Dickens (1812-1876) David Copperfield

For a start, there is no point reading this chapter unless you have read the one on IAS 32. This chapter covered covered the issue of a company raising finance, and the need to classify the financial instrument as either a liability (debt finance) or equity (shares).

IAS 39 does not address accounting for equity instruments issued by the reporting enterprise, but it does deal with accounting for financial liabilities, and therefore classification of an instrument as liability or as equity is critical. **IAS 32 Financial instruments: presentation** addresses the initial classification question.

So ... what's it trying to achieve?

The standard establishes the principles for recognising and measuring financial instruments. It also provides rules and treatments for hedge accounting.

---

* Balance Sheet = Statement of financial position (see page 18)

Classification of financial liabilities

Once you have decided it is a financial liability and IAS 39 applies, we then have a further classification issue.

IAS 39 recognises two classes of financial liabilities:

- financial liabilities at fair value through profit or loss
- other financial liabilities measured at amortised cost using the effective interest method.

Most financial liabilities are measured on the balance sheet* using the standard amortised cost method. However the fair value through the profit and loss account method may be appropriate if you are looking at liabilities created by a derivative contract (forward contracts, futures, options and swaps).

Transactional example

Aidan Inc wishes to raise finance. It decides to issue bonds with a nominal value of $200,000 for a cash injection of $157,763. It agrees to pay an annual coupon rate of 4% (i.e. $200,000 x 4% = $8,000 each year) and it will be required to repay $200,000 in five years time.

Note. In a transaction like this, because the amount borrowed is $157,763 and the amount to be paid is $200,000, the difference is effectively 'back-loaded' interest. The effective 'real' interest rate is 9.5%.

IAS 32 would classify this as a debt instrument – a liability, as we have an obligation to transfer economic benefit – both interest and on redemption. As it is a liability not equity, IAS 39 also applies.

As it is not a derivative instrument but a loan, this will be classified by IAS 39 as 'other financial liability' to be measured at amortised cost.

Initial recognition

Financial assets and liabilities should be recognised when the company becomes party to the contractual provisions of the instrument. The asset or liability is measured at fair value – the actual transaction price on the reporting date, i.e. George would:

Dr Cash $157,763

    Cr Liability account $157,763

Subsequent measurement – amortised cost

This financial liability would then be measured at 'amortised cost', This means that, instead of using the coupon rate of interest in the income statement, we apply substance over form and charge the effective rate of interest (9.5 %). The first year's income statement is charged with $157,763 x 9.5% = $14,988 interest payable.

We are effectively divorcing the charge in the income statement with the amount going through the cash flow statement. The difference is what is called 'rolled up interest' and is added to the loan account, i.e. Aidan would:

Dr Income statement – interest payable $14,988

Cr Cash $8,000 (4% x $200,000)

Cr Loan account – 'rolled up interest' $6,988

At the balance sheet* date the liability would show as $164,751 (157,763 + 6,988).

We would commonly use an 'amortised cost table' to show this:

Period	Amount borrowed	Interest (at 9.5%) for income statement	Cash repayment 4% (200,000)	Rolled up interest	Bal c/fwd – liability for balance sheet*
	$	$	$	$	$
1	157,763	14,988	(8,000)	6,988	164,751

For many questions, you only need one row in your table. If all you are asked for is an extract from this year's accounts, you now have information for both the income statement and the balance sheet*. You might be asked to show the accounting over the life of the financial instrument however, and that would simply require that you completed the table. See below:

Period	Amount borrowed	Interest (at 9.5%) for income statement	Cash repayment 4% (200,000)	Rolled up interest	Bal c/fwd – liability for balance sheet*
	$	$	$	$	$
1	157,763	14,988	(8,000)	6,988	164,751
2	164,551	15,651	(8000)	7,651	172,402
3	172,402	16,378	(8,000)	8,378	180,780
4	180,780	17,174	(8,000)	9,174	189,954
5	189,954	18,046	(8,000)	10,046	200,000

The redemption amount in year 5 is $200,000, which leaves a liability of nil when paid.

* Balance Sheet = Statement of financial position (see page 18)

Classification of financial assets

Remember, for every company that raises finance somebody must be providing it. These companies are purchasing 'investments'. IAS 39 applies to financial assets as well as financial liabilities.

 IAS 39 recognises four classes of financial assets:

- financial assets at fair value through profit or loss
- held-to-maturity investments
- loans or receivables
- available-for-sale financial assets.

A **financial asset** or **financial liability** at fair value through profit or loss is a financial instrument that meets either of the following conditions:

- it is classified as held for trading; or
- upon initial recognition it was designated as fair value through profit or loss (proposed restrictions).

Held-to-maturity investments are non-derivative fixed-term investments that the entity has the intent and ability to hold to maturity.

(Very strict tainting rules ensure that only instruments to be held to maturity are classified as held-to-maturity).

Loans or receivables are non-derivative financial assets with fixed or determinable payments that are not quoted in an active market and which are not classified as fair value through profit or loss.

(Financial assets where there is a substantial risk of non-recovery cannot be classified as loans or receivables).

Available-for-sale financial assets are non-derivative financial assets that are not classified as any of the above three items.

Initial recognition

Financial assets and liabilities should be recognised when the company becomes party to the contractual provisions of the instrument. The asset or liability is measured at fair value – the actual transaction price on the reporting date.

Subsequent measurement

The following table summarises how financial assets and liabilities are measured and how changes in value are recognised.

Item	Measurement on balance sheet*	Gains/losses
Assets/at FV through profit or loss	FV	Income statement
Available for sale	FV	Equity until derecognition of the asset, then recycled to income statement
Held-to-maturity	Amortised cost	n/a
Loans and receivables	Amortised cost	n/a

* Balance Sheet = Statement of financial position (see page 18)

Sorry but you need to know ... DEFINITIONS

Financial instrument

Any contract that gives rise to both a financial asset of one enterprise and a financial liability or equity instrument of another enterprise.

Financial asset

Any asset that is:

- cash
- a contractual right to receive cash or another financial asset from another enterprise
- a contractual right to exchange financial instruments with another enterprise under conditions that are potentially favourable; or
- an equity instrument of another enterprise.

Financial liability

A liability that is a contractual obligation:

- to deliver cash or another financial asset to another enterprise; or
- to exchange financial instruments with another enterprise under conditions that are potentially unfavourable.

A **financial asset or financial liability** at fair value through profit or loss is a financial instrument that meets either of the following conditions:

- it is classified as held for trading; or
- upon initial recognition it was designated as fair value through profit or loss (proposed restrictions).

Held-to-maturity investments are non-derivative fixed-term investments that the entity has the intent and ability to hold to maturity.

(Very strict tainting rules ensure that only instruments to be held-to-maturity are classified as held-to-maturity.)

Loans or receivables are non-derivative financial assets with fixed or determinable payments that are not quoted in an active market and which are not classified as fair value through profit or loss.

(Financial assets where there is a substantial risk of non-recovery cannot be classified as loans or receivables.)

Available-for-sale financial assets are non-derivative financial assets that are not classified as any of the above three items.

Derivatives

> ## Note
>
> *Note how broad the definition is of a financial instrument …*
>
> *'Any contract that gives rise to both a financial asset of one enterprise and a financial liability or equity instrument of another enterprise.'*

This means that if the question you are looking at has a company that has taken out any of the following derivative contracts:

* forwards
* futures
* options
* swaps

then IAS 39 will apply to these contracts as well as stuff like investments in shares and issuing loan notes.

Derivative contracts will need to be measured at the balance sheet*. They will be deriving their value from some underlying transaction – movements in the forex rate or the interest rate perhaps. As at the balance sheet* date the contract could be in a favourable position – a derivative asset may exist, or indeed it may be in an unfavourable positive – a derivative liability may exist. The basic accounting rule is to classify derivative contracts as 'Fair Value through P&L. However there is a possibility that the company might employ an alternative mechanism we call 'hedge accounting'.

Sometimes a company only has a derivative instrument as part of a 'hedging strategy'. If this is the case basic accounting may not give the fairest presentation.

Hedge accounting

To be allowed to hedge account an entity must formally designate a hedging relationship between a hedged item (the asset/liability, future transaction or foreign subsidiary) being protected and the hedging instrument (always a derivative unless protecting foreign exchange risk where it may be a primary instrument, a loan).

The hedge can be one of three types.

* Fair value   Hedged item is an asset or liability or a firm commitment.
* Cash flow   Hedged item is a forecast future transaction (or a firm commitment for foreign exchange transactions).
* Net investment   Hedged item is a foreign subsidiary.

---

* Balance Sheet = Statement of financial position (see page 18)

To hedge account (see below) the following criteria must be met:

- formal documentation at the inception of the hedge
- designation between the hedged item and the hedging instrument is documented.
- hedge is expected to be highly effective at inception and on-going
- effectiveness can be measured
- for cash flow hedges – transaction must be highly probable
- the hedge is assessed on an on-going basis, and effective throughout the period.

An effective hedge is when the gain or loss on the hedged item is offset by an opposite gain or loss on a hedging instrument between 80% and 125%.

 A mnemonic **(DEAD)** works well here – remember it if you are asked the criteria for hedge accounting in the exam:

D **Document the hedge formally at its inception**

E **Effectiveness of the hedge must be expected**

A **Assessment of the hedge is assessed on an on-going basis (80–125%)**

D **Designation between the hedged item and hedging instrument at the outset**

The hedge accounting treatment is as follows.

Fair value hedge

Both the hedged item and the hedging instrument are revalued to fair value, and the opposite gains and losses are recognised directly in the income statement.

Cash flow hedge

The hedging instrument is revalued to fair value and the gain or loss is taken to a separate reserve. When the hedged item is recognised the separate reserve is recycled to the income statement, or if it is a non-monetary asset or liability the recycling can be to the cost of the hedged item.

Net investment hedge

The hedging instrument (usually a loan) is revalued to fair value with any gain or loss recognised in reserves to offset against the gain or loss on the foreign subsidiary. The offset is limited to the gain or loss recognised on the subsidiary.

And the really important stuff ... accounting practice

Recognition and Derecognition

Financial assets and liabilities should be recognised when the company becomes party to the contractual provisions of the instrument.

Financial assets should be derecognised when the risks and rewards associated with the asset have been transferred to another party. If it is unclear whether risks and rewards have been transferred, financial assets are derecognised if control has been transferred.

Financial liabilities are only derecognised when they are extinguished.

Gains and losses on derecognition should be recognised in the income statement.

Measurement

The following table summarises how financial assets and liabilities are measured and how changes in value are recognised.

Item	Measurement on balance sheet*	Gains/losses
Assets/at FV through profit or loss	FV	Income statement
Derivatives (not hedging)	FV	Income statement
Derivatives (not hedging)	FV	(see special rules)
Available for sale	FV	Equity until derecognition of the asset, then recycled to income statement
Held-to-maturity	Amortised cost	n/a
Loans and receivables	Amortised cost	n/a
Other financial liabilities	Amortised cost	n/a

Financial assets must be reviewed for impairment annually and written down through the income statement if impaired. If an available for sale investment is impaired, any losses previously recognised in reserves must be recycled to the income statement.

* Balance Sheet = Statement of financial position (see page 18)

Conclusion

IAS 39 is a very important topic for more advanced accounting students. Most companies raise finance. It is imperative that financial liabilities can be accounted for. As you move through your studies you need to be just as comfortable preparing the accounts for the providers of finance, i.e. dealing with financial assets becomes key. Derivatives are more common than students think. Even small companies in the real world get involved in forward contracts – not a subject to be ignored.

IAS 40 – Investment property

Introduction

> **"An investment in knowledge pays the best interest."**
>
> **Benjamin Franklin (1706–1790)**

Well, although the idea in the quote is lovely, many companies like many individuals decide instead to invest in property. We, as accountants, do have to recognise that the IAS 16 basis of accounting for property may not be appropriate when the property is not being used to operate/trade from, but is instead held for its investment potential. The requirement for depreciation seems a bit silly in this case.

Not all properties are the same then?

Exactly – we have to have an alternative treatment for some properties, if the accounts are to present fairly. IAS 40 gives companies that opportunity.

So ... what's it trying to achieve?

IAS 40 prescribes the accounting treatment for investment property and the related disclosure requirements.

A company may only use IAS 40 to account for a property when the definition of an investment property is met. Otherwise another accounting standard must be applied – maybe IAS 16 or indeed IAS 2, if the asset is in fact 'inventory (see transactional example)

---

* Balance Sheet = Statement of financial position (see page 18)

Transactional example

Munchkin Inc has got the following properties and it is not sure which accounting standard is applicable.

- *Factory held by Munchkin Inc for use in production of its goods.*
- *Land held by Munchkin Inc, unused at present, no plans to sell.*
- *An empty building owned by Munchkin Inc and to be leased out using an operating lease.*

A factory held by a company for use in production should not be accounted for under IAS 40, because it is owner-occupied. It is a non-current asset – property per IAS 16.

The land however would qualify as an investment property under IAS 40, as indeed would the empty building leased out under an operating lease.

 A common mistake is to treat an owner-occupied building as an investment property because of its capital appreciation potential.

Sorry but you need to know ... DEFINITIONS

Investment property is property (land or a building – or part of a building – or both) held (by the owner or by the lessee under a finance lease) to earn rentals or for capital appreciation or both, rather than for:

(a) use in the production or supply of goods and services or for administrative purposes; or

(b) sale in the ordinary course of business.

Properties held under operating leases may be investment properties if, and only if, the property meets the other criteria to be classified as an investment property, and the fair value model is followed.

Owner-occupied property is property held (by the owner or by the lessee under a finance lease) for use in the production or supply of goods and services or for administrative purposes.

And the really important stuff ... accounting practice

Investment properties should be recognised as assets when, and only when:

(a) it is probable that the future economic benefits will flow to the enterprise; and

(b) the cost can be measured reliably.

Investment properties should initially be measured at cost.

 Subsequent measurement of investment properties should follow the **preferred fair value model** or the alternative cost model.

Fair value model	Cost model
• The investment properties are revalued to fair value at each balance sheet* date	• The investment properties are held using the benchmark method in IAS 16 (cost)
• Gains or losses on revaluation are recognised directly in the income statement	• The properties are depreciated like any other asset
• The properties are not depreciated	

Transfers into and out of investment property should only be made when supported by a change of use of the property.

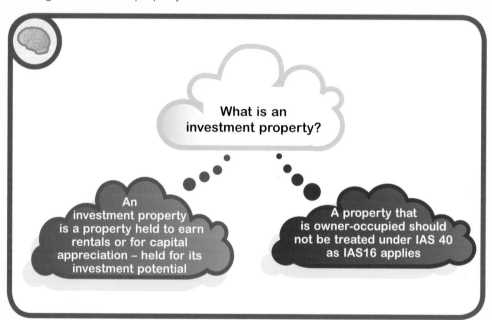

What is an investment property?

An investment property is a property held to earn rentals or for capital appreciation – held for its investment potential

A property that is owner-occupied should not be treated under IAS 40 as IAS16 applies

* Balance Sheet = Statement of financial position (see page 18)

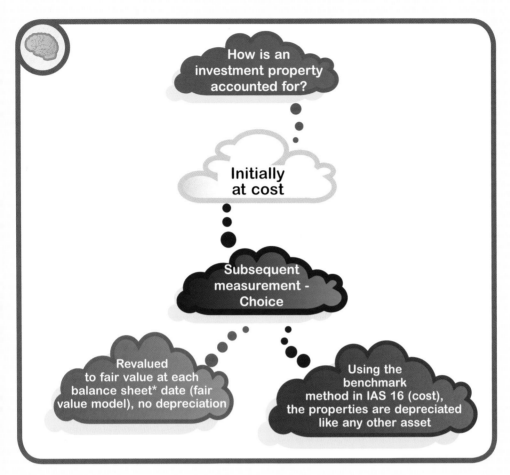

Disclosures

Key disclosures include:

- whether the fair value or cost model has been followed
- if following the fair value model whether any assets held under operating leases have been classified as investment properties
- the methods and significant assumptions in determining fair values
- the extent of valuations performed by an independent professionally qualified valuer
- the amounts recognised for:
  - rental income
  - direct operating expenses
- reconciliations of the movement in the investment property on the balance sheet* (for both property held under the fair value and the cost models).

There are other specific disclosures for properties held under both the fair value or cost models.

Conclusion

Again this is a standard that is not an 'exam dealbreaker'. It is likely to be part of a bigger exam question rather than a full blown question.

IFRS 5 – Discontinued operations and presentation of assets held for sale

Introduction

> "Ah! this is the one we use when companies decide to stop doing the stuff they used to do ... isn't it?"
>
> **Anon accounting student**

Well to be fair that quote just about sums it up – companies stop doing stuff they used to do. For most sets of accounts that you prepare you will use IAS 16 to account for property, plant and equipment. If, however, you are looking at a question where you are told the company has committed to stop doing stuff, 'discontinues an activity' or plans to sell a building, for example then you may also have to consider whether IFRS 5 will apply. The questions you would need to ask include:

- is the building available for immediate sale?
- is it being actively marketed at a price that makes the sale highly probable?

If the answer to both is yes, then an alternative treatment of the asset may be available under IFRS 5.

So some owned assets are accounted for under IAS 16, some under IAS 40, and now you're telling us some are under IFRS 5 ... big sigh!!

---

* Balance Sheet = Statement of financial position (see page 18)

Sorry you are right: most owned assets are accounted for under IAS 16, fewer are treated as 'investment properties' under IAS 40 and fewer still, but still relevant, are those 'held for sale' under IFRS 5.

Under IAS 16 the building will be depreciated over its remaining useful economic life (UEL) in the usual way. If, however, IFRS 5 applies and it gets classed as 'held for sale', the building will not need to be depreciated.

So ... what's it trying to achieve?

IFRS 5 was the first exposure draft issued by the IASB in its convergence project with US GAAP. As such its requirements are driven by US GAAP. Its aim is to give guidance on the presentation of non-current assets held for sale and to give rules on discontinued operations.

Transactional example

The board of Alfie Inc approved a plan to sell its head office site, both land and buildings. A new head office has been acquired and the staff have moved across. The old site, including renovated vacant buildings are being offered for sale via a local real estate dealer. The board is not sure how to deal with the old head office in the accounts.

Under IFRS 5, a non current asset should be classified as 'held for sale' if its carrying amounts will be recovered principally through a sale transaction rather than its continuing use. The criteria which have to be met are:

M	Management committed to a plan
A	Actively trying to find a buyer and marketing assets
A	Assets available for immediate sale
S	Sale is highly probable, and
S	Sale expected to complete within one year of classification.

Remember the acronym – **MAASS** or maybe you prefer mnemonics:

Management accountant available – seriously sexy!!

Non-current assets held for sale should not be depreciated. The assets should be measured at the lower of carrying amount and fair value, less costs to sell.

Be careful with these transactions. Just having gone to an estate agent/ real estator doesn't make it held for sale – it will have to be priced so it is realistically expected to sell in order to meet the criteria. This is a controversial standard as it is believed it can be used for manipulation – with regard to non-depreciation of assets.

Sorry but you need to know ... DEFINITIONS

A **component of an entity** is operations and cash flows that can be clearly distinguished, operationally and for financial reporting purposes, from the rest of the entity.

A **disposal group** is a group of assets to be disposed of, by sale or otherwise, together as a group in a single transaction, and liabilities directly associated with those assets that will be transferred in the transaction. The group includes goodwill acquired in a business combination if the group is a cash-generating unit to which goodwill has been allocated in accordance with IAS 36.

And the really important stuff ... accounting practice

Non-current assets held for sale

Non-current assets held for sale, and assets and liabilities to be disposed of together in a single transaction (a disposal group) should be separately presented on the balance sheet*. The assets and liabilities in a disposal group should not be offset however.

The IFRS gives the same criteria for distinguishing assets held for sale or a disposal group as in SFAS 144 (i.e. the US equivalent accounting standard):

- management committed and actively marketing assets
- assets available for immediate sale
- very unlikely to withdraw from the plan and
- sale expected to complete within one year of classification.

Non-current assets held for sale should not be depreciated.

The assets should be measured at the lower of carrying amount and fair value less costs to sell.

* Balance Sheet = Statement of financial position (see page 18)

Discontinued operations

A discontinued operation is a component of an entity:

- that either has been disposed of or is classified as held for sale,
- whose operations and cash flows have been, or will be, eliminated from the on-going operations of the entity as a result of the disposal transaction; and
- in which the entity will have no significant continuing involvement after the disposal transaction.

A component of an entity may be a segment (under IFRS 8), a cash-generating unit (IAS 36) or a subsidiary.

The revenue, expenses, pre-tax profit or loss and the income tax expense of the discontinued operations should be separately presented on the face of the income statement or in the notes to the accounts. The face of the income statement must include, as a minimum, the profit or loss of discontinued operations.

The cash flows from operating, investing and financing should be separately disclosed on the face or in the notes.

Components of an entity that are abandoned are subject to the same disclosure requirements as those disposed when the abandonment occurs. Assets abandoned (as opposed to components of an entity) are not discontinued operations.

Conclusion

The analysis regarding discontinued activities is key if users of accounts are to be presented with relevant information. When a company discontinues an activity, a purchaser of shares needs to know about it if the results are to be understandable.

* Balance Sheet = Statement of financial position (see page 18)

IFRS 7 – Financial instruments: disclosures

Introduction

> "The Board believes that the introduction of IFRS 7 will lead to greater transparency about the risks that entities run from the use of financial instruments. This, combined with the new requirements in IAS 1, will provide better information for investors and other users of financial statements to make informed judgements about risk and return."
>
> Sir David Tweedie, IASB Chair

IFRS 7 is a companion standard to IAS 32 and 39. As it is purely a disclosure standard, it is not going to be a major issue in its own right – basically you just need an awareness of what it's all about.

So ... what's it trying to achieve?

IFRS 7 introduces new requirements to improve the information on financial instruments that is given in entities' financial statements. It replaces IAS 30 Disclosures in the **Financial Statements of Banks** and **Similar Financial Institutions** return.

IFRS 7 applies to all risks arising from all financial instruments, except those covered by another more specific standard such as interests in subsidiaries, associates and joint ventures, post-employment benefits, share-based payment and insurance contracts. Although IFRS 7 applies to all entities, the extent of disclosure required depends on the extent of the entity's use of financial instruments and of its exposure to risk.

Disclosures

The IFRS requires disclosures about the significance of financial instruments for an entity's financial position and performance. These disclosures incorporate many of the requirements previously in IAS 32 (whose title has been shortened to reflect the change). The IFRS also requires information about the extent to which the entity is exposed to risks arising from financial instruments, and a description of management's objectives, policies and processes for managing those risks. Together, these disclosures provide an overview of the entity's use of financial instruments and the exposures to risks they create.

Qualitative and quantitative information about exposure to risks arising from financial instruments is required, including specified minimum disclosures about credit risk, liquidity risk and market risk. The qualitative disclosures describe management's objectives, policies and processes for managing those risks. The quantitative disclosures provide information about the extent to which the entity is exposed to risk, based on information provided internally to the entity's key management personnel.

IFRS 7 includes mandatory application guidance that explains how to apply the requirements in the IFRS. It is accompanied by Implementation Guidance that describes how an entity might provide the disclosures required by the IFRS.

IFRS 7 is effective for annual periods beginning on or after 1 January 2007. Earlier application is encouraged.

Conclusion

When you are studying financial instruments it is probably best if you study IAS 32, IAS 39 and IFRS 7 all together as they relate to the same topic.

---

* Balance Sheet = Statement of financial position (see page 18)

3

Group accounts

"Things should be made as simple as possible but not any simpler."

Albert Einstein (1879-1955)

Introduction

Accountancy is really two quite separate topics. We tend to think of the double-entry bookkeeping records, leading to the individual company separate financial statements, as the 'real' accounts of a company. However, once we have a group of companies we may have to prepare from these 'real' accounts a set of consolidated financial statements. This is because the individual company accounts are not adequate for 'fair presentation' of the results of such groups.

A separate body of accounting standards exists for these group or consolidated accounts.

For those interested in group accounts:

- IAS 27 Consolidated and separate financial statements
- IFRS 3 Business combinations
- IAS 28 Investments in associates
- IAS 31 Interests in joint ventures

"In individuals insanity is rare; but in groups, parties, nations and epochs it is the rule."

Friedrich Nietzsche (1844-1900)

Note

Many books on accounting standards start by giving you the aims and definitions from the standard. This book deliberately does not structure the chapters in that style. Instead the issue is generally explained, with the sort of transactions that the standard relates to being introduced. We do get to the aims and definitions and, for those of you who already feel comfortable with the standard, you may like to turn first to the definitions box – re-affirm those and then read the chapter.

---

* Balance Sheet = Statement of financial position (see page 18)

(23) IAS 27 – Consolidated and separate financial statements

Introduction

> **"I believe I was extremely greedy. I've lost my moral compass and did things I regret."**
>
> **Andrew Fastow, Chief Financial Officer (CFO) of Enron**

Andy Fastow was the Chief Financial Officer of Enron, the most famous bankruptcy of all time. One of the 'things' that Andy Fastow 'did' (he went to prison for six and a half years by the way) was to set up a deliberate network of over 4,000 companies that, despite being controlled entities in substance, were not included in the consolidated financial statements of Enron. This was because they were deliberately established to fall outside the US GAAP definition of a subsidiary. This was a deliberate plan to mislead the readers of the main Enron accounts about the amount of cash that Enron was borrowing and to cover up the true level of its debt.

Consolidated accounts are pretty important then?

Absolutely! All companies may be separate legal entities but often one company owns enough shares to appoint the board of another company. This means that, although the second company is a separate legal entity, in substance it is merely like a division of the first. The two companies together are commercially a 'single entity'. Just preparing separate financial statements will not present fairly. We call the company that owns the shares the 'parent' and the second company the 'subsidiary'. All subsidiaries should have their accounts consolidated with those of the parent. Only in this way is the true commercial reality being reflected.

So ... what's it trying to achieve?

IAS 27 prescribes which companies are subsidiaries, exclusions from consolidation and the consolidation procedures to be adopted by companies.

---

* Balance Sheet = Statement of financial position (see page 18)

Transactional example

Aston acquired 45% of the voting shares of Villa on 1 March 20X6. The other shares are owned by MJ (25%) and AJ (30%). MJ and AJ are both represented on the board as they are institutional investors. Aston has the power to appoint four board members and AJ and MJ the power to appoint three each. To change the capital structure of the company all ten directors must vote in favour of the proposal. However from a day-to-day operating policy point of view, it is the four directors appointed by Aston who have the effective power. You have to decide whether Aston is required to consolidate Villa with its own accounts.

A typical error that students make in questions concerning consolidation relates to determining the status of the company. Students often apply a blanket percentage approach, i.e if it is above 50% they consolidate and if it is below they don't. Remember the decision should be made by ability to control, not the percentage held. Here Villa should be consolidated because Aston has effective control through its control, over the board of directors and decision making. Although the full board retains some powers, these are limited.

Sorry but you need to know ... DEFINITIONS

Consolidated financial statements are the financial statements of a group presented as those of a single economic entity.

Control is the power to govern the financial and operating policies of an entity so as to obtain benefits from its activities.

A **group** is a parent and its subsidiaries.

A **parent** is an entity that has one or more subsidiaries.

A **subsidiary** is an entity, including an unincorporated entity such as a partnership, that is controlled by another entity.

And the really important stuff ... accounting practice

Scope and exclusion from consolidation

A parent shall present consolidated accounts subject to some limited exemptions mainly for unlisted parents that are themselves wholly owned subsidiaries.

Subsidiaries can only be excluded from consolidation if control is intended to be temporary, they are expected to be sold within the next 12 months, and where management is actively seeking a buyer. Subsidiaries in this position are treated as 'held for trading' in accordance with IAS 39.

Consolidation procedures

Intra-group (intra=within) balances and transactions must be eliminated in full.

If they have different year-ends the parent and subsidiary accounts can be consolidated if they are within three months of each other.

Parents and subsidiaries must use uniform accounting policies.

Minority interests should be presented in equity, but separate from the parent shareholder's equity. Minority interests should also be separately presented in the income statement.

If an investment ceases to be a subsidiary it should be accounted for as an associate, or under IAS 39. Its carrying amount on the date it ceases to be a subsidiary is regarded as its cost on initial measurement under IAS 39.

Separate financial statements

In the separate financial statements of a parent company a subsidiary, associate or jointly controlled entity may be accounted for either:

* at cost; or
* in accordance with IAS 39.

Conclusion

Once consolidated accounts are on your syllabus they tend be examined at every sitting. Once you are happy with identifying a subsidiary, you really need to get very familiar with IFRS 3, the companion standard which shows the method to be used for business combinations. You then need to make sure you don't underestimate how much practice this subject will take.

* Balance Sheet = Statement of financial position (see page 18)

(24) IFRS 3 – Business combinations

Introduction

> **"The success combination in business is – do what you do better … and do more of what you do."**
>
> David Joseph Schwartz

IFRS 3 is a companion standard to IAS 27. Once you can identify that you have got a subsidiary you then clearly need to be able to account for one. As we saw in Chapter 23, if one company owns more than 50% of the ordinary shares of another company this will usually give the first company 'control' of the second company.

This is because the first company, that is referred to as the holding or parent company (H say), has enough voting power to appoint all the directors of the second company that we call the subsidiary (S say). H is, in effect, able to manage S as if it were merely a department of H, rather than a separate entity. In strict legal terms H and S remain distinct, but in economic substance (commercial reality) they can be regarded as a single unit (a 'group').

The key principle underlying group accounts is the need to reflect the economic substance of the relationship.

To reflect the true economic substance of a group of companies we need to produce group accounts in addition to the individual accounts prepared for each company within the group. One of the main methods of doing this is to prepare 'consolidated' accounts using the 'purchase' method and this is the main thrust of this chapter.

Consolidated accounts present the group as though it were a 'single economic entity'.

So ... what's it trying to achieve?

The objective of IFRS 3 is to specify how to account when one entity combines with another.

The single entity concept

Business combinations consolidate the results and net assets of group members so as to display the group's affairs as those of a single economic entity. As already mentioned, this conflicts with the strict legal position that each company is a distinct entity. Applying the single entity concept is a good example of the accounting principle of showing economic substance over legal form.

The group as a single entity

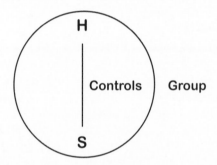

The mechanics of consolidation

When one company buys shares in another company the cash paid is recorded as an investment in the acquiring company's balance sheet*.

A standard group accounting question will present you with the accounts of the parent company and the accounts of the subsidiary and will require you to prepare consolidated accounts. Consolidated balance sheet* questions should be approached using the following set of standard workings.

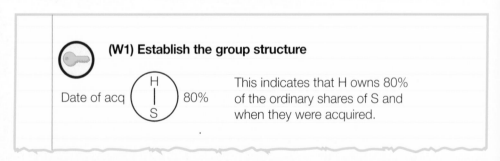

(W1) Establish the group structure

Date of acq   H
                | 80%
                S

This indicates that H owns 80% of the ordinary shares of S and when they were acquired.

* Balance Sheet = Statement of financial position (see page 18)

(W2) Net assets of subsidiary

sheet*	At date of acquisition $	At the balance (B/S) date $
Share capital	X	X
Reserves:		
Retained earnings	X	X
	X	X

 (W3) Goodwill on acquisition

	$
Cost of shares acquired	X
Less: Share of net assets at acquisition (see W2)	(x)
	X
Less: Impairments to date	(x)
	X

 (W4) Minority interest

	$
Share of net assets at balance sheet date (see W2)	X

 (W5) Group retained earnings

	$
H reserve (100%)	X
S – group share of post-acquisition reserves	X
Less: Goodwill impairments to date (W3)	X
	X

Other group reserves

	$
H reserve (100%)	X
S group share of post-acquisition reserves	X
	X

These five workings are really key to consolidation of a balance sheet*, so use the revise/cover/test approach.

This simply means you need to learn the five workings, then cover them up and see if you can correctly write them out without looking at the answers. Then you need to apply them to past exam questions.

Pre-acquisition reserves

The reserves that exist in a subsidiary company at the date when it is acquired are called its 'pre-acquisition' reserves. These are capitalised at the date of acquisition by including them in the goodwill calculation. We really need to look at some numbers.

? Transactional example

Draft balance sheet's of Harriet and Sophie on 31 December 20X1 are as follows:*

	Harriet	Sophie
	$000	$000
Non-current assets	90	100
Investment in Sophie at cost	110	
Current assets	50	30
	250	130
Equity and liabilities		
Capital and reserves		
Ordinary share capital $1	100	100
Retained earnings	120	20
	220	120
Current liabilities	30	10
	250	130

Harriet had bought 80% of the ordinary shares of Sophie on 1 January 20X1 when the retained earnings of Sophie's had a balance of $10,000. No impairment of goodwill has occurred to date.

Required:

Prepare a consolidated balance sheet as at 31 December 20X1.*

First set out your answer booklet – you need a page for the consolidated balance sheet* and then a separate page for the workings as shown below.

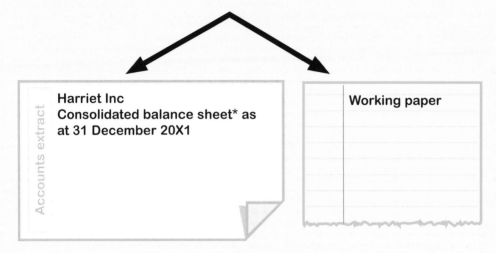

We are going to start with the working paper – use the five core workings from p172.

Workings

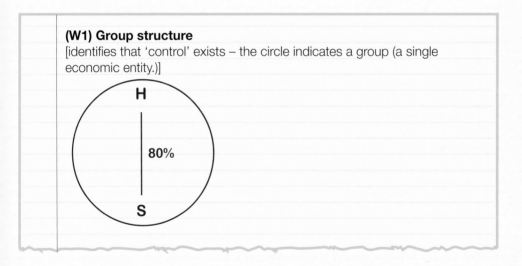

(W2) Net assets of Sophie

(Current balance sheet* date is easy – tick off from Sophie's balance sheet* in the question, and always assume a company's capital structure is unchanged since the date the company was incorporated unless the question tells you otherwise, i.e. share capital is usually the same at both dates.)

	At date of acquisition $000	At balance sheet date $000
$1 shares	100	100
Reserves	10	20
	110	120
	Take this to (W3)	Take this to (W4)

(The reserves at the date of acquisition are ascertained by reading the supporting information in the question. If the reserves are NOT given in the supporting information, you will find there is enough information to allow you to calculate it.)

(W3) Goodwill

(Pick up the purchase consideration from the parent company's (Harriet) balance sheet* – tick it off.)

	$000
Purchase consideration	110
For 80% of net assets acquired **(apply the group percentage to the net assets at the date of acquisition)** (W2) (80% × $110,000)	(88)
Goodwill **(becomes an intangible asset on the consolidated balance sheet* unless it is impaired)**	22

(W4) Minority interests

(If the group owns 80% of the shares, then third parties **(who we call a minority interest)** own the other 20%.)

	$000
20% of net assets at balance sheet* date ($120,000)	24

(The minority interest account only appears on a consolidated balance sheet*, not an individual company balance sheet*.)

---

* Balance Sheet = Statement of financial position (see page 18)

(W5) Group retained earnings
(Always include 100% of any earnings that relate to the parent company –
but think carefully about the subsidiary.)

	$000
100% Holding co/parent co. *(Tick it off as you use it!)*	120

10
Pre-acquisition

20
Subsidiary

Post-acquisition
10 × 80%   8

                                                                           ───
                                                                           128

[The subsidiary's reserves cannot just be added to those of the parent
because if any existed at the date of acquisition they have already been
taken in the goodwill calculation. You must therefore exclude those (we call
them pre-acquisition) reserves, so we are looking to bring in just our share
of the reserves created since the date of acquisition (we call them post-
acquisition).]

You would then be in a position to put together the answer. Start with the goodwill
from Working 3. It appears on the consolidated balance sheet*,unless it has been
impaired.as an intangible asset. Do not forget to cross reference to your workings! Any
numbers that are not already 'ticked' are then combined. Your answer should now
look like this:

Harriet group consolidated balance sheet* as at 31 December 20X1

Assets	$000
Non-current assets	
Intangible assets (W3)	22
Tangible assets (90 + 100)	190
	───
	212
Current assets (50 + 30)	80
Total assets	───
	292

*Balance sheet**

Harriet group consolidated balance sheet* as at 31 December 20X1

Equity and liabilities	$000
Capital and reserves	
$1 shares (100% parent company only)	100
Retained earnings (W5)	128
Shareholders' capital	228
Minority interest (W4)	24
	252
Current liabilities (30 + 10)	40
Total equity and liabilities	292

Sorry but you need to know ... DEFINITIONS

Goodwill is the future economic benefit arising from assets that are not capable of being individually identified and separately recognised.

Intangible assets follow the definition in IAS 38.

Minority interest is that portion of the profit or loss and net assets of a subsidiary attributable to equity interests that are not owned, directly or indirectly through subsidiaries, by the parent.

What if the goodwill is impaired?

We saw in Chapter 18 that the rule is 'assets must not be carried at more than their recoverable amount'. If the goodwill is impaired, it must not be shown as an asset, as it is not recoverable.

If an exam question tells you the goodwill is fully impaired, instead of taking it to the balance sheet*, it becomes a negative adjustment to group reserves (remember an impairment loss on goodwill is a cost in the consolidated income statement).

If the question above had told you the goodwill was fully impaired, Working 3 and Working 5 would now look like this:

---

* Balance Sheet = Statement of financial position (see page 18)

(W3) Goodwill

	$000
Purchase consideration	110
For 80% of net assets acquired	
(W2) (80% x $110,000)	(88)
Goodwill	22
Impaired to date	(22)
Intangible for balance sheet*	nil

(W5) Group retained earnings

	$000
100% Holding co/parent co.	120

10
Pre-acquisition

20
Subsidiary

Post-acquisition
10 × 80% 8

	128
Less: Goodwill impaired to date	(22)
	106

So the balance sheet* would look like this:

Harriet group consolidated balance sheet* as at 31 December 20X1

Assets	$000	$000
Non-current assets		
Intangible assets (W3)		nil
Tangible assets (90 + 100)		190
		190
Current assets (50 + 30)		80
Total assets		270

Harriet group consolidated balance sheet* as at 31 December 20X1

	$000	$000
Equity and liabilities		
Capital and reserves		
$1 shares (100% parent company only)		100
Retained earnings (W5)		106
Shareholders' capital		206
Minority interest (W4)		24
		230
Current liabilities (30 + 10)		40
Total equity and liabilities		270

Remember the goodwill may only be partially impaired so it may have a partial write off through Working 5 and a partial intangible on the balance sheet*.

Inter-company transactions

The single entity concept

A common mistake in 'consolidation' questions is to fail to understand the true objective of group accounts is to present the group as a single entity. Hence the effects of transactions between group members need to be eliminated as the group has not transacted with any third party.

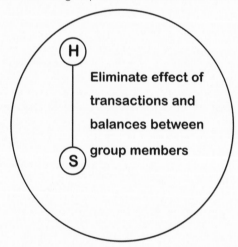

Reflecting the group as a single entity means that items which are assets in one group company and liabilities in another need to be cancelled out; otherwise group assets and liabilities could be overstated.

---

* Balance Sheet = Statement of financial position (see page 18)

Intra-group balances result from, for example:

- loans and debentures between group companies
- intra-group trading
- dividends declared in the year but not yet paid by S to H.

To eliminate such balances, cancel the credit balance in one company against the debit balance in the other, before summing net assets line-by-line.

 Transactional example

Draft balance sheets* of Henry and Suzi on 31 March 20X7 are as follows.

	Henry $000	Suzi $000
Tangible non-current assets	100	140
Investment in Suzi at cost	180	
Current assets		
Inventory	30	35
Trade receivables	20	10
Cash	10	5
	340	190
Equity and liabilities		
Capital and reserves		
Share capital: Ordinary $1 shares	250	100
Share premium	–	30
Retained earnings	–	20
	250	150
Non-current liabilities		
10% loan notes	65	–
Current liabilities	25	40
	340	190

Notes:

1. *Henry bought 80,000 shares in Suzi in 20X1 when Suzi's reserves included a share premium of $30,000 and retained earnings of $5,000.*

2. *Henry owes Suzi $8,000 and this is reflected in both their accounts.*

3. *No impairment of goodwill has occurred to date.*

Required:

Prepare a consolidated balance sheet* as at 31 March 20X7.

> **Note**
>
> *Because of the inter-company debt you will have to:*
>
> Dr Group payables $8,000
>
> Cr Group receivables $8,000 (deduct $8,000 from both lines)

Henry group consolidated balance sheet* as at 31 March 20X7

	$000	$000
Assets		
Non-current assets		
Intangible assets (W3)		72
Tangible assets (100 + 140)		240
		312
Current assets		
Inventory (30 + 35)	65	
Trade receivables (20 + 10 – 8)	22	
Cash (10 + 5)	15	
		102
		414
Equity and liabilities		
Capital and reserves		
Share capital (100% parent only)		250
Retained earnings (W5)		12
		262
Minority interests (W4)		30
		292
Non-current liabilities		
10% loan notes		65
Current liabilities		
Payables (25 + 40 – 8)		57
		414

(W1) Group structure

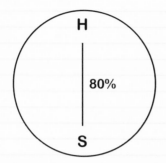

(W2) Net assets of Suzi
(Note all reserves go into this working.)

	At date of acquisition $000	At balance sheet date $000
Share capital	100	100
Share premium	30	30
Retained earnings	5	20
Net assets	135	150

(W3) Goodwill

	$000
Purchase consideration	180
For 80% of net assets ($135,000) acquired	(108)
Goodwill	72

(W4) Minority interests

	$000
20% of net assets at balance sheet* date (150,000)	30

(W5) Group retained earnings

	$000
100% H	Nil

S 20,000 — Pre-acquisition 5,000

15,000 × 80%
Post-acquisition ... 12

Group retained earnings	12

Group share premium account

	$000
100% H	Nil

S 30,000 — Pre-acquisition 30,000

Nil × 80%
Post-acquisition ... Nil

Group share premium	Nil

The consolidated income statement

Control and ownership

An income statement shows the profit generated by resources disclosed in the related balance sheet*.

- H's individual income statement includes dividend income receivable from S.
- The consolidated income statement (CIS) shows all income generated by the group's resources (i.e. by the net assets shown in the consolidated balance sheet*).

To reflect this we must prepare the CIS on a basis consistent with the consolidated balance sheet*. In particular, the CIS must show incomes generated from the net assets under H's control.

To do this, we include in the CIS all of S's income and expenses (100%), line by line, down to and including net profit for the period (profit after tax). This is the case even if the equity share in S is less than 100%.

To reflect the ownership in S we must then show the amounts attributable to the 'equity holders of the parent' (the parent's shareholders) and the amount attributable to the 'minority interest'.

* Balance Sheet = Statement of financial position (see page 18)

If S has paid dividends to H these should be cancelled against H's investment income. Indeed, this is just one example of intra-group transactions that must be eliminated from the consolidated accounts. We have already dealt with such transactions in the consolidated balance sheet* (e.g. unrealised profit in closing inventories). We now look at the impact of intra-group transactions on the CIS.

Intra-group transactions

Intra-group transactions are those which take place within the group and do not involve outside entities. An equivalent term is inter-company transactions (inter = between): transactions between members of the group, not involving outsiders.

The objective of consolidated accounts is to display the group as a single entity. Intra-group transactions have a nil effect on the group as a whole and must be excluded from the consolidated accounts. We have just seen one example of this: payment of a dividend by S to H. Similarly, if S pays loan interest to H this too must be excluded.

The effect of this on the CIS is any dividend income shown in the CIS must arise from trade investments, not investments in S or H.

The minority interest in S is calculated on the profit after tax and before dividends. The figure therefore includes the minority's share of S's dividends and S's retained earnings.

Inter-company trading must also be eliminated from the CIS. Such trading will be included in the sales revenue of one group company and the purchases of another. To cancel these transactions on consolidation:

- add across H and S sales revenue and cost of sales to get the consolidated figure
- deduct the value of the inter-company sale from consolidated sales revenue and cost of sales.

If any items sold by one group company to another are included in closing inventories, their value must be adjusted to the lower of cost and net realisable value to the group. This is consistent with our treatment of inventories in the consolidated balance sheet*.

Transactional example

Below are the income statements of the Binbrook Group, as at 31 December 20X8.

	Binbrook $000	Earlswood $000
Revenue	385	100
Cost of sales	(185)	(60)
Gross profit	200	40
Distribution costs	(10)	(10)
Administration expenses	(40)	(5)
Profit from operations	150	25
Tax	(50)	(12)
Profit after tax	100	13

You are also given the following information:

- *Binbrook acquired 45,000 ordinary shares in Earlswood. Earlswood has 50,000 $1 ordinary shares*

- *Binbrook sold $10,000 of goods to Earlswood. None was in inventory as at the year end.*

Draft a consolidated income statement for Binbrook for the year ended 31 December 20X8.

Note

We are going to combine the results of the two companies, making sure we exclude any internal transactions. As we do not own 100% of the shares in Earlswood we will need to express a minority interest in the profits of Earlswood – two figures exist for minority interest, the balance sheet* one is based on net assets and the income statement one based on profit – don't confuse the two.

See below:

---

* Balance Sheet = Statement of financial position (see page 18)

Binbrook group

Consolidated income statement for the year ended 31 December 20X8

	$000
Revenue (385 + 100) – 10	475
Cost of sales (185 + 60) – 10	(235)
Gross profit (200 + 40)	240
Distribution costs (10 + 10)	(20)
Administration expenses (40 + 5)	(45)
Profit from operations	175
Taxation (50 + 12)	(62)
Profit after tax	113
Amount attributable to:	
Equity holders of the parent	111.7
Minority interests (10% of Earlswood's profit after tax)	1.3

(W1) Group structure

$$\frac{45,000}{50,000} = 90\%$$

Fair values

The accounting problem

So far in dealing with the acquisition of a subsidiary we have assumed that the net assets shown in the subsidiary's balance sheet* are stated at fair value. This is not always the case, owing to the limitations of historical cost accounting. It is important that the financial results reported following acquisition accurately show the performance of the new management.

Therefore IFRS 3 requires that at the date of acquisition the identifiable assets and liabilities and contingent liabilities of the subsidiary that meet its recognition criteria must be stated at fair value on that date.

Group accounting questions may therefore include a requirement to put through fair value adjustments. The fair values not the book values will be used in the calculation of goodwill

You will also have taken account of the impact of these adjustments on the post-acquisition reserves and assets and liabilities in the consolidated balance sheet*.

Accounting treatment

The parent should recognise separately at fair value the acquiree's identifiable assets, liabilities and contingent liabilities at the acquisition date only if they satisfy the following criteria at that date:

- for an asset other than an intangible asset, it is probable that any associated future economic benefits will flow to the acquirer, and its fair value can be measured reliably
- for a liability other than a contingent liability, it is probable that an outflow of resources embodying economic benefits will be required to settle the obligation, and its fair value can be measured reliably
- in the case of an intangible asset or a contingent liability, its fair value can be measured reliably.

Identifiable assets and liabilities recognised in the accounts are those of the acquired entity that existed at the date of acquisition. The following specifically do not meet the criteria listed above and therefore must be dealt with as post-acquisition items:

- changes resulting from the acquirer's intentions or future actions
- changes resulting from post-acquisition events
- provisions for future operating losses or reorganisation costs incurred as a result of the acquisition.

Calculating fair values

IFRS 3 offers guidelines in determining the fair values of specific classes of assets and liabilities:

- marketable securities (i.e. those traded on an active market) should be valued at current market value
- non-marketable securities should be valued at estimated value. Looking at comparable securities of similar quoted enterprises may be helpful
- receivables should be valued at the present value of amounts expected to be received. Discounting is unlikely to be necessary for short-term receivables
- inventories:
  - finished goods should be valued at selling prices less the sum of disposal costs and a reasonable profit allowance
  - work in progress should be valued at ultimate selling prices less the sum of completion costs, disposal costs and a reasonable profit allowance
  - raw materials should be valued at current replacement costs
- property, plant and equipment should be valued at market value. If there is no evidence of market value, depreciated replacement cost should be used.
- intangible assets as per IAS 38
- payables should be valued at the present value of amounts expected to be paid. As with receivables, discounting will not be necessary for short-term payables.

Contingent assets and pension surpluses or deficiencies are not normally recognised except on acquisition. Acquisition makes it necessary to identify and recognise all assets and liabilities provided they can be reliably valued. If this is not done, reporting of post-acquisition performance will be distorted.

The fair value exercise should be completed, if possible, by the date on which directors approve the first post-acquisition financial statements of the acquirer. If this is not possible there is a 12-month window to make fair value adjustments to the assets, liabilities and therefore goodwill. After this 12-month period, changes may only be made if errors occurred in accordance with IAS 8.

The mechanics of dealing with fair value adjustments

To process a fair value adjustment in a consolidation question you must consider the impact both at the acquisition and the balance sheet* date.

At acquisition put an adjustment into the net assets working of the subsidiary to bring the net assets to fair value.

At the balance sheet* date, any adjustments remaining from the acquisition must be accounted for both on the face of the consolidated balance sheet* and in the net assets working as shown in the comprehensive illustration below.

(W2) Net assets	At date of acquisition $000	At balance sheet date $000
Ordinary share capital + Reserves	X	X
Fair value adjustments:		
Land *(no dep'n to consider from acq to B/S date)*	X	X
Other tangibles *(depreciate the FV adj from acq to B/S date using policy given)*	X	X
Intangible assets meeting the IAS 38 criteria *(amortise the FV adj from acq to B/S date using policy given)*		
Inventory *(probably sold by the B/S date so no adj)*	X	–
Long-term payables *(discount to present value if an interest rate is given at acq and B/S date)*	X	X
Contingent liabilities *(include in the net assets of sub eventhough they would not normally be included in the FS)*	x/(x)	x/(x)
Net assets at fair value	xx	xx

* Balance Sheet = Statement of financial position (see page 18)

> **Note**
>
> **Other factors to consider:**
> Common accounting policies (it may be necessary to bring the subsidiary in line with group policy on such items as capitalisation of finance costs).

The cost of the acquisition

The cost of acquisition includes the following elements:

- cash paid
- fair value of any other consideration (which can often be in the form of shares)
- professional fees and similar incremental costs incurred directly in making the acquisition.

Issue costs of shares or other securities must be deducted from the proceeds of the issues not included in the cost of the acquisition.

Deferred consideration should be discounted, using a rate at which the acquirer could obtain similar borrowing (see example below).

Any contingent consideration should be included if the payment is probable and can be measured reliably. Adjust the cost of acquisition and goodwill when estimates are revised.

Where contingent consideration involves the issue of shares there is no liability (obligation to transfer economic benefits). Recognise this as part of the shareholders' funds under a separate caption representing shares to be issued.

 Transactional example

John Inc acquired 60% of the ordinary share capital of Robbie Inc four years ago, when the balance of Robbie Inc's reserves were $1,000,000.

At the date of acquisition the total of the fair value of the net assets of Robbie was $5,000,000.

There were three fair value adjustments at the date of acquisition, one for $200,000 related to inventory that has since been sold, one for land which the company still holds of $200,000, and the other fair value adjustment relating to plant with an original estimated life of ten years, which was two years old at the date of acquisition.

Goodwill arising on consolidation is capitalised and no impairment has occurred.

* Balance Sheet = Statement of financial position (see page 18)

	John Inc	Robbie Inc
Income statements	$000	$000
Revenue	10,000	10,000
Operating costs	(8,000)	(9,000)
Operating profit	2,000	1,000
Tax	(500)	(400)
Profit for the year	1,500	600
Balance sheet*s		
Net assets	9,000	7,000
Investment in Robbie Inc	5,000	
	14,000	7,000
Ordinary shares	8,000	3,000
Reserves	5,000	3,000
Liabilities	1,000	1,000
	14,000	7,000

Required:

Prepare the consolidated income statement and balance sheet* for the John Inc group.

First you would set up your answer booklet – leave a page for preparation of the balance sheet* and a page for preparation of the income statement.

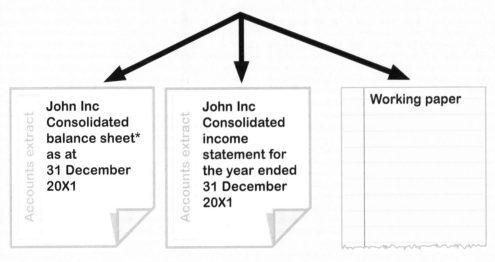

Then prepare a working paper. First do the standard balance sheet* workings. However, this time as we have got fair value adjustments we will have to be prepared to adjust the (W2) net assets to fair value as per the requirements of IFRS 3.

(W1) Group structure

John
|
Robbie   60%   4 years ago

(W2) Net assets at fair value

(This will need a bit of thinking about – first put a basic working together at book value but note you are given fair value information. You will have to put through fair value adjustments – set up a skeleton working as below:)

	Net assets at acquisition $	Net assets at B/S date $
Share capital	3,000	3,000
Reserves	1,000	3,000
Net assets at book value	4,000	6,000
Fair value adjustments		
	——	——
	——	——

You are told the net assets at fair value at the date of acquisition were $5,000. This becomes your bottom line in the date of acquisition column – see below – it's a bit like fitting a jigsaw of numbers together.

(W2) Net assets at fair value

(your skeleton working now looks like this:)

	Net assets at acquisition $	Net assets at B/S date $
Share capital	3,000	3,000
Reserves	1,000	3,000
Net assets at book value	4,000	6,000
Fair value adjustments		
	——	——
Net assets at fair value	5,000	
	(told in question)	
	——	——

You then need to read what assets it relates to: it could be land (easy as non-depreciating); inventory (usually easy as inventory is a current asset and is usually gone by the balance sheet* date) and property, plant and equipment (depreciating non-current assets need most thinking about due to the time lapse between the date of acquisition and the balance sheet* date). Complete the date of acquisition column from the information in the question as below.

(W2) Net Assets at fair value

(skeleton working continued)

	Net assets at acquisition $	Net assets at B/S date $
Share capital	3,000	3,000
Reserves	1,000	3,000
Net assets at book value	4,000	6,000
Fair value adjustments		
Land *(doesn't depreciate)*	200	
Inventory *(current asset – gone at balance sheet* date)*	200	–
Plant *(depreciating asset)*	600	
	–	
	5,000	

You can now complete the current balance sheet* date column. If you have a fair value adjustment on a depreciating asset you will need to know how many years have elapsed between the date of acquisition and the current balance sheet* date, so you can adjust the fair value – **WATCH THE DATES!!** Here the date of acquisition was four years previously and there is a depreciating fair value adjustment on an asset (plant) which had a useful economic life of eight years (10 – 2) at the date of acquisition. It now, therefore has a remaining useful economic life of four years (8 – 4). The working can now be completed – see below.

(W2) Net assets at fair value (complete working)

	Net assets at acquisition $	Net assets at B/S date $
Share capital	3,000	3,000
Reserves	1,000	3,000
Net assets at book value	4,000	6,000
Fair value adjustments		
Land *(doesn't depreciate)*	200	200
Inventory *(current asset – gone at balance sheet* date)*	200	–
Plant *(depreciating asset)*	600	300 (600 × 4/8)
	–	
	5,000	6,500

Note

The fair value adjustment on land is the same in both columns, on inventory it has gone by the balance sheet* date and on the plant it is in both columns but at a reduced amount to reflect the elapse of time. These fair value figures are then the figures used in the other workings. Your next step will be to calculate goodwill at (W3) based on the fair value of the net assets at the date of acquisition.

(W3) Goodwill

	$
Cost of investment	5,000
For 60% × 5,000 (net assets at the date of acquisition at fair value)	(3,000)
Goodwill	2,000

Calculate minority interest for the balance sheet* also using the net assets at fair value, but this time use the balance sheet* date figure.

(W4) Minority interest

	$
40% (6,500)	2,600

When you calculate group reserves in a question with a depreciating fair value adjustment, you need to calculate post-acquisition profit by using the 'CHANGE IN NET ASSETS' approach. If you consider the net assets at fair value at the current balance sheet* date (i.e. $6,500), and deduct the net assets at the date of acquisition at fair value (i.e. $5,000), the difference must be reserves created in the post-acquisition period (unless new share capital was introduced). This is a quick and easy way of doing the calculation – essential when you have a depreciating fair value adjustment in the question, and will work for all questions. See example below:

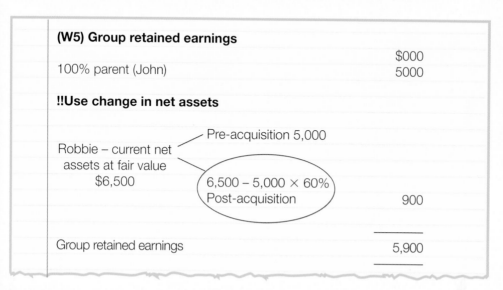

(W5) Group retained earnings

	$000
100% parent (John)	5000

!!Use change in net assets

Robbie – current net assets at fair value $6,500

Pre-acquisition 5,000

$6,500 – 5,000 × 60%
Post-acquisition — 900

Group retained earnings	5,900

Note

To use movement on reserves line will work but will take longer as you will have to make adjustments.

i.e. Robbie's reserves are currently $3,000 but would need adjusting for the $300 relating to depreciation on the plant ($3,000 – $300) = $2,700. The $1,000 that existed at the date of acquisition would need increasing due to the inventory fair value ($1,000 + 200) = $1,200. $2,700 – $1,200 = $1,500 × 60% = $900. We get the same answer either way but it is quicker to work with net assets. If the fair value adjustment is the same in both columns such as land, then it cancels out and so is a non-issue.

You can now prepare the consolidated balance sheet*!! **Check the net assets at fair value at current balance sheet* date. You need to remember to bring in the fair values to the consolidated balance sheet*.** You do **the whole thing** by reference to fair values when they come up.

---

* Balance Sheet = Statement of financial position (see page 18)

John group balance sheet*

	$
Goodwill (W3)	2,000
Assets 9,000 + 7,000 + 300	
(FVA – plant) + 200 (FVA – land) =	16,500
	18,500
Share capital (100% parent)	8,000
Reserves (W5)	5,900
Minority interest (W4)	2,600
(40% × 6,400)	
Liabilities 1,000 + 1,000	2,000
	18,500

When you put together the income statement, remember you will have an expense that doesn't exist in the real company accounts – the additional depreciation expense re Robbie's plant (the depreciating fair value adjustment. A one year (current year effect) charge will need to be shown as an expense in the income statement $[(600 \times 1/8) = 75]$ based on the eight years remaining useful economic life. This will also need to be reflected at the minority interest line as it relates to the subsidiary. The income statement will look like this:

Group income statement

Revenue 10,000 + 10,000	20,000
Operating costs (8,000 + 9,000)	
+ 75 additional depreciation	(17,075)
Operating profit	2,925
Tax 500 + 400	(900)
Profit after tax	1950
Minority interest	(210)
40% (600 –75) *(Robbie's profit after tax*	
– additional dep'n expense)	
Profit for the year	1740

And the really important stuff ... accounting practice

All business combinations must be accounted for under the purchase method. The pooling of interests method (merger method) that was available in IAS 22 has been abolished.

---

* Balance Sheet = Statement of financial position (see page 18)

If a business combination is by exchange of shares and control passes to the party that has not issued the shares, the acquisition is a reverse acquisition. The controlling party (the legal subsidiary) is treated as the acquirer.

The cost of a business combination is the aggregate of:

- the fair values of assets given, liabilities incurred, and equity instruments issued; plus
- costs directly attributable to the business combination.

Contingent costs are included when probable.

The acquirer recognises separately the acquiree's identifiable assets, liabilities and contingent liabilities if they satisfy the following criteria:

- for assets other than intangibles, it is probable that economic benefits will flow and they can be measured reliably
- for liabilities (other than contingent liabilities), it is probable that an outflow of economic benefits will be required and they can be measured reliably
- it is an intangible (including in-progress R&D) that meets the criteria in IAS 38 and is not the value of the assembled workforce (it is presumed in IAS 38 that these can be measured reliably if they have a finite life)
- for contingent liabilities, its fair value can be measured reliably.

Goodwill should initially be measured at cost, being the cost of the business combination (above) less the fair value of the subsidiary's identifiable net assets (above).

Positive goodwill is not amortised but instead is subject to an annual impairment review (following IAS 36).

Negative goodwill is immediately recognised as income in the income statement.

Disclosures

An acquirer should disclose information that enables users of its financial statements to evaluate the nature and financial effect of business combinations that were effected:

(a) during the reporting period

(b) after the balance sheet* date but before the financial statements are authorised for issue.

Conclusion

If group accounts are on your syllabus they will be a very important part of most exams. In fact, once they are on your syllabus it is quite rare for them to go unexamined. You must make sure you practise many questions set previously by your examiner to ensure you understand the standard to which you are being examined. There are many different potential complications in group accounting questions. Find out which ones your examiner includes and … **practise, practise, practise!!**

IAS 28 – Investments in associates

Introduction

> **"Goodness is the only investment that never fails."**
>
> **Henry David Thoreau (1817–1867)**

So … what's it trying to achieve?

IAS 28 attempts to give guidance on when a parent has an associate and also the accounting treatments required in order to show a fair presentation when accounting for the interest in an associate.

 Transactional example

ACF Inc acquires 30% of the voting rights of Arden Inc on 8 March 20X7. It appoints three directors to the board, which consists of eight members. ACF is also the sole supplier of raw materials to Arden and has a contract to supply certain expertise regarding the maintenance of Arden's equipment.

ACF is likely to be exercising significant influence over Arden. As well as owning 30% of the vote and appointing three directors, it has influence as sole supplier and in the form of the maintenance contract. Arden will be treated as an associated company and should be accounted for using the equity method.

Note

A common error is to treat an associate as if it were a subsidiary and to add it into the parent company figures.

Sorry but you need to know ... DEFINITIONS

An **associate** is an entity, including an unincorporated entity such as a partnership, over which the investor has significant influence and that is neither a subsidiary nor an interest in a joint venture.

Significant influence is the power to participate in the financial and operating policy decisions of the investee but it is not control or joint control over those policies.

And the really important stuff ... accounting practice

Consolidated accounts

A parent company must decide whether it has significant influence. The standard makes a presumption that significant influence exists where the parent has at least 20% of the voting rights.

If a parent company has significant influence it must use the equity method of accounting for its interest in the associate in the consolidated accounts unless the investment is held exclusively for resale.

The equity method requires that:

* the consolidated income statement shows the parent's share of the profit or loss of the associate as a separate line
* the consolidated balance sheet* shows the parent's share of the associate's net assets plus unamortised goodwill as a single entry in non-current assets. This can also be calculated by adding together the cost of the investment and any post-acquisition profits
* the consolidated cash flow statement shows dividends from associates as either investing or operating activities.

It is not usual to recognise associates as negative amounts in the balance sheet* of the parent company.

Separate parent accounts

Follow the rules in IAS 27 for separate financial statements.

Conclusion

Although associates are not examined as frequently as subsidiaries, this is still a very important skill – you must be prepared to use the equity method of accounting.

* Balance Sheet = Statement of financial position (see page 18)

26 IAS 31 – Interests in joint ventures

Introduction

> **"Joint ventures, like marriage, stand a better chance when they benefit both sides."**
>
> **Anon**

It is quite common for two parties to get together to undertake an activity. When the activity that is undertaken is subject to joint control, with both parties having to unanimously consent to the decisions relating to the activity, we have usually got a joint venture.

So ... both the parties are obtaining equal benefits?

Well, the key thing is that no one party (venturer) should be in a position to control the activities.

It is important that there is a contractual arrangement to establish this joint control. This could be by contract or via discussions (minuted) between the venturers, or they may be set out in the articles of the entity, but it should usually be in writing.

So ... what's it trying to achieve?

IAS 31 defines what a joint venture is and the accounting method required for the different types of joint venture.

Transactional example

Golcar Inc and Longwood Inc decide to form a joint venture. Each company is to own 50% of the equity shares and provides equal numbers to the management board. There is an understanding that the shares in the joint venture cannot be sold unless first offered to the other shareholder. How will this venture be accounted for?

The structure of this arrangement means that joint control will exist, with each venturer having to consult the other before decisions can be made. Both will account for it as a joint entity, either choosing proportional consolidation or the equity method of accounting.

Note

A common mistake is to consolidate the entity as if it were a subsidiary, on the basis of 'well it's nearly controlled!!'.

 ## Sorry but you need to know ... DEFINITIONS

 A **joint venture** is a contractual arrangement whereby two or more parties undertake an economic activity that is subject to joint control.

 Proportionate consolidation is a method of accounting whereby a venturer's share of each of the assets, liabilities, income and expenditure of a jointly controlled entity is combined line-by-line with similar items in the venturer's financial statements or reported as a separate line in the venturer's financial statements.

And the really important stuff... accounting practice

IAS 31 distinguishes between three different forms of joint venture – the jointly controlled asset, jointly controlled operation and the jointly controlled entity.

A jointly controlled asset occurs when venturers each contribute to a shared asset(s) (often under joint ownership) but do not form any new companies, partnerships or other entities, e.g. could be oil companies sharing a pipeline. Each venturer accounts for its share of the joint asset line-by-line in its financial statements.

---

* Balance Sheet = Statement of financial position (see page 18)

A jointly controlled operation occurs when each venturer uses its own assets and incurs its own expenses in contributing to a joint product. For example a number of venturers each might supply a part of a completed aircraft (engines, wings, etc) in return for a proportion of the proceeds from selling an aeroplane. Each venturer accounts for its own costs, assets and liabilities and takes a proportion of the sale proceeds, all line-by-line in the financial statements.

 A jointly controlled entity occurs when a new corporation, partnership or other entity is formed to run the joint venture. There are two methods of accounting for a joint entity.

- Benchmark (preferred)   Proportionate consolidation
- Allowed alternative   Equity accounting

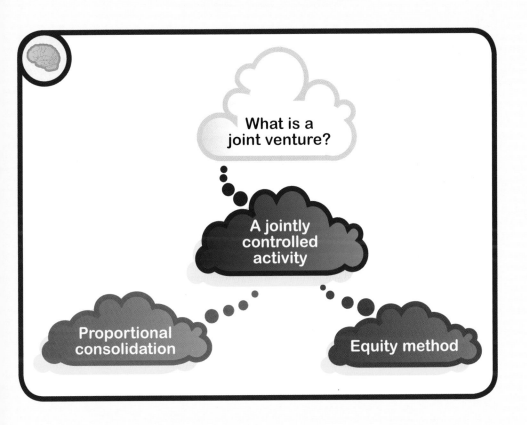

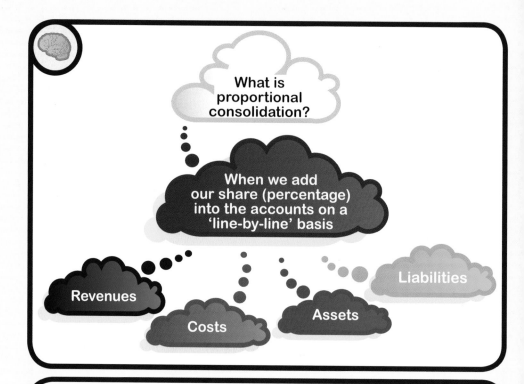

Note

Equity method is the same as we use for an associate – one line accounting.

Disclosures

Some of the key disclosures for joint ventures are:

- the venturer's share of any contingent liabilities (of the venturer or of the venture) of joint ventures separated from the other contingent liabilities in the accounts
- capital commitments of the venturer in relation to the joint venture, and its share of the capital commitments of the joint venture itself
- a listing of all joint ventures and, if no separation is made of the results and net assets of the joint venture on the face of the primary statements, the aggregate amounts of each of current assets, long-term assets, current liabilities, long-term liabilities, income and expenses related to its interest in the joint venture
- the method used to recognise interests in joint entities.

Conclusion

When you are doing group accounts, it is key that you can deal with subsidiaries and associates as they are examined so frequently. Remember that once you can do an associate, the equity method you use is then a transferable skill and is allowable for joint ventures also.

* Balance Sheet = Statement of financial position (see page 18)

Seriously advanced!!

"Only the little people pay taxes."

Leona Helmsley, hotel owner and prison inmate

Introduction

Once you start to get to final financial reporting/corporate reporting papers, you get to tackle companies that offer final salary pension schemes, foreign currency payment, share-based payment and the like.

For the seriously advanced!! – there are eleven 'red' standards:

- IAS 19   Employee benefits
- IAS 21   The effects of changes in foreign exchange rates
- IAS 24   Related party disclosures
- IAS 29   Financial reporting in hyper-inflationary economies
- IAS 34   Interim financial reporting
- IAS 41   Agriculture
- IFRS 1   First-time adoption of International Financial Reporting Standards
- IFRS 2   Share-based payment
- IFRS 4   Insurance contracts
- IFRS 6   Exploration for and evaluation of mineral assets
- IFRS 8   Operating segments

"The one serious conviction that a man should have is that nothing is to be taken too seriously."

Nicholas Butler (1862-1947)

* Balance Sheet = Statement of financial position (see page 18)

IAS 19 – Employee benefits

Introduction

> **"Research indicates that employees have three prime needs: interesting work, recognition for doing a good job, and being let in on things that are going on in the company."**
>
> **Zig Ziglar – Employee**

Well it is true that employees want interesting work, recognition and to be 'in the know'… but as accountants we recognise they also expect to be paid! – not just salaries and wages but also other benefits such as pensions. If only it were so easy that they wanted merely the non-financial rewards of things like recognition!

It's four prime needs really then?

Absolutely – employees do expect remuneration. We need an accounting standard because employee remuneration is not only the simple stuff like salaries and wages, but also the not so simple stuff like post-retirement benefits – pensions. These schemes can be easy to account for (defined contribution) or they can be a complex accounting issue (defined benefit). This is the stuff covered by IAS 19.

Defined contribution plans

These are not a problem. They relate to post-employment benefit plans where the enterprise pays fixed amounts into a separate fund and has no legal or constructive obligation if the fund has insufficient assets to pay all employee benefits. (These are often referred to as 'money purchase schemes'.) As the company pays the contribution into the scheme we will debit the income statement. Furthermore as the company has made no further promises as to the level of pension that the employee will receive, there is no balance sheet* impact – no further liability exists.

---

* Balance Sheet = Statement of financial position (see page 18)

Defined benefit plans

These are the problem – post-employment benefit plans other than defined contribution plans. (These are very variable but often relate to what is known as 'final salary schemes'.) These are difficult schemes to account for – the company is making promises to the employees about a level of pension which will be based on some pre-agreed formula. This is commonly based upon their final salary, the number of years they work for the employer and a pre-agreed fraction.

For example, it could be that, if you retire earning $60,000 after working for 30 years, you might be entitled to an annual pension of $30,000. This would be the case if your employer were offering you a scheme based on a fraction of 60, which is quite common. This would give you a pre-agreed formula – final salary × number of years worked/60.

($60,000 × 30/60 = $30,000) pension to be paid every year, between the date of retirement and the date you die. Note that even your death will often not cancel this liability completely as many schemes promise to pay a widow/widower benefit to your other half, when you die, until they die – the liability can be vast.

This sort of promise will therefore have a balance sheet* implication. The company has now opened itself up to an obligation of an unknown amount – the level of liability will be dependent on factors like staff turnover and mortality rates. If your workforce tends to have a long life expectancy and to stay in employment with you for their entire career, this could clearly be a massive liability.

In order to account for such a promise, the company will use the services of an actuary who will model the expected liabilities, taking into account all factors including the time value of money. Note that the employees may not be due to retire for many years so the present value of the liability can be significantly different to the total estimate of the liability.

The actuary will then usually advise the company to contribute cash each year into a pension fund to buy assets, from which this future liability will be funded. This means we are accounting for a fund of assets as well as the projected liability. (We do occasionally see some companies that operate an 'unfunded' scheme – these companies only have a liability to account for; they pay the pensions directly out of current year income when employees retire.)

So ... what's it trying to achieve?

IAS 19 prescribes the accounting and disclosure requirements for employee benefits. The standard requires a liability to be recognised if employee benefits are to be paid in the future and an expense when the enterprise receives service from an employee in return for benefit.

Transactional example

Let us assume that Bowser makes up its financial statements to 31 December each year. The company offers its staff a defined benefit (final salary pension scheme). It employs the services of an actuary to model the liability and advise upon contributions to an asset fund. To keep the computations simple, all transactions are assumed to occur at the year-end. The present value of the obligation and the market value of the plan assets were both $1,000 at 1 January 20X1. The following information is available from the actuary re the model.

	20X1	20X2
Discount rate at start of year	*10%*	*9%*
Expected rate of return on plan assets		
at start of year	*12%*	*11%*
	$	*$*
Current service cost	*180*	*140*
Benefits paid	*150*	*180*
Contributions paid	*90*	*100*
Present value of obligations at 31 December	*1,100*	*1,380*
Market value of plan assets at 31 December	*1,190*	*1,372*

The balance sheet*

The focus of IAS 19 is to ensure that the balance sheet* reflects the position the company is in with regard to its promises to employees. If the obligation (liability) is the same as the fund of assets, there will be no impact on the balance sheet*. The liability and asset are presented net on the balance sheet*. This would have been the case at the start of the year. Obligations are measured at $1,000 which is the same as the market value of the assets. As long as this continues to be the case there will no impact on the balance sheet* (see below).

Balance sheet* (extract) as at 31st December 20X0

	$
Pension fund assets	1,000
Pension fund liabilities	(1,000)
	─────
Net pension	nil

If there is a difference, however, the company will have to show either a net pension asset or a net pension liability on its balance sheet*. This is the case at 31 December 20X1.

* Balance Sheet = Statement of financial position (see page 18)

20X1 accounts

Balance sheet* (extract)	$
Present value of obligation, 31 December	1,100
Fair value of assets, 31 December	1,190
Net pension fund asset	90

Balance sheet

The income statement

Note that none of the figures in the income statement are the actual cash flows; we are using the information provided by the actuary, i.e. modelled figures.

Current service cost is the increase in the present value of the scheme liabilities expected to arise from employee service in the current period.

Interest cost is the expected increase during the period in the present value of the scheme liabilities because the benefits are one period closer to settlement.

Remember always apply the model percentage rates to opening balances.

Past service cost is the increase in the present value of the scheme liabilities related to employee service in prior periods arising in the current period as a result of the introduction of, or improvement to, retirement benefits.

The income statement charge for the period is made up from the current service cost, the interest cost, the expected return on plan assets, maybe any actuarial gains and losses recognised, past service costs recognised, and the effect of curtailments and settlements. We will consider past service costs and actuarial gains in a little while.

First we have to learn the key impact on the income statement – as illustrated below for Bowser.

Income statement (extract) for the year ended 31 Dec 20X1

Operating expense	$
Current service cost (a debit)	180
Finance cost	
Interest cost (1,000 × 10%) (a debit)	100
Expected return on plan assets (1,000 × 12%) (a credit)	(120)

Remember, none of the figures in the income statement are the actual cash flows; we are using the modelled figures.

Impact on reserves

We now need to calculate how the model worked compared to actuals to determine what, if any, actuarial gains and losses have arisen. These calculations can be done by comparing the expected obligations and asset values at the end of each period with the actual obligations or asset values.

Let us explore the change in the liability – we usually expect it to increase. This is because of two reasons; firstly we have benefited from the employees for an additional year, and secondly, as staff get older and we get nearer to the liability being paid, we would expect the present value to be increasing.

Remember the debits in the income statement are not credited to cash but to the liability account (a balance sheet* account) as shown below.

Pension fund liability a/c (skeleton)

	$		$
		Bal b/fwd *(per 20X0 balance sheet*)*	1,000
		Current service cost *(per 20X1 income statement)*	180
		Interest cost (1,000x10%) *(per 20X1 income statement)*	100
			1,280

If the scheme is mature, i.e if people have reached the age of retirement, this account will need to reflect the benefits paid out in the year. NB. A common error made by students is to make the benefits paid out a cash flow of the company. The company accounts will only show one cash flow – the contribution to the fund each year. If the company contributes cash to the fund each year and was then to pay the pensions directly too, you will be double counting. The benefits are being paid out of the pension fund assets – therefore you will have a contra entry for benefits paid out:

Dr Pension fund liability
Cr Pension fund assets

A separate set of accounts is maintained by the pension fund, which holds the assets in trust.

Pension fund liability a/c (skeleton continued)			
	$		$
Benefits paid out	150	Bal b/fwd	1,000
(from example)		*(per 20X0 balance sheet*)*	
		Current service cost	180
		(per 20X1 income statement)	
		Interest cost	100
		(1,000 × 10%)	
		(per 20X1 income statement)	
			1,280

The figure that we take to the balance sheet* is not the balance on the account but the actual present value of the liability as recalculated by the actuary – in our example it is now $1,100. If you look at our 'T' account, it is showing a balance of 1,130 (1,000 + 180 + 100 − 150 = 1,130). As the liability is actually lower than we had anticipated, we have made an actuarial gain of 30 (1,130 − 1,100). Actuarial gains or losses are taken to reserves with the £1,100 carried to the balance sheet* as below:

Pension fund liability a/c (complete)

	$		$
Benefits paid out *(from example)*	150	Bal b/fwd *(from 20X0 balance sheet*)*	1,000
		Current service cost *(from 20x1 income statement)*	180
		Interest cost	100
Actuarial gain on liabilities *(goes to reserves)*	30	(1000 × 10%) *(from 20X1 income statement)*	
Bal c/fwd *(from 20X1 balance sheet*)*	1,100		
	1,280		1,280
		Bal b/fwd	1,100

As we are also accounting for a fund of assets we will need a second ledger to show the movement on the asset account.

Pension fund assets (skeleton)

	$		$
Balance b/fwd *(per the 20X0 balance sheet*)*	1,000	Benefits paid out *(per the liability account)*	150
Expected return on the assets *(per the 20X1 income statement)*	120		

The contributions paid into the fund by the company are then debited to the asset account and credited to cash (the only cash flow for the company).

Pension fund assets (skeleton continued)

	$		$
Balance b/fwd 150 *(per the 20X0 balance sheet*)*	1,000	Benefits paid out *(per the liability account)*	
Expected return on the assets *(per the 20X1 income statement)*	120		
Contributions *(cash paid)*	90		

* Balance Sheet = Statement of financial position (see page 18)

Again the actual outcome on the asset account can be different to what we had planned. If we get a stock market or property boom, our assets invested in shares or buildings may have a higher fair value than we had planned – an actuarial gain will arise. If the stock market or property values fall we can make an actuarial loss. These actuarial gains and losses are accounted for in reserves. Here we can see we are expecting the asset balance to be 1,000 + 120 + 90 − 150 = 1,060. The actual fair value of the assets at 31 December 20X1 is measured at 1,190. We again have made an actuarial gain, this time of 130 (1,190 − 1,060 = 130). This is again taken to reserves. (see below). This enables us to carry the 1,190 to the balance sheet*.

Pension fund assets a/c (complete)

	$		$
Balance b/fwd	1,000	Benefits paid out	150
(per the 20X0 balance sheet)*		*(per the liability account)*	
Expected return on the assets	120		
(per the 20X1 income statement)			
Contributions	90		
(cash paid)			
Actuarial gain on assets	**130**		
(taken to reserves)			
		Bal c/fwd	1,190
		(figure from 20X1 balance sheet)*	
	1,340		1,340
Bal b/fwd	1,190		

We can see with both the assets and liabilities the actual outcome can be different to the model – in respect of the liabilities, if retired employees start to live longer than the actuaries model had estimated, our liabilities will be bigger than expected and an actuarial loss will arise. If we get a stock market boom, our assets invested in shares may have a higher fair value than we had planned – an actuarial gain will arise.

What to do with the actuarial gains and losses that are now in reserves?

A number of options exist.

Transactional example (continued)

Let us assume the policy of Bowser is to recognise actuarial gains and losses above the 10% threshold in the income statement over the ten-year remaining working lives of the employees.

This means we might be able to make a reserve transfer to the income statement, subject to – the 10% corridor rule.

10% corridor – what's that then?

The limits of the '10% corridor' need to be calculated in order to establish whether actuarial gains or losses exceed the corridor limit and therefore could be recognised in the income statement. Actuarial gains and losses can be recognised in the income statement if they exceed the 10% corridor, and they are recognised by being amortised over the remaining service lives of employees.

The limits of the 10% corridor are set (at the first day of each year) at the greater of:

(a)   10% of the present value of the obligation before deducting plan assets; and
(b)   10% of the fair value of plan assets.

	20X1
Limit of '10% corridor' (at 1 January)	100
(10% 1000)	
Actuarial gains and losses unrecognised	
(1 January)	–
Actuarial gain (loss) recognised over 10 years	
Cumulative unrecognised gains (losses)	–
(1 January)	
Gains (losses) on the obligation *(per above)*	30
Gains (losses) on the assets *(per above)*	130
Cumulative gains (losses) before amortisation	160
Amortisation in the period	–
Cumulative unrecognised gains (losses)	160
(31 December)	

As we had a nil balance b/fwd re unrecognised gains and losses, we cannot release anything to current period income statement. We do however now have unrecognised actuarial gains of 160. We will initially record them in reserves. In the 20X2 period we may be able to release some of this to the income statement – subject to the 10% corridor.

To illustrate this we need to move on to the 20X2 accounting period. First of all let's show the impact on the balance sheet*.

Balance sheet* (extract) for the year ended 31 December 20X2

	20X2
	$
Present value of obligation, 31 December	1,380
Fair value of assets, 31 December	1,372
Net pension liability	(8)

Now let us look at the 20X2 income statement.

Income statement (extract)

Income statement

	20X2 $
Current service cost *(per example)*	140
Interest cost (9% 1,100)	99
(apply %age to opening bal of liabilities)	
Expected return on plan assets (11%1,190)	(131)
Recognised actuarial (gains) losses (see below)	(4)
Income statement charge	104

The reason why we now have an additional credit of (4), (see above), is because we have applied the 'corridor approach' to the unrecognised gain we had in last year's reserves.

Last year's reserves
Unrecognised actuarial gains (losses)   160

10% corridor

As we have already discussed, the limits of the '10% corridor' need to be calculated in order to establish whether actuarial gains or losses exceed the corridor limit and therefore need recognising in the income statement. Actuarial gains and losses are recognised in the income statement if they exceed the 10% corridor, and they are recognised by being amortised over the remaining service lives of employees.

The limits of the 10% corridor are set (at 1 January each year) at the greater of:
(a) 10% of the present value of the obligation before deducting plan assets; and
(b) 10% of the fair value of plan assets.

	20X2
Limit of '10% corridor' (at 1 January) (10%1,190)	119
Actuarial gains and losses unrecognised (1 January)	160
Actuarial gain (loss) to be recognised over 10 years	41
Figure for income statement (119 – 160)/10 years (rounded)	4

This is therefore released from reserves to the income statement.

Again actuarial gains or losses will arise on the current period as follows [you may find it helpful to post two 'T' accounts **(ledger accounts)** with the double entry or alternatively to use two schedules] (see over page).

* Balance Sheet = Statement of financial position (see page 18)

Alternative presentation
(for those who don't like T accounts!)

Change in the obligation

	20X1	20X2
	$	$
Present value of obligation, 1 January	1,000	1,100
Interest cost	100	99
Current service cost	180	140
Benefits paid	(150)	(180)
Actuarial (gain)/loss on obligation (balancing figure)	(30)	221
Present value of obligation, 31 December	1,100	1,380

Change in the assets

	20X1	20X2
Fair value of plan assets, 1 January	1,000	1,190
Expected return on plan assets	120	131
Contributions	90	100
Benefits paid	(150)	(180)
Actuarial gain/(loss) on plan assets (balancing figure)	130	131
Fair value of plan assets, 31 December	1,190	1,372

The actuarial gains /losses can be summarised as follows:

Unrecognised actuarial gains and losses in reserves

	$		$
Loss on liabilities *(per liability ledger or schedule)*	221	Balance brought forward (30 + 130)	160
		Gain on assets *(per asset ledger or schedule)*	131
Bal c/fwd	70		
	291		291
Release to income Statement	4	Bal b/f	70
Bal c/fwd	66		

... OR ...

* Balance Sheet = Statement of financial position (see page 18)

	20X1 $	20X2 $
Cumulative unrecognised gains (losses) (1 January)	–	160
Gains (losses) on the obligation	30	(221)
Gains (losses) on the assets	130	131
Cumulative gains (losses) before amortisation	160	70
Amortisation in the period	–	(4)
Cumulative unrecognised gains (losses) (31 December)	160	66

In the exam, therefore, it is much easier to choose the alternative approach of recognising actuarial gains and losses immediately in reserves. If you choose this accounting policy you will not have to worry about the corridor. Some exam questions however, will tell you to use the corridor approach.

Past service cost

Occasionally some exam questions may mention a 'past service cost'. Past service cost is the increase in the present value of the scheme liabilities related to employee service in prior periods arising in the current period as a result of the introduction of, or improvement to, retirement benefit.

Past service costs are recognised in the income statement over the period to which they vest. A cost becomes vested once an employee is entitled to receive a pension benefit unconditionally. Most past service costs vest immediately and are treated the same as current service costs. There may be occasion though when a 'spread forward' treatment is the best answer.

Sorry but you need to know ... DEFINITIONS

Employee benefits are all forms of consideration given by an enterprise in exchange for services rendered by employees.

Defined contribution plans are post-employment benefit plans where the enterprise pays fixed amounts into a separate fund and has no legal or constructive obligation if the fund has insufficient assets to pay all employee benefits. (These are often referred to as 'money purchase schemes'.)

Defined benefit plans are post-employment benefit plans other than defined contribution plans. (These are very variable but often relate to what is known as 'final salary schemes'.)

Actuarial gains/losses are changes in actuarial deficits or surpluses that have arisen because (a) events have not coincided with actuarial assumptions made for the last valuation or (b) the actuarial assumptions have changed.

Current service cost is the increase in the present value of the scheme liabilities expected to arise from employee service in the current period.

Interest cost is the expected increase during the period in the present value of the scheme liabilities because the benefits are one period closer to settlement.

Past service cost is the increase in the present value of the scheme liabilities related to employee service in prior periods arising in the current period as a result of the introduction of, or improvement to, retirement benefits.

And the really important stuff ... accounting practice

Short-term benefits

An enterprise should recognise all short-term benefits at undiscounted amounts as liabilities (reduced by anything paid in the period) and as expenses. This generally means salaries and wages are debited to the income statement and credited to cash, with an accrual being made for anything outstanding at the balance sheet* date.

Pensions

Defined contribution schemes

Defined contribution schemes are accounted for by recognising a cost in the income statement equal to the contributions payable to the scheme for the period. Again we make a debit in the income statement and a credit to cash with an accrual if anything is outstanding at the balance sheet* date.

Defined benefit schemes

The scheme assets are valued at fair value (usually market value).

The scheme liabilities are measured using the projected unit credit method, discounted at the current rate of return on high quality corporate bonds.

---

* Balance Sheet = Statement of financial position (see page 18)

The balance sheet* recognises the total of:

Market value of scheme assets	x
Less: Present value of the obligations of the fund	(x)
Balance sheet* asset (liability)	x(x)

Actuarial gains and losses above the 10% corridor should be recognised in the income statement over the maximum of the average remaining working lives of the employees. Any shorter period of recognition is also acceptable (including for those within the 10% corridor).

The 10% corridor is the greater of:

(a) 10% of the market value of the assets; and

(b) 10% of the present value of the obligations of the fund.

As an alternative to the use of the 10% corridor, a company is allowed to recognise actuarial gains and losses immediately in reserves.

The income statement charge for the period is made up from the current service cost, the interest cost, the expected return on plan assets, any actuarial gains and losses recognised, and past service costs recognised and the effect of curtailments and settlements.

Past service costs are recognised in the income statement over the period to which they vest. A cost becomes vested once an employee is entitled to receive a pension benefit unconditionally.

Significant disclosures are required for pensions that explain assumptions used by actuaries, the make up of pension assets, liabilities and charges, and a history of actuarial gains and losses.

Other long-term employee benefits

These are accounted for as for pensions except that actuarial gains and losses and past service costs are recognised immediately in the income statement.

Conclusion

Accounting for employee benefits can be very easy. If all the company offers in addition to salaries and wages is a defined contribution pension scheme, then it is basically a case of Dr Income statement, Cr Cash.

However, if the company offers a defined benefit pension scheme, it is a different thing altogether. There is a complete divorce between what goes in the income statement and the cash flow. The emphasis is on the balance sheet*. The accruals concept is still bedrock though – the scheme **IS** being expensed in appropriate periods. It takes a while to adjust to the entries required, but once you are familiar with 'the model' these are nice questions to answer.

IAS 21 – The effects of changes in foreign exchange rates

Introduction

> "To the optimist the glass is half full,
> to the pessimist the glass is half empty,
> to the accountant the glass is twice as big as it
> needs to be."
>
> **Traditional**

Even the smallest of companies will find themselves having to account for changing foreign exchange (forex) rates. Companies will export their goods, import their inventory, source plant from overseas, for example. Inevitably this will mean they have to record a transaction in their books, which is in a different currency to their own accounting currency. An accounting standard is essential in this area if we are going to record these transactions in a consistent manner.

It's about importing and exporting stuff then?

Well … hmm … yes … BUT it also covers the issue of foreign subsidiaries as well as your basic individual company transactions. It is therefore relevant to some group accounting questions – it's really a standard of two halves!!

Individual company issues

This section gives guidance to companies that enter into a transaction where the currency is not that of their primary economic environment e.g. an Australian company that buys plant from Europe, a UK company that imports inventory from China, or a French company exporting its cars to Africa. These transactions will all need translating into the 'functional currency' – i.e, the accounting currency.

---

* Balance Sheet = Statement of financial position (see page 18)

Group accounting issues

The company you are preparing group accounts for may have a foreign operation. This is when an entity that is a subsidiary, associate, joint venture or branch of a reporting entity, prepares its accounts in a currency other than those of the reporting entity. Again we will have a translation issue.

So ... what's it trying to achieve?

IAS 21 explains the standard accounting practice for translating foreign transactions (and foreign operations) and for presenting the exchange differences that arise.

Transactional example

Let us assume Aston plc has a year end of 31 December 20X1.
On 25 October 20X1 Aston plc buys goods from a Swedish supplier for SwK 286,000.

On 16 November 20X1 Aston plc pays the Swedish supplier in full.

The goods remain in inventory at the year end.

Exchange rates

25 October 20X1	*$1 = SwK 11.16*
16 November 20X1	*$1 = SwK 10.87*
31 December 20X1	*$1 = SwK 11.02*

This illustrates the issue – what rate of exchange do we use to record this transaction? Well initially we record it at the 'spot rate' – the rate of exchange as at the date we entered into the transaction. At 25 October 20X1 the spot rate is $1= Swk 11.16. We will therefore record the initial purchases/payables as at that rate.

Journal entries		$	$
25 October 20X1	Dr Purchases (W1)	25,627	
	Cr Payables		25,627

Workings
(W1) SwK 286,000 ÷ 11.16 = $25,627

When we come to pay for the goods on 16 November the forex rate has moved – inevitably we make a gain or a loss. Forex gains and losses are taken through the income statement as shown below.

			$	$
16 Nov 20X1	Dr	Payables	25,627	
	Dr	Income statement		
		– other operating expense	684	
	Cr	Cash (W2)		26,311
Workings				
(W2)		SwK 286,000 ÷ 10.87 = $26,311		

(It is actually costing us $26,311 we recorded the liability originally at $25,627 and this is now cleared to zero). The difference is taken as an expense through the income statement – a forex loss has occurred.

Balance sheet* date

At the year-end, closing balances should be translated as follows:

- monetary items (cash, bank, receivables, payables, loans) at closing rate, i.e the rate of exchange as at the balance sheet* date
- non-monetary items at historic rate, i.e do not retranslate but leave on balance sheet* at original translation as at date we entered into the transaction.

Here the inventory is unused as at the balance sheet* date. The goods will remain in stock at the year end at $25,627.

Unsettled items

However If the payable had been outstanding at the balance sheet* date, this would have been retranslated to the closing rate and the forex gain/loss arising would be routed through the income statement.

Sorry but you need to know ... DEFINITIONS

Closing rate is the spot rate at the balance sheet* date.

Foreign operation is an entity that is a subsidiary, associate, joint venture or branch of a reporting entity, the activities of which are based or conducted in a country or currency other than those of the reporting entity.

Functional currency is the currency of the primary economic environment in which the entity operates.

Presentation currency is the currency in which the financial statements are presented.

And the really important stuff ... accounting practice

Translation of transactions into functional currency

Translation rules	Exchange difference treatment
(1) All transactions in the period should be translated at the rate in force on the date of the transaction (actual rate). (2) At the year-end closing balances should be translated: • monetary items at closing rate • non-monetary items at historic rate. (3) It is not acceptable to use forward contract rates.	(1) All exchange differences are to be recognised in the income statement.

Foreign operations

(a) The following rules apply to foreign operations with a different functional and presentation currency.

Translation rules	Exchange differences
(1) All net assets should be translated at the closing rate. (2) Goodwill and fair value adjustments must be made in the local currency. (3) The income statement must be translated at average rate.	(1) Arise on the restatement of opening net assets from opening to closing rate, and retained profit from average rate to closing rate. (2) The parent's percentage of the total exchange difference is shown as a movement in a separate item in equity (exchange difference reserve).

(b) If the functional currency of the subsidiary is not the same as its local currency the transactions must be translated into functional currency following the rules for translating individual transactions.

(c) On disposal of a foreign operation any exchange differences recorded in the separate item of equity should be recycled and made part of the profit or loss on disposal.

---

* Balance Sheet = Statement of financial position (see page 18)

Disclosure

- Exchange differences recognised in the income statement.
- Exchange differences recognised in equity.
- Differences in presentation and functional currency with reasons for those differences.
- Changes in functional currency.

Conclusion

Even the smallest companies enter into foreign currency transactions. Many lower level accountancy exam papers are very unreal as they ignore IAS 21 altogether. In the real world, this is a vital standard. Higher level exam papers will therefore commonly include foreign transactions somewhere. It is vital that you learn the rules for both individual and group transactions.

* Balance Sheet = Statement of financial position (see page 18)

IAS 24 – Related party disclosures

Introduction

> "Ah … this is the one that always makes me think about birthdays – relations and parties."
>
> **Accountancy student**

 Well unfortunately it's not about 'party parties', with or without your relations! When readers of accounts are trying to analyse the performance of a company, one of the big dangers is the presence of related party transactions. These transactions can have a completely distorting effect on the accounts. This topic is not just important in so far as you may get a written question on related party transactions, but you have to watch for the issue in interpretation of accounts questions.

Why the big fuss?

The presence of related party transactions in a set of accounts can seriously undermine the fair presentation of the company's results. If you ignore the issue you can make a seriously bad investment decision!! ... For example …

You decide that you want to buy a coffee/sandwich shop in the city centre. Your target businesses are those in tower blocks with many different office workers employed in the building. You identify two businesses close to each other, both up for sale, and you obtain their accounts. On comparison, one is clearly more profitable than the other, despite the sale price being the same. It seems like a no brainer … you offer for the more profitable shop and the deal is done.

However, what the owner didn't tell you was that her dad owned the office block and she paid no rent. It was not surprising that she made profit – she was benefiting from a related party transaction. When we look at accounts we assume that transactions are 'arms-length', unless the accounts tell us differently. We need to have 'non-arms' length transactions spelt out clearly. That is all IAS 24 requires – it's a disclosure standard.

So ... what's it trying to achieve?

IAS 24 tries to ensure that attention is drawn to the possibility that the financial position and performance of the enterprise may have been affected by the existence of related parties and transactions and balances with those related parties.

Transactional example

Smudge Inc is a manufacturer of pet accessories and has provided an interest-free loan to a company owned by the finance director of Smudge Inc. Would this need to be disclosed as a related party transaction?

Yes, this loan would need to be disclosed in the accounts because the finance director is a member of the key management personnel of the entity and is therefore a related party.

The loan is a related party transaction and would need disclosure. The fact that it is interest free will warrant disclosure since Smudge would not normally provide unrelated parties with interest-free loans.

Sorry but you need to know ... DEFINITIONS

A **related party** is related to an entity if:

(a) directly, or indirectly through intermediaries, the party
   (i)   controls, or is controlled by, or is under common control with, the entity
   (ii) has an interest in the entity that gives it significant influence over the entity
   (iii) has joint control over the entity
(b) the party is an associate
(c) the party is a joint venture
(d) the party is a member of the key management personnel of the entity or its parent
(e) the party is a close member of the family and any individual referred to in (a) or (d)
(f) the party is an entity that is controlled, jointly controlled or significantly influenced by, or for which significant voting power in such entity resides with, directly or indirectly, any individual referred to in (d) or (e); or
(g) the party is a post-employment benefit plan of the entity, or of any entity that is a related party of the entity.

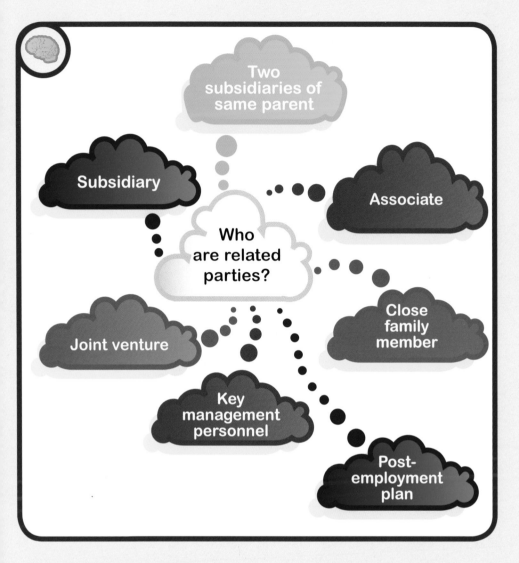

A **related party transaction** is a transfer of resources, services or obligations between related parties, regardless of whether a price is charged.

And the really important stuff ... accounting practice

Relationships between parents and subsidiaries shall be disclosed regardless of whether any transactions have occurred with the related party. The disclosure should include the parent and ultimate parent company if different.

Disclosure is required of key management personnel compensation in total grouped in various types of benefit.

* Balance Sheet = Statement of financial position (see page 18)

Disclosures

If a related party transaction has been entered into, the following disclosures should be made:

- a description of the relationship
- a description of the transactions
- the amounts involved
- other elements of the transactions necessary for an understanding of the financial statements
- balances with related parties at the balance sheet* date (and any provision for doubtful debts from related parties)
- amounts written off in the period on debts due to or from related parties.

No disclosure of related party transaction is required in 100% owned subsidiary company individual company accounts.

Note – the name of the related party is NOT a required disclosure.

Conclusion

 Although IAS 24 is nobody's favourite accounting standard, it is really essential. Miss the issue of related party transactions at your peril – it is a good way of messing up a ratios question!!

---

* Balance Sheet = Statement of financial position (see page 18)

IAS 29 – Financial reporting in hyperinflationary economies

Introduction

> **"Bankers know that history is inflationary and that money is the last thing a wise man will hoard."**
>
> **William J Durant**

Historic cost accounting has little value if a country is experiencing what we term 'hyperinflation'. Hyperinflation is not actually defined by IAS 29. When a country suffers from the general characteristics (see page 233) of a hyperinflationary economy, presenting financial information in historic cost terms presents a distorted picture.

There are many examples of countries who have suffered this problem:

- 1922 Germany 5,000%
- 1985 Bolivia >10,000%
- 1989 Argentina 3,100%
- 1990 Peru 7,500%
- 1993 Brazil 2,100%
- 1993 Ukraine 5,000%
- 2007 Zimbabwe 11,000%.

So – we are going to have to do something other than report historical terms?

Absolutely, adjustments to the financial statements will be necessary.

So ... what's it trying to achieve?

IAS 29 prescribes the rules about restating the financial statements of companies for the effects of hyperinflation. This ensures that the users of the financial statements get better information as the financial statements can be influenced by very high levels of inflation.

Transactional example

Holland Inc operates in an hyperinflationary economy. The accounts are prepared to 31 December and for the year ended 31 December 20X5 its balance sheet* is as follows:

Balance sheet* at 31 December 20X5

	Krams (m)
Property, plant and equipment	450
Inventory	1,350
Cash	175
	1,975
Share capital (issued 20X1)	200
Retained earnings	1,175
Non-current liabilities	250
Current liabilities	350
	1,975

The movement of the general price index (GPI) has been as follows:-

	31 December
20X1	100
20X2	130
20X3	150
20X4	240
20X5	300

The property, plant and equipment was purchased on 3 December 20X3 and there is six months' inventory held. The non-current liability was a loan raised on 31 March 20X5.

Holland will need to restate the property, plant and equipment, the inventory and the share capital. Retained earnings become a balancing figure. The monetary items do not need restating.

Balance sheet*

Restated balance sheet*	Krams (m)
Property, plant and equipment (450 × 300/150) current GPI/GPI in year of purchase	900
Inventory (1350 × 300/270) note bought six months ago (300 + 240/2=270)	1,500
Cash (monetary item)	350
	2,750
Share capital (200 × 300/100) (current GPI/GPI in year of issue)	600
Retained earnings (balance)	1,550
Non-current liabilities (monetary item)	250
Current liabilities (monetary item)	350
	2,750

Note

The inventory has been restated on the assumption that the index has increased proportionately over time.

And the really important stuff ... accounting practice

There is no prescriptive definition in the standard about what constitutes hyperinflation, but typical characteristics are:

(a) the general population prefers to keep its wealth in non-monetary assets
(b) the general population regards monetary amounts in terms of a relatively stable foreign currency
(c) sales and purchases on credit are at prices compensating for inflation
(d) interest rates, wages and prices are linked to a price index
(e) the cumulative inflation rate over three years is approaching or exceeds 100%.

* Balance Sheet = Statement of financial position (see page 18)

The financial statements of companies in hyperinflationary economies should be stated in terms of the measuring unit current at the balance sheet* date. The comparative amounts should also be restated to the measuring unit current at the balance sheet* date.

The gain or loss on the net monetary position should be included in net income and separately disclosed.

The restatement should be done using a general price index.

The above rules apply to both individual company financial statements and consolidated financial statements.

Disclosures

(a) The fact that the financial statements and comparatives have been restated.
(b) Whether the financial statements are based on a historical cost or current cost approach.
(c) The identity and level of the price index at the balance sheet* date, and the movement in the index in the current and previous period.

Conclusion

Financial Reporting in hyperinflationary economies is quite a rare problem, for both the real world and in the exam hall – however IAS 29 exists to give guidance should you need it.

---

* Balance Sheet = Statement of financial position (see page 18)

IAS 34 – Interim financial reporting

Introduction

> **"Maybe it should, but IAS 34 does not detail which entities should publish interim financial reports or how frequently they should be published."**
>
> Anon

Before you go any further with this chapter, just stop and check that you do actually need to know this standard. Even at the higher levels many accounting syllabuses exclude this accounting standard. Check with your tutor or list of examinable documents. There is a good chance you can miss this one out!! ... yippee! (or maybe not ...)

So ... what's it trying to achieve?

IAS 34 prescribes the minimum content of an interim financial report and the principles for recognition and measurement in complete or condensed financial statements for an interim period. The standard does not prescribe the companies that should produce interim reports.

Sorry but you need to know ... DEFINITIONS

Interim period is a financial reporting period shorter than a full financial year.

Interim financial report means a financial report containing either a complete set of financial statements or a set of condensed financial statements for an interim period.

And the really important stuff ... accounting practice

Contents of an interim report

The minimum contents prescribed by the standard are:

- a condensed balance sheet*
- a condensed income statement
- a condensed cash flow statement
- a condensed statement of changes in equity or STRGL equivalent; and
- a selected explanatory notes.

The condensed information must at least have the same headings and subtotals as were in the latest annual financial statements published.

Basic and diluted EPS should be presented in the interim report.

Periods covered

The interim statements should cover the following periods:

- a balance sheet* as of the end of the current interim period and a comparative balance sheet* as of the end of the immediately preceding financial year
- an income statement for the current period and cumulatively for the current financial year to date, with comparative income statements for the comparable interim periods (current and year-to-date) of the immediately preceding financial year
- a statement showing changes in equity cumulatively for the current financial year to date, with a comparative statement for the comparable year-to-date period of the immediately preceding financial year; and
- cash flow statement cumulatively for the current financial year to date, with a comparative statement for the comparable year-to-date period of the immediately preceding financial year.

The type of notes to be disclosed include changes in accounting policy, changes in outstanding debt or equity, dividends, segment information, subsequent events and changes in contingencies.

Special disclosure is also required regarding unusual events and transactions in the interim period.

Conclusion

For most accounting syllabuses this is not even planned for examination. If it is on your syllabus though, it does become a current issue following debate about corporate collapses. However, note that an entity that does not comply with IAS 34 does not compromise its compliance with International Financial Reporting Standards (IFRS) in its annual financial statements.

* Balance Sheet = Statement of financial position (see page 18)

IAS 41 – Agriculture

Introduction

> ## "You mean we have an accounting standard on 'accounting for cows?"
>
> **Accountancy student**

Well, it's a bit broader than that, but essentially – 'yes'.

> ## So … what's it trying to achieve?
>
> IAS 41 prescribes the accounting treatments and disclosures for agricultural activity.

When an agricultural business has biological assets such as a dairy herd to account for, using IAS 2 *'Accounting for inventory'* does not give relevant information. Instead IAS 41 would apply, which would require the herd to be measured at each balance sheet* date at fair value less estimated point of sale costs except where fair value cannot be measured reliably.

Any gains or losses should be included in net profit or loss in the period in which it arises. The standard encourages companies to separate the changes in fair value less estimated point of sale costs between that due to physical changes and the portion attributable to price changes.

Transactional example

The Smart Dairy has an inventory of 70,000 milk-producing cows and 35,000 heifers which are being raised to produce milk.

The herds comprise at 31 May 20X6:

50,000 – 3-year-old cows (all purchased on or before 1 June 20X5)
25,000 – Heifers (average age 1.5 years old – purchased 1 December 20X5)

No animals were born or sold in the year.

The per unit values less estimated point of sales costs were as follows:
20X5 data

2-year-old animal at 1 June 20X5	*$50*
1-year-old animal at 1 June 2005 and 1 December 20X5	*$40*

20X6 data

3-year-old animal at 31 May 20X6	*$60*
1.5-year-old animal at 1 May 20X6	*$46*
2-year-old animal at 31 May 20X6	*$55*
1-year-old animal at 31 May 20X6	*$42*

For the year to 31 May 20X6, let us consider how the herd would be accounted for.

First of all we need the fair value of the herd at the start of the year:

	$000
Fair value at 1 June 20X5 50,000 × $50	2,500

Then consider any purchases:

I December purchases 25,000 × $40	1,000

Then add on increase due to price fluctuation (fair value)

50,000 × $(55 − 50)	250
25,000 × $(40 − 42)	50

Then add on increase due to physical change

50,000 × $(60 − 55)	250
25,000 × $(46 − 42)	100
	────
	4,150

Made up value less point of sale costs at 31 May 20X6

50,000 × 60	3,000
25,000 × 46	1,150
	────
	4,150

Sorry but you need to know ... DEFINITIONS

Agricultural activity is the management by an enterprise of the biological transformation of biological assets for sale, into agricultural produce, or into additional biological assets.

A biological asset is a living animal or plant.

Harvest is the detachment of produce from a biological asset or the cessation of a biological asset's life processes.

Biological transformation comprises the processes of growth, degeneration, production or procreation that cause qualitative or quantitative changes in a biological asset.

Agricultural produce is the harvested product of the enterprise's biological assets.

And the really important stuff ... accounting practice

An enterprise should recognise a biological asset or agricultural produce when, and only when:

- the enterprise controls the asset as a result of past events
- it is probable that future economic benefits will flow to the enterprise; and
- the fair value or cost of the asset can be measured reliably.

Biological assets should be measured initially and at each balance sheet* at fair value less estimated point of sale costs.

Harvested produce should also be measured at fair value less point of sale costs at the point it is harvested.

Any gains or losses generated by measuring at fair value should be recognised in the income statement immediately.

Biological assets should be separately presented on the face of the balance sheet*.

* Balance Sheet = Statement of financial position (see page 18)

Disclosures

Significant disclosures are required for biological assets including reconciliations of the changes in biological assets over the period.

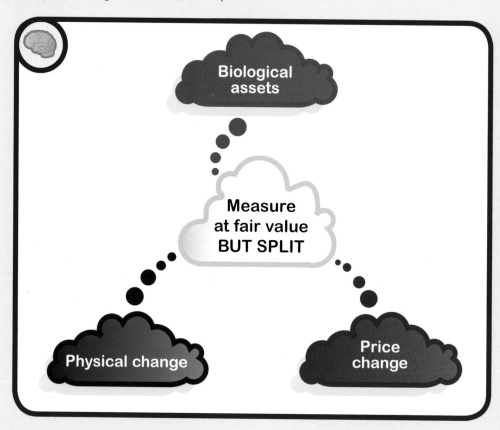

Conclusion

IAS 41 is very specific to a certain industry and as such is not examined very frequently. However, when faced with biological assets, students will need to know the difference between using IAS 2 – value at lower of cost or NSP – and the very different answer you get with IAS 41.

* Balance Sheet = Statement of financial position (see page 18)

IFRS 1 - First-time adoption of International Financial Reporting Standards

Introduction

"In terms of the largest companies included in the Fortune 500 list, 176 prepare their accounts under US GAAP and 200 under IFRS, 81 under Japanese GAAP."

Michael Prada, Chair of the Technical Committee of IOSCO, February 2006

So ... what's it trying to achieve?

IFRS 1 aims to ensure that an entity's first IFRS financial statements and its interim reports during its first period provide high quality and transparent information where the costs of producing the information do not outweigh the benefits the information provides.

Transactional example

Sardinia Inc presented its financial statements, under its local GAAP annually as at 31 December each year. The most recent financial statements were presented to 31 December 20X6. Sardinia Inc decided to adopt IFRS as of 31 December 20X7 and to present one-year comparative information for the year 20X6. Sardinia needs to consider when it should prepare its first balance sheet* to IFRS.

Well, Sardinia Inc will need an 'opening balance sheet*', prepared as at 1 January 2006. Note that the more comparative periods it wants to give, the earlier will be the date of the opening balance sheet*.

Sorry but you need to know ... DEFINITIONS

The **date of transition** to IFRS is the beginning of the earliest period for which an entity presents full comparative information under IFRS in its first IFRS financial statements.

The **previous GAAP** is the basis of accounting that a first-time adopter used immediately before adopting IFRS.

The **reporting date** is the end of the latest period covered by financial statements or by an interim report.

And the really important stuff ... accounting practice

An entity must prepare an opening balance sheet* at its transition date to IFRS as a basis for preparing the current and comparative financial statements.

In preparing the opening balance sheet* the entity should follow all accounting standards relevant at its first reporting date (full retrospective application) subject to certain optional exemptions detailed below.

The exemptions from fully retrospective application are:

Property, plant and equipment	A 'frozen' revaluation in previous GAAP is allowed as a deemed cost on transition to IFRS.
Business combinations	The rules in IFRS 3 can be applied from any previous business combination as long as all since that date follow the rules.
	Without any retrospective application, positive goodwill is frozen and subject to annual impairment review, and negative goodwill must be written back to retained earnings.
Employee benefits	On transition any actuarial gains and losses can be recognised within the pension asset or liability even if a spreading policy is adopted for those that arise after the transition date.

* Balance Sheet = Statement of financial position (see page 18)

Exchange difference reserve	It is not required to recognise exchange differences arising before transition as a separate reserve if they were not recognised separately under previous GAAP. The exchange differences would not be recycled on disposal of the foreign subsidiary.
Financial instruments	Very complex rules, but the main issue is that IAS 32 and 39 do not need to be followed in the comparative periods for first-time adopters in 2005.

Any estimates made under previous GAAP should be brought forward into the first IFRS financial statements without adjustment, unless they are so incorrect as to make the accounts not show a fair presentation.

Disclosures

In the first IFRS financial statements the following extra disclosures are required:

- full balance sheet* reconciliations from previous GAAP to IFRS for the beginning of the first reporting period and at the date of transition to IFRS
- full income statement reconciliation for the comparative period income statement
- full explanations of the adjustments made in the above reconciliations.

Conclusion

This was a very important standard for students around 2005 when many countries adopted IFRS for the first time. It is now less important as IFRS is becoming established.

IFRS 2 – Share-based payments

Introduction

> **"... demand for greater transparency ... particularly in regard to employee share options."**
>
> **Sir David Tweedie, IASB Chair**

When senior staff negotiate an employment package, it is not usually just salary and pension, but often includes share options. Traditional accounting methods did not expense this part of employee remuneration as there was no associated cash flow. IFRS 2 has brought in a radical new approach.

So ... what's it trying to achieve?

IFRS 2 prescribes the accounting treatment when enterprises undertake share-based payment transactions. It requires an entity to reflect the effect of share-based payments in its income statement.

Transactional example

Bonofi granted 2,000 share options to each of its three directors on 1 January 20X7 subject to the directors being employed on 31 December 20X9. The options vest on 31 December 20X9. The fair value of each option on 1 January 20X7 is $10 and it is anticipated that all of the share options will vest on 31 December 20X9. The options will only vest if the company's share price reaches $14 per share. It is anticipated that there will only be two directors employed on 31 December 20X9. The directors are unsure as to how the share options will be accounted for in the accounts for the year ended 31 December 20X7.

---

* Balance Sheet = Statement of financial position (see page 18)

Directors' share options

IFRS 2 requires that, when a company grants share options to its employees, an expense is arising. The employees are benefiting from a form of remuneration and the company is benefiting from their labour. The expense will have to be calculated based on the fair value of the directors' share options at the date they were granted – 1 January 20X7. The fair value will need to be used. Share option pricing models such as Black-Scholes are available. The market-based condition, i.e. the increase in the share price, can be ignored for the purpose of the calculation. However, the employment condition must be taken into account.

Expense arising

The options will be treated as follows:

2,000 options × 2 Directors × \$10 × 1year/3 years = \$13,333. Equity will be increased by this amount and an expense shown in the income statement for the year ended 31 December 2007.

Dr Income statement
Cr Other equity

Sorry but you need to know ... DEFINITIONS

Vesting conditions are conditions that must be satisfied for the counterparty to become entitled to receive cash, other assets or equity instruments under a share-based payment arrangement.

Vesting period is the period during which all the specified vesting conditions of a share-based arrangement are to be satisfied.

Share-based payment arrangements are agreements between the entity and a third party (including an employee) to enter into a share-based payment transaction.

And the really important stuff... accounting practice

Equity-settled (company will issue shares in the future/ has issued share now)

For goods and services (other than employee service) the fair value in the income statement is the fair value of the goods or services received. For employee service it is the fair value of the equity instruments issued at their grant date.

The fair value of options at the grant date will usually be measured by using a pricing model (such as Black-Scholes), and must take into account:

- exercise price of the option
- life of the option
- current price of the underlying shares
- expected volatility of the share price
- dividends expected on the shares; and
- risk-free interest rate.

The charge must be recognised over the vesting period using the 'truing-up' method from US GAAP (SFAS 123). This method bases the charge on the number of options that vest. (Options vest even if they are not subsequently exercised.)

The credit entry is recognised as a separate item of equity.

Cash-settled (company will pay cash based on the share price)

The charge is the fair value of the expected cash payment spread over the period to which the liability is settled.

The fair value must be remeasured at each balance sheet* date.

The credit entry is made as a liability.

Cash or equity settled

If the supplier has the choice of settlement the company treats the charge as the issue of a compound instrument. This means that it is recognised as a liability and an equity option.

If the entity has the choice the instrument is either treated as equity-settled or cash-settled dependent on the likelihood of settlement method.

---

* Balance Sheet = Statement of financial position (see page 18)

Disclosures

An entity must disclose information that enables users of the financial statements to understand the nature and extent of share-based payment arrangements that existed during the period.

Conclusion

IFRS is a frequently examined topic for the more advanced student. Consequently it is very much a transaction that it is worth getting familiar with.

IFRS 4 – Insurance contracts

Introduction

> "There are worse things in life than death. Have you ever spent the evening with an insurance salesman?"
>
> **Woody Allen**

Before you read on you need to check whether this is actually examinable – it often isn't as it is so specific. Please check with your tutor or list of examinable documents.

So ... what's it trying to achieve?

IFRS 4 provides guidance on accounting for insurance contracts issued by companies. In particular the standard requires:

(a) limited improvements to accounting by insurers for insurance contracts
(b) improved disclosures for insurance contracts in the financial statements of insurers.

Sorry but you need to know ... DEFINITIONS

An **insurance contract** is a contract under which one party (the insurer) accepts significant insurance risk from another party (the policyholder) by agreeing to compensate the policyholder if a specified uncertain future event (the insured event) adversely affects the policyholder.

Insurance liability is an insurer's net contractual obligations under an insurance contract.

Insurance assets are an insurer's net contractual rights under an insurance contract.

Scope

(a) The IFRS applies to:

- insurance contracts; and
- financial instruments with a discretionary participation feature.

(b) The IFRS applies to embedded derivatives in insurance contracts with the exception of a policyholder's option to surrender an insurance contract early.

(c) Some insurance contracts contain an insurance and a deposit element. If the contract does include these separate parts, it is acceptable to separate the parts and account for them separately provided the information is available to split.

And the really important stuff … accounting practice

The standard exempts an insurer from the normal accounting policy requirements in IAS 8 for both insurance contracts that it issues and reinsurance contracts that it holds.

The standard does not exempt insurers from some requirements:

- no recognition of catastrophe or equalisation provisions
- insurers must carry out a liability adequacy test
- insurers shall remove a liability only when it is extinguished
- no offsetting of insurance liabilities and reinsurance assets, or income and expenses from insurance and reinsurance contracts
- impairment tests are required for reinsurance assets
- no changes in accounting policy are required but if policies are changed some restrictions on new policies are enforced
- no measurement of liabilities on an undiscounted basis
- no measurement of contractual rights at an amount exceeding their fair value
- no use of non-uniform policies.

Discretionary participation features (such as with-profits elements in policies) can be separated out from the guaranteed element of policies, but it is not compulsory. Discretionary features can be treated as a liability or a separate component of equity.

Disclosures

An insurer should disclose information about the following:

- information that identifies and explains the amounts in its financial statements arising from insurance contracts
- the amount, timing and uncertainty of cash flows that arise under insurance contracts.

There is detail in the standard about the necessary disclosures under each of these main sections.

* Balance Sheet = Statement of financial position (see page 18)

Conclusion

This one you may be able to ignore – don't forget to check – it is commonly not examinable!!

---

* Balance Sheet = Statement of financial position (see page 18)

 **IFRS 6 – Exploration for and evaluation of mineral resources**

Introduction

> **"We shall never cease from exploration**
> **And the end of all our exploring**
> **Will be to arrive where we started**
> **And know the place for the first time."**
>
> **TS Eliot (1888-1965)**

IFRS 6 is another standard that is often excluded from syllabus. Please check with your tutor or examinable document list before reading any further.

The exploration industry (particularly the oil and gas industry) has faced serious issues as a result of the move to International Financial Reporting Standards (IFRS). In particular the impact of IAS 36 *'Impairment of assets,'* with its requirement to consider cash-generating units at the lowest possible level. For this industry it can mean an individual petrol station is a separate cash-generating unit.

Also, with regards to the costs involved in exploration, evaluation and extraction of mineral resource assets, prior to IFRS 6 there was a complete lack of consistency in their treatment. Some countries had a GAAP that failed to deal with the issue at all and, where national standards did exist, the allowed accounting practices were diverse. Some countries required capitalisation of these expenses, others required immediate write-off to income and others were allowed a choice.

So what was the norm?

Most of the major companies in this sector use the 'successful efforts' method. This means the costs incurred in finding, acquiring and developing reserves are capitalised on a 'field by field' basis. What this means is that, when a commercially-viable mineral reserve is discovered, the capitalised costs are allocated to the discovery. If a discovery is not made, the expenditure is charged as an expense.

So what was the other method called?

Well some companies have used the 'full cost' approach, where all costs are capitalised. Prior to IFRS 6, on a move to IFRS companies would have to default to the IASB 'Framework' which would have forced a change in practice. IFRS 6 has therefore been issued as an interim standard and is intended to be a short-term solution to the problem.

So ... what's it trying to achieve?

IFRS 6 is designed to provide some limited guidance to companies but does not aim to harmonise accounting practice in these areas.

Transactional example

Emily Inc is adopting IFRS. It has always applied an accounting policy of capitalisation of exploration costs. Will the move to IFRS affect this policy?

IFRS 6 permits entities to continue to use their existing accounting policies, provided they comply with paragraph 10 of IAS 8 *'Accounting policies, changes in accounting estimates and errors'*. What this means is that the information provided must be relevant and reliable, although it is not in full compliance with the definition of an asset in the IASB Framework. IFRS 6 therefore is allowing an exemption from the Framework.

Criteria to be used

IAS 8 paragraph 10 sets out the criteria for determining whether a policy is relevant and reliable. You need to learn this.

---

* Balance Sheet = Statement of financial position (see page 18)

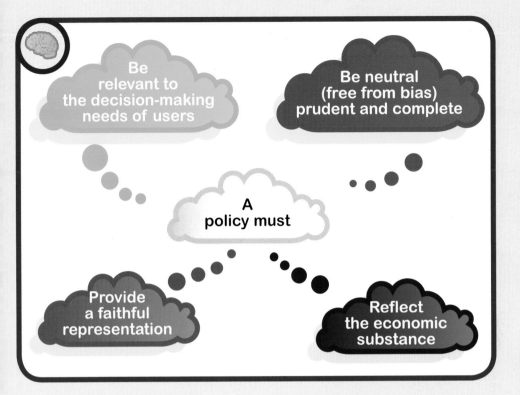

Emily Inc can change its accounting policy for exploration and extraction assets but only if the result brings it closer to the principles of the IASB Framework. The change must result in a policy that is more reliable and no less relevant or more relevant and no less reliable than the previous policy. Emily may therefore have an asset on the balance sheet* that does not meet the IASB Framework definition of an asset. The capitalisation criteria may not require the demonstration of future economic benefits. Following IFRS 6, therefore, may result in earlier capitalisation than would be the case under the IASB Framework.

Tangible or intangible?

Recognised exploration and evaluation assets can be classified as either tangible or intangible assets under IFRS 6. Assets recognised in respect of licences and surveys should be classified as intangible assets. Subsequent costs incurred during the exploration and evaluation phase should be capitalised in accordance with this same policy. Basically the entity can retain the accumulated cost as an exploration asset until there is sufficient information to determine whether there will be commercial cash flows or not.

Application of IAS 16 and IAS 38

These standards will apply to these assets. Initially the assets are recognised using the cost model as normal. Subsequently Emily Inc will have a choice of using the cost model or adopting the revaluation model as described in IAS 16 and IAS 38. Depreciation and amortisation is not calculated for the assets because the economic benefits that the assets represent are not consumed until the production phase.

The trigger for an impairment test on these assets

IFRS 6 is very clear with regards to the impairment testing of these assets. Emily will have to test for impairment if the carrying value (book value) of the asset may not be recoverable.

You must learn the circumstances and facts that indicate a possible impairment and will trigger an impairment test:

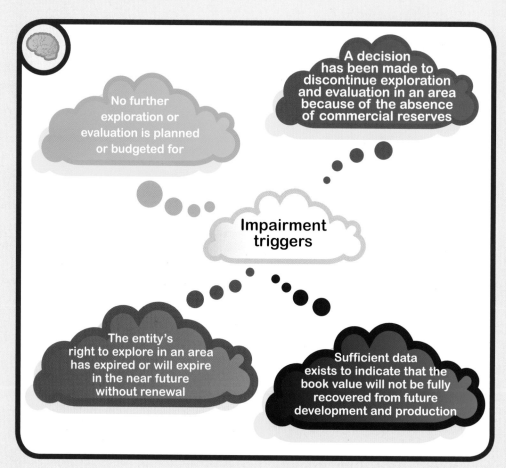

 Note

Note a common error is to read the information – the company has a lack of sufficient data to determine whether the carrying amount of the exploration and evaluation asset is likely to be recovered in full from successful development or by sale, – **as meaning an impairment test must be performed. This would actually NOT trigger an impairment test**.

* Balance Sheet = Statement of financial position (see page 18)

The impairment test

As this type of asset does not generate cash inflows it will have to be tested for impairment as part of a 'cash-generating unit' – a larger group of assets. Emily will need an accounting policy for allocating these assets to groups of cash-generating units (CGUs). **Note that a CGU is also referred to as an IGU – ' income-generating unit' – it means the same thing**. The policy will need to be applied consistently. IAS 36 will then apply in testing the CGU for impairment, subject to certain special requirements.

Special requirements?

The limitation specified in IFRS 6 is that the CGU to which the assets are allocated should not be larger than a segment of the entity. You may remember that IAS 36 specifies that an CGU is the smallest unit for which independent cash flows can be identified. Without this special exemption, it could mean that each individual extraction unit (such as an oil rig) would be classified as a CGU. IFRS 6 is therefore allowing some flexibility for these companies when defining a CGU.

At what point does IFRS 6 stop being relevant to the asset?

If Emily Inc has demonstrated the technical and commercial feasibility of extracting a mineral resource, the assets fall outside IFRS 6 and are reclassified according to other appropriate standards. An impairment test must be performed at this point, i.e. before reclassification.

Sorry but you need to know ... DEFINITIONS

Exploration for and evaluation of mineral resources

The search for mineral resources, including minerals, oils, natural gas and similar non-regenerative resources after the entity has obtained legal rights to explore in a specific area, as well as the determination of the technical feasibility and commercial viability of extracting the mineral resource.

And the really important stuff ... accounting practice

The standard permits a company to continue with its existing accounting policies for mineral resources, and exempts them therefore from the normal requirements for setting accounting policies of IAS 8.

Impairment tests must be performed on exploration and evaluation assets if circumstances suggest the asset may have impaired.

Disclosure

Exploration and development costs that are capitalised are classified as non-current assets in the balance sheet*, and should be separately disclosed on the face, distinguished from production assets where material.

The classification as 'tangible' or 'intangible' established during the exploration phase, should be continued through to the development and production phases.

Details of the amounts recognised in the financial statements, including:

- accounting policies; and
- the amounts of assets, liabilities, income, expenditure and cash flows.

Conclusion

IFRS 6 is not aiming to or achieving consistency of accounting treatment in this area. In fact it allows companies using very different accounting policies to claim adherence to IFRS GAAP. It is exempting such companies from applying the Framework in a similar way to IFRS 4 *'Insurance contracts'*. It was argued that it was too harsh to force those entities that use capitalisation in their accounts to switch to expensing, even though IAS 38 requires that they treat these costs as costs not assets. There was also a problem with those companies that exist solely to carry out exploration. Once the exploration is complete they then sell the rights to the minerals found. Prior to IFRS 6, with an application of the Framework and IAS 36 to their transactions, they would only ever have costs and no substantial assets would appear on their balance sheet*. The IASB accepted these arguments and issued IFRS 6.

IFRS 6 is a very likely exam question where it is on your syllabus as it presents examiners with a useful industry-based scenario, is very current and allows discussion of the conflict between the Framework and some standards.

---

* Balance Sheet = Statement of financial position (see page 18)

IFRS 8 – Operating segments

Introduction

> ## "You might be an accountant if ... you have no idea that GAP is also a clothing store!"
>
> **Traditional**

Well we are nearly at the end of IFRS GAAP now (feel free to cheer!). So what is IFRS 8 about? Well, when a business operates in a variety of different types (classes) of business or in different geographical locations, the external reporting (per IAS 1) of just totals for stuff like profit and revenue is not actually that useful to investors. If meaningful comparisons are to be made, the informed investor would require further detail on performance and sales within specific businesses.

So it's like taking the revenue line, etc and doing a pie chart – segmenting it?

Yep, you've got it – it's just for listed companies and it requires disclosures of certain totals, broken down and reconciled (sort of like a pie chart, i.e. segmented by type of operation). Only then is the reader of the accounts getting a complete and understandable picture of the company's operations.

 Sorry but you need to know ... DEFINITIONS

A **reportable segment** is an operating segment or aggregations of operating segments that meet specified criteria.

An **operating segment** is a component of an entity about which separate financial information is available that is evaluated regularly by the chief operating decision maker in deciding how to allocate resources and in assessing performance.

So … what's it trying to achieve?

IFRS 8 requires an entity to report financial and descriptive information about its reportable segments. It requires an entity to adopt the 'management approach' to reporting on the financial performance of its operating segments. Generally this means that, the information to be reported would be what management uses internally for evaluating segment performance, and for deciding how to allocate resources to operating segments.

And the really important stuff … accounting practice

Financial information is required to be reported on the basis that it is used internally for evaluating operating segment performance and deciding how to allocate resources to operating segments.

The definition of an operating segment includes a component of an entity that sells primarily or exclusively to other operating segments of the entity, if the entity is managed that way.

The standard requires reconciliations of total reportable segment revenues, total profit or loss, total assets, total liabilities and other amounts disclosed for reportable segments to corresponding amounts in the entity's financial statements.

Disclosures

Reconciliations of total reportable segment:

- revenues
- profit or loss
- assets
- liabilities
- other amounts.

---

* Balance Sheet = Statement of financial position (see page 18)

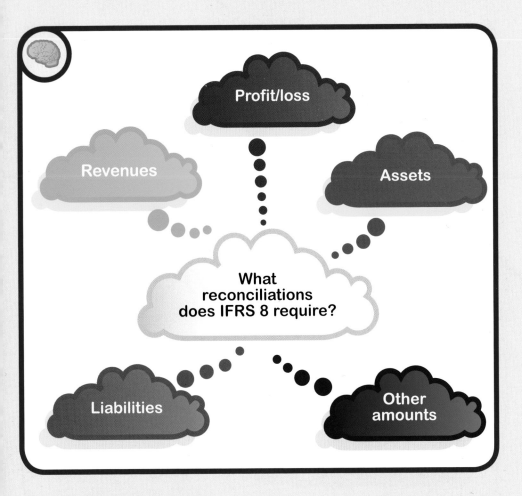

Further Disclosures

- An explanation of how segment profit or loss and segment assets and liabilities are measured for each reportable segment.
- Information about the revenues derived from its products or services (or groups of similar products and services), about the countries in which it earns revenues and holds assets, and about major customers, regardless of whether the information is used by management in making operating decisions.
- Descriptive information is required about the way the operating segments were determined, the products and services provided by the segments, differences between the measurements used in reporting segment information and those used in an entity's financial statements, and changes in the measurement of segment amounts from period to period.

A summary of the disclosures required

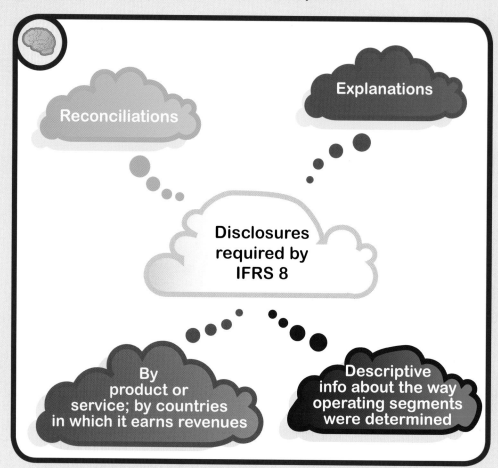

Reconciliations

Explanations

Disclosures required by IFRS 8

By product or service; by countries in which it earns revenues

Descriptive info about the way operating segments were determined

Conclusion

IFRS 8 is merely about providing extra analysis and disclosure. As such questions on this topic are usually 'gifts' – particularly for somebody who likes numbers – practice a few and enjoy. Don't forget to refer to the Framework document if you are asked: 'Why are companies required to prepare segmental information? Go back to Chapter 1 – remember the mnemonic ACCURATE – apply these key words to your answer and you will score well.

* Balance Sheet = Statement of financial position (see page 18)

And so they lived happily ever after ... or did they?

Unfortunately the area of accounting standards is one that is subject to frequent change. No sooner do we learn them and a new standard replaces the old one. If you want to check if the position has changed or is due to change, have a look at

www.astudentsguideto.com.

> **"Knowledge is a comfortable and necessary retreat and shelter for us in advanced age, and if we do not plant it while young it will give us no shade when we grow old."**
>
> Phillip Chesterfield (1694–1773)

Index

Index

	Page
Accruals	7
Agriculture	237
Asset – definition	9
Associates	199
Balance sheet	16
Borrowing costs	122
Business combinations	171
Cash flow statements	30
Changes in accounting policies	48
Consistency	7
Consolidated and separate financial statements	168
Comparability	7
Construction contracts	86
Contingent assets	72
Contingent liabilities	72
Disposals of non-current assets held for sale	158
Earnings per share (EPS)	129
Employee benefits	208
Events after the balance sheet date	55
Exploration for and evaluation of mineral assets	251
Financial instruments: disclosures	163

Financial instruments: disclosure and presentation   125

Financial instruments: recognition and measurement   144

Financial statements   12

Foreign exchange rates   222

Fundamental errors   48

Going concern   7

Government grants   118

Hyper inflationary economies   231

IAS 1   Presentation of financial statements   12

IAS 2   Inventories   25

IAS 7   Cash flow statements   30

IAS 8   Accounting policies, changes in accounting estimates and errors   48

IAS 10   Events after the balance sheet date   55

IAS 11   Construction contracts   86

IAS 12   Income taxes   95

IAS 16   Property, plant and equipment   59

IAS 17   Leases   107

IAS 18   Revenue   67

IAS 19   Employee benefits   208

IAS 20   Accounting for government grants and disclosure of government assistance   118

IAS 21   The effects of changes in foreign exchange rates   222

IAS 23   Borrowing costs   122

IAS 24   Related party disclosures   227

IAS 27   Consolidated and separate financial statements   168

IAS 28   Investments in associates   199

IAS 29 Financial reporting in hyper inflationary economies   231

IAS 31 Investments in joint ventures   201

IAS 32 Financial instruments: disclosure and presentation   125

IAS 33 Earnings per share   129

IAS 36 Impairment of assets   139

IAS 37 Provisions, contingent liabilities and Contingent Assets   72

IAS 38 Intangible assets   78

IAS 39 Financial instruments: recognition and measurement   144

IAS 40 Investment property   154

IAS 41 Agriculture   237

IFRS 2 Share-based payment   244

IFRS 3 Business combinations   171

IFRS 4 Insurance contracts   248

IFRS 5 Disposals of non-current assets held for sale   158

IFRS 6 Exploration for and evaluation of mineral assets   251

IFRS 7 Financial instruments: disclosures   163

IFRS 8 Operating segments   257

Impairment of assets   139

Income statement   19

Income taxes   95

Insurance contracts   248

Intangible assets   78

Inventories   25

Investments in associates   199

Investments in joint ventures   201

Investment property   154

Joint ventures   201

Leases   107

Liabilities – definition   9

Mineral assets   251

Non-current assets held for sale   158

Operating segments   257

Pensions   208

Presentation of financial statements   12

Property, plant and equipment   59

Provisions, contingent liabilities and contingent assets   72

Related party disclosures   227

Relevance   7

Reliability   7

Retirement benefits   208

Revenue   67

Share-based payment   244

Statement of changes in equity   22

Subsidiaries   168

Taxes   95

Understandability   7

Q 1. Can you write out the format for the income statement?

Remember in some exams you are given it!!

Really Cute Guys (or gals) Distract Accountants, Preventing Infatuated Fools Passing The Paper

	20X2	20X1
Revenue (Really)	x	x
Cost of sales (Cute)	(x)	(x)
Gross profit (Guys/Gals)	x	x
Distribution costs (Distract)	(x)	(x)
Administrative expenses (Accountants)	(x)	(x)
Profit from operations (Preventing)	x	x
Investment income (Infatuated)		
Finance cost (Fools)	(x)	(x)
Profit before tax (Passing)	x	x
Tax expense (The)	(x)	(x)
Profit after tax (Paper)	x	x

Just starting out?

Q **2. What about the statement of financial position (balance sheet*)?**

XYZ- Statement of financial position(balance sheet*) as at 31 December 20X2

(in thousands of currency units)	20X2	20X2	20X1	20X1
Assets				
Non-current assets				
Current assets				
Total assets		X		X
Equity and liabilities				
Equity attributable to the holders of the parent				
Share capital				
Retained earnings				
Non-current liabilities				
Current liabilities				
Total equity and liabilities		X		X

* Balance Sheet = Statement of financial position (see page 18)

i.e. all the debits in the top half and all the credits in the bottom half.

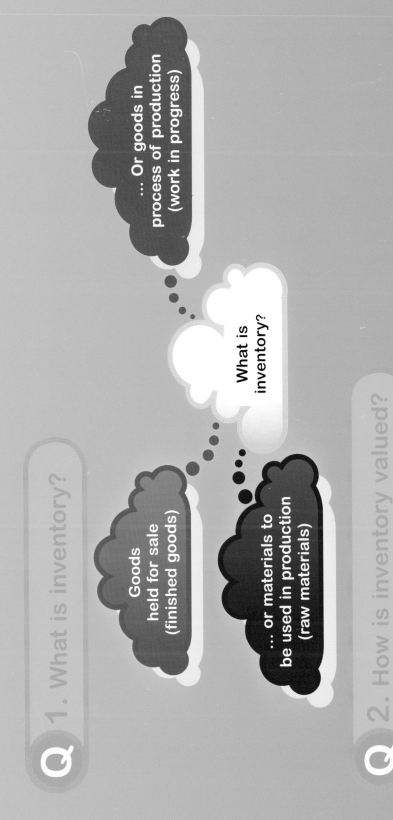

IAS 2 – Inventory

Q 1. What is inventory?

Goods held for sale (finished goods)

… or materials to be used in production (raw materials)

What is inventory?

… Or goods in process of production (work in progress)

Q 2. How is inventory valued?

Inventories should be valued at total of the lower of cost (all costs incurred in bringing to present location and condition) and net realisable value of separate items of stock, or of groups of similar items.

IAS 2 – Inventory

Q 3. What is net realisable value?

Net realisable value is the estimated selling price (ordinary course of business) less estimated completion and selling costs.

Q 4. Which cost formulae are acceptable and which aren't?

Last-in, first-out (LIFO) is not acceptable.

First-in, first-out (FIFO) and weighted average cost formulae are acceptable.

IAS 7 – Cash flow statements

- Operating activities.
- Investing activities.
- Financing activities.

Q 1. What are the three headings required by IAS 7?

Q 2. Can you remember the format for cashflow from operating activities?

Cash flows from operating activities

Profit from operations (**P**lainly)	x
Adjustments for:	
Depreciation (**D**edicated)	x
Disposal of property, plant and equipment (gain)/ loss (**D**octors)	(x)/x
Operating cash flows before working capital changes	x
Inventories increase/decrease (**I**nspire)	(x)/x
Receivables increase/decrease (**R**eal)	(x)/x
Payables decrease/increase (**P**eople)	(x)/x
Cash generated from operations	xx

Plainly **D**edicated **D**octors **I**nspire **R**eal **P**eople

Q 3. Can you remember how to work out the tax paid figure in a cash flow statement? (note – primary working)

(Working 2)

Tax account

ß Cash paid in year	x	Bal b/fwd – Current tax	x
(for the cash flow statement)		Bal b/fwd – Deferred tax	x
Bal c/fwd – Current tax	**x**	Income Statement –	
Balance c/fwd – Deferred tax	**x**	tax for the year	x
	xx		xx

IAS 7 – Cash flow statements

Q 4. Can you remember how to work out cash flow from purchase of property, plant and equipment? (Note: a primary working)

(Working 4)

Non-current assets/property, plant and equipment

Bal b/fwd (from opening balance sheet*)	x	Depreciation	x
= Additions in period	xx	NBV of asset sold	x
		Bal c/fwd (from closing balance sheet*)	x

Q 5. What about the proceeds from disposal?

(Working 3)

Proceeds from disposal of equipment

NBV of asset sold (what you expected to get)	x
= Proceeds from sale (figure for cash flow statement)	Add: Profit made on disposal (taken to income statement) i.e. you got more than expected x
	xx

Note, If you can do these, you can apply the principle to other cashflows.

IAS 8 – Accounting policies, changes in accounting estimates and errors

Q 1. What is the difference between a change in accounting policy and a change in accounting estimate?

A change in accounting policy

A change in the specific principles, bases, conventions, rules and practices applied by an entity

A change in accounting estimate

An adjustment of the carrying amount of an asset or a liability, or the amount of periodic consumption of an asset. A change in an accounting estimate is not a change in policy or correction of errors

IAS 8 – Accounting policies, changes in accounting estimates and errors

Q 2. Give five examples of changes in accounting policy.

A REAL

A – Asset measurement changed from depreciated historic cost to revaluation

R – Revenue recognition policy is changed

E – Expenses reclassified from cost of sales to admin

A – A new accounting standard forces change

L – Legislation changes

Q 3. Give three examples of changes in accounting estimate.

PUB

P – Provisions for warranty obligations

U – Useful lives of property, plant and equipment

B – Bad debts

Q 4. If a company has made a material change to an accounting policy in preparing its current financial statements, what disclosures are required?

The reasons for the change.

The amount of the adjustment in the current period and in comparative information for prior periods.

IAS 10 – Events after the reporting period

Q 1. What are 'events after the reporting period'?

They are events, both favourable and unfavourable, that occur between the balance sheet* date and the date of approval of the accounts.

This is not a difficult standard but it is important right from your earliest accounting exams and therefore a cloud diagram works well.

Q 2. What are the two types of event?

Two types of event

Adjusting

Non-adjusting

* Balance Sheet = Statement of financial position (see page 18)

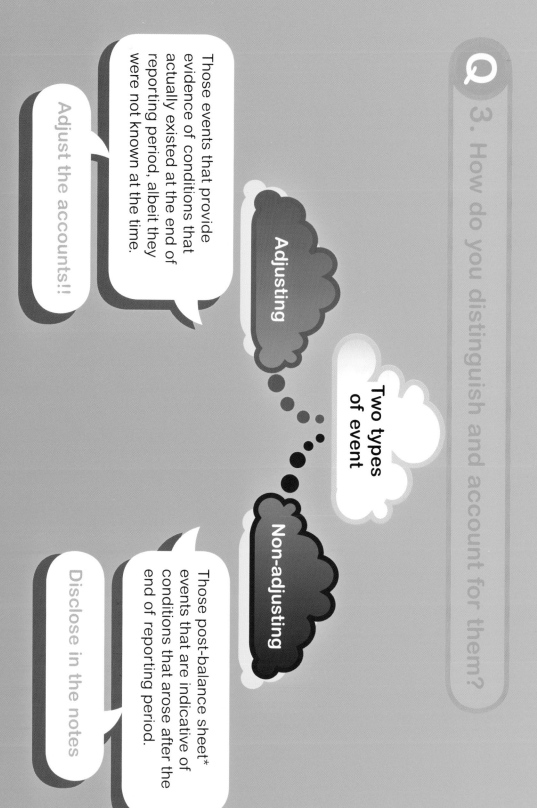

IAS 10 – Events after the reporting period

Q 3. How do you distinguish and account for them?

Two types of event

Adjusting

Those events that provide evidence of conditions that actually existed at the end of reporting period, albeit they were not known at the time.

Adjust the accounts!!

Non-adjusting

Those post-balance sheet* events that are indicative of conditions that arose after the end of reporting period.

Disclose in the notes

IAS 16 – Property, plant and equipment

Q 1. Which assets are covered by IAS 16?

Property, plant and equipment:
- are held for use in the production or supply of goods and services, for rental to others, or for administrative purposes; and
- are expected to be used during more than one period.

Q 2. What is depreciation?

Depreciation is the systematic allocation of the depreciable amount (cost or valuation less residual value) of an asset over its useful economic life.

Q 3. What is meant by 'fair value'?

Fair value is the amount for which an asset could be exchanged between knowledgeable, willing parties in an arms length transaction.

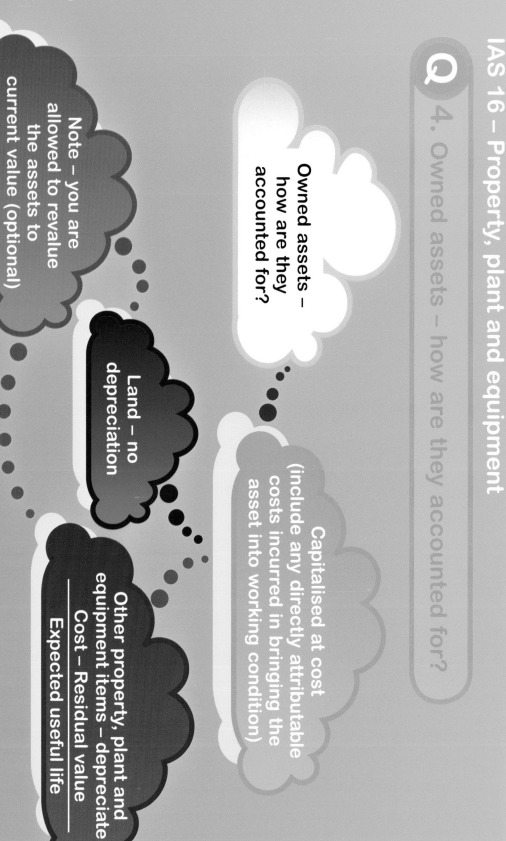

IAS 18 – Revenue

Q 1. How is revenue measured?

Revenue should be measured at the fair value of the consideration received or receivable.

If revenue is deferred it should be measured at present value.

In a barter transaction the revenue should be the fair value of the goods received and, only if unreliable, the fair value of the goods given up.

Q 2. When should revenue be recognised for sale of goods?

When should revenue be recognised for sale of goods?

Measured reliably

Costs incurred can be measured reliably

No retained involvement or control over the goods

Risks and rewards transferred to buyer

Probable economic benefits will flow

¿Just starting out?

IAS 18 – Revenue

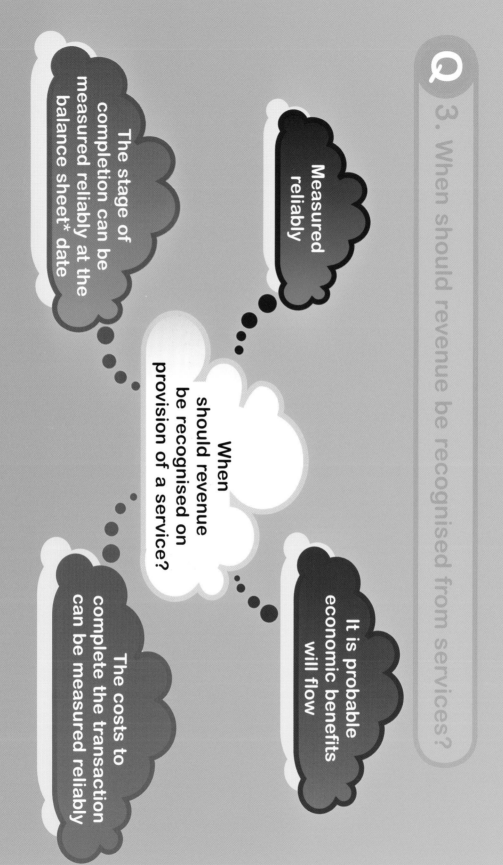

Measured reliably

The stage of completion can be measured reliably at the balance sheet* date

When should revenue be recognised on provision of a service?

It is probable economic benefits will flow

The costs to complete the transaction can be measured reliably

* Balance Sheet = Statement of financial position (see page 18)

IAS 37 – Provisions, contingent assets and contingent liabilities

Q 1. What is a provision?

A provision is a liability of uncertain timing or amount.

A liability is a present obligation of an entity to transfer economic benefits as a result of past transactions or events.

Q 2. What is a contingent liability?

A contingent liability is a possible obligation that arises from past events whose outcome is based on uncertain future events, or an obligation that is not recognised because it is not probable or cannot be measured reliably.

Q 3. What is a contingent asset?

A contingent asset is a possible asset that arises from past events and whose existence will only be confirmed by uncertain future events not wholly within the control of the enterprise.

Just starting out?

IAS 37 – Provisions, contingent assets and contingent liabilities

Q 4. When should provisions be recognised?

Has a present obligation (either legal or constructive).

Provide only when all conditions are met.

It is probable that a transfer of economic benefits will be required to settle the obligation.

The obligation can be measured reliably.

Q 5. How should a provisions be accounted for?

When deciding if a provision should be recognised an entity should determine whether the future expenditure can be avoided. If the future expenditure can be avoided no provision should be made.

Q 6. How should contingent liabilities be accounted for?

Contingent liabilities should not be recognised in the financial statements. However disclosure should be made unless the possibility of the transfer of economic benefits is remote.

Q 7. How should contingent assets be accounted for?

Contingent assets should not be recognised, and disclosure is only allowed if the possible profit is considered probable. Virtually certain profits could be recognised in the financial statements.

IAS 38 – Intangible assets

Q 1. What is an intangible asset?

An intangible asset is an identifiable non-monetary asset without physical substance. Assets are identifiable because they are separable, or because they are identifiable through legal or contractual rights.

Q 2. When should intangibles be recognised on a balance sheet*?

Intangibles should be recognised if, and only if, the following criteria are met:
- It is probable that the future economic benefits will flow to the enterprise; and
- The cost of the asset can be measured reliably.

Q 3. When can you capitalise internally generated intangibles?

The generation of the asset is classified into:
- a research phase (never capitalise)
- a development phase (may be capitalised but criteria need to be met):

(a) technically feasible (totally)
(b) intention to complete and use or sell the asset (important)
(c) ability to use or sell the asset (always)
(d) existence of a market or demonstration of usefulness of intangible (employ)
(e) availability of technical, financial or other resources to complete the asset (attractive)
(f) measure the cost reliably (men).

Totally important – always employ attractive men!!

* Balance Sheet = Statement of financial position (see page 18)

IAS 38 – Intangible assets

Q 4. What about purchased intangibles?

For purchased intangibles the probability criteria is always met (because a price has been paid) and therefore they are recognised on the balance sheet*, albeit subject to an impairment review.

For intangibles acquired in a business combination there is an assumption that the probability criteria is met, and there is always information to measure the cost separately from goodwill. This means the following sorts of intangibles (plus others) must be recognised separately from goodwill:

- customer lists
- in progress R&D
- employment contracts below market rate
- order or production backlogs.

Q 5. Once intangibles are on the balance sheet*, what then?

Intangible assets should be amortised over their useful economic lives. If no amortisation is charged because the life is indefinite, the asset must be subject to an annual impairment review.

Intangibles can be revalued only if an active market exists for the asset (very rare).

IASB Framework

Asset –
a resource controlled by the entity as a result of past events and from which future economic benefits are expected to flow to the entity

Liability –
a 'present obligation of the entity arising from past events, the settlement of which is expected to result in an outflow from the entity of resources embodying economic benefits'

Equity –
the residual interest in the assets of the entity after deducting all of its liabilities

Expenses –
decreases in economic benefits during the accounting period in the form of outflows or depletions in assets or incurrences of liabilities that result in decreases in equity, other than those relating to distributions to equity participants

Income –
increases in economic benefit during the accounting period in the form of inflows or enhancements of assets or incurrences of liabilities that result in increases in equity, other than those relating to distributions to equity participants

Just starting out?

IASB Framework

Q 2. Give four examples of qualitative characteristics of financial statements

Comparability
Understandability
Relevance
Reliability

Q 3. According to the 'Framework', what characteristics make financial information reliable?

Faithful representation
Neutrality
Prudence

Q 4. Which two 'bedrock' assumptions underlie the preparation and presentation of financial statements?

Accruals
Going concern

IAS 11 – Construction Contracts

Q 1. What is a construction contract?

A construction contract is a contract specifically negotiated for the construction of an asset or a combination of assets that are closely interrelated or interdependent in terms of their design, technology and function or their ultimate purpose or use.

Q 1. What are the two methods of calculating completion percentage on a project?

The percentage completion can be calculated by:

$$\text{Work certified method} = \frac{\text{Work certified to date}}{\text{Contract price}}$$

Invent a project you have quoted a price to build. Imagine it ¾ built Now think of the money you are do to get under the contract , that is one way of measuring the degree of completion. The work certified method conjures positive imagery- a building nears completion/loads of money to earned.

You mean there's more?

COST METHOD = $\dfrac{\text{Cost to date}}{\text{Total contract costs}}$

The cost method creates more negative imagery cash going out of your bank whilst you undertake the project
And under the line even more cash yet to be paid out- a sad face

Revenue and costs on contracts should be recognised over the period of the contract. Profit should also be recognised over the period of the contract as long as it can be assessed with reasonable certainty.

3. How are losses recognised?

Losses on contracts must be recognised in full as soon as they are foreseen.

IAS 12 – Income taxes

Q **1. When does deferred tax arise?**

Deferred tax is provided in full on all temporary differences (a balance sheet* calculation approach), except for any relating to non-deductible goodwill and assets purchased that are ineligible for capital allowances.

> We have a 'temporary difference' if the figure on the balance sheet* – the Net Book Value (NBV) – is different to its 'tax base', i.e. its tax written down value (WDV) – the amount that can be set against future tax bills.

Q **2. Can you set out the temporary difference working which is key for all deferred tax questions?**

> Deferred tax provision required for balance sheet*
>
> | | 20X1 |
> | --- | --- |
> | | $000 |
> | Cost-depreciation (NBV) | x |
> | Tax value (WDV) | x |
> | Temporary difference | xx |
> | Closing deferred tax liability [xx × tax rate] | x |

Q **3. What are the accounting entries?**

To achieve this we
Dr Income statement
– transfer to deferred tax
Cr Balance sheet*
– provision for deferred tax

> Unless we are reducing an existing provision for deferred tax when instead we
> Dr Balance sheet*
> – provision for deferred tax
>   Cr Income statement
>   – -transfer from deferred tax

You mean there's more?

IAS 12 – Income taxes

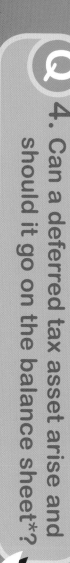

Q 4. Can a deferred tax asset arise and should it go on the balance sheet*?

Deferred tax assets can be created (mainly for tax losses) provided it is probable that the asset will be recovered.

Q 5. How is deferred tax measured?

Deferred tax must not be discounted to present value.

The tax rate used should be the one when the differences reverse, however, based on legislation enacted or substantially enacted by the balance sheet* date.

Q 6. Where does it go in the format?

Deferred tax is always presented as a non-current item on the balance sheet*.

If the item giving rise to the deferred tax is in reserves (for example, a revaluation of an asset), then the deferred tax should be recognised in reserves.

IAS 17 – Leases

Q 1. What are the two types of lease?

Finance lease

Operating lease

Q 2. Can you define them both?

A finance lease is a lease that substantially transfers the risks and rewards of ownership to the lessee.

An operating lease is a lease other than a finance lease.

Q 3. How do you decide if it is a finance lease or an operating lease?

What are the indicators of whether the risks and rewards of ownership have passed to the lessee?

Land leases are operating leases unless legal title passes at the end of the lease term. Leases of land and buildings must be treated as two leases

The lease transfers legal title at the end or there is a bargain purchase option for the lessee

The present value of guaranteed minimum lease payments is substantially all of the fair value of the asset at the start of the lease

The lessee has the use of the asset for the substantial majority of its economic life

You mean there's more?

IAS 17 – Leases

Q 4. How do you account for a finance lease?

Finance lease assets are capitalised (brought on balance sheet*) at their fair value, or the present value of the guaranteed minimum lease payments if lower than fair value, and a lease creditor is set up for the same amount.

The non-current asset should be depreciated over the shorter of the useful economic life of the asset and the lease term.

Interest is allocated to the lease creditor and charged to the income statement using either the interest rate implicit in the lease or, occasionally, the sum-of-digits method. As the rental payments are made the lease creditor falls.

Q 5. Can you draw a leasing table for an in arrears lease?

Balance b/fwd	Interest	Cash paid	Balance c/fwd

In numeric questions we use a leasing table to sort the numbers for us. You will need to first of all ascertain whether the lease payments are made in advance or in arrears. This is vital as it will change the calculations.

Q 6. Can you draw a leasing table for an in advance lease?

Balance b/fwd	Cash paid	Capital outstanding	Interest	Balance c/fwd

The rentals are charged to the income statement on a straight-line basis over the lease term (unless another systematic basis is more appropriate).

Q 7. How are operating leases accounted?

No asset or liability arises except for normal accruals and prepayments.

IAS 20 – Accounting for government grants and disclosure of government assistance

Q 1. How are government grants accounted for, if they relate to current or future costs?

Government grants should be recognised in the income statement to match them against the expenditure to which they contribute.

For current/future costs – in the period that the costs are recognised.

Grants towards future expenditure will be treated as deferred income when they are received and credited to income statement to match against the expenditure.

Q 2. How are government grants accounted for, if they relate to past costs?

For past costs incurred – immediately in the income statement.

You mean there's more?

IAS 20 – Accounting for government grants and disclosure of government assistance

Q 3. What are the two methods re non-current assets?

Non-current asset grants

Deducted from the cost of the asset – depreciate the net amount

Treated as deferred income (a liability) in the balance sheet* and released to the income statement over the useful economic life. This is matched against depreciation

Grants can only be recognised when the conditions for their receipt have been complied with.

Provision must be made for the repayment of grants if this is likely to happen.

IAS 23 – Borrowing costs

Q 1. What are the two possible accounting treatments for borrowing costs?

Borrowing costs?

Borrowing costs directly attributable to the purchase, construction or production of a qualifying asset are capitalised

Benchmark treatment is that borrowing costs should be recognised as an expense in the period they are incurred

IAS 23 – Borrowing costs

Q 2. What is a qualifying asset?

An asset that necessarily takes a substantial period of time to get ready for its intended use or sale.

Q 3. What are the rules attached to the alternative treatment?

Finance costs must be capitalised for the period of construction, and must cease when all activities necessary to get the asset to its intended use have been completed. Capitalisation must also cease during periods when construction is suspended.

IAS 32 – Financial instruments: presentation and disclosure

Q 1. What is a financial instrument?

Any contract that gives rise to both a financial asset of one enterprise and a financial liability or equity instrument of another enterprise.

Q 2. What is a financial asset?

Cash

A financial asset

A contractual right to receive cash or another financial asset from another enterprise (e.g. receivables!)

An equity instrument of another enterprise (e.g. an investment in shares)

A contractual right to exchange financial instruments with another enterprise under conditions that are potentially favourable (e.g. a forward contract when the market has moved favourably)

You mean there's more?

* Balance Sheet = Statement of financial position (see page 18)

IAS 32 – Financial instruments: presentation and disclosure

You mean there's more?

Q 3. What is a financial liability?

To deliver cash or another financial asset to another enterprise (e.g. payables/loans)

A liability that is a contractual obligation

To exchange financial instruments with another enterprise under conditions that are potentially unfavourable (e.g. forward contract where the market has moved against the contract)

Q 4. What is an equity instrument?

Any contract that evidences a residual interest in the assets of an enterprise after deducting all of its liabilities.

Q 5. How do we present financial instruments?

Equity and liabilities should be presented on the balance sheet* following the substance of the instruments. If an instrument contains an obligation to pay out cash it is a financial liability. Preference shares are therefore often financial liabilities.

Compound instruments issued (those with both debt and equity elements) such as convertible debentures are 'split' accounted. This means the proceeds are recognised as debt and a separate equity option. The debt is measured by discounted cash flows and the equity is the residual of the proceeds.

Interest, dividends, gains and losses treatment follow the presentation on the balance sheet*. If a preference share is treated as a debt instrument, any dividends paid on that share are treated as interest charges.

* Balance Sheet = Statement of financial position (see page 18)

* Balance Sheet = Statement of financial position (see page 18)

IAS 33 – Earnings per share

Q 1. How do you calculate earnings per share?

The basic EPS calculation is simply $\dfrac{\text{Earnings}}{\text{Shares}}$

Q 2. What do we mean by 'earnings'?

Profit available to the ordinary shareholders … profit after tax – minority interests – preference dividend.

Q 3. What do we mean by 'shares'?

Actually under the line is a 'weighted average number of shares'

Q 4. Can you calculate a weighted average number of shares? – you must learn this.

Q 5. What do you do if it's a rights issue of shares?

When a rights issue takes place shares are issued at less than full market price. We treat this as a combination of a bonus issue and an issue at full market price. We will therefore need to calculate the rights issue bonus fraction by using share prices.

Actually under the line is a 'weighted average number of shares'

Date	Actual number of shares	Fraction of year	Total
1 January 20X4	8,280,000	$\dfrac{6}{12}$	4,140,000
30 June 20X4	11,592,000	$\dfrac{6}{12}$	5,796,000
Number of shares in EPS calculation			9,936,000

(dates and numbers for illustrative purposes only)

You mean there's more?

You mean there's more?

IAS 33 – Earnings per share

Q 6. What is the rights issue bonus fraction?

Diluted earnings per share

Rights issue bonus fraction = $\dfrac{\text{Actual cum rights price}}{\text{Theoretical ex rights price}}$

Actual cum rights price = Price of share with rights attached immediately before rights issue.

Theoretical ex rights price = Expected share price immediately after rights issue (weighted average of actual cum rights price and exercise price of rights issue shares).

Q 7. What circumstances give rise to a 'diluted' calculation?

- Shares not yet ranking for dividend.
- Convertible debt or preference shares in issue.
- Options granted to subscribe for new shares.

Rights issue bonus fraction
(numbers for illustration)

	$	$
5 shares at	1.80	9.00
1 share at	1.20	1.20
6 shares		10.20

10.20/6 = $1.70

Therefore rights
issue bonus fraction = $\dfrac{\$1.80}{\$1.70}$

Q 8. What is the formula for diluted EPS?

$\dfrac{\text{Earnings + Notional earnings}}{\text{Number of shares + Notional extra shares}}$

For convertible instruments By adding the maximum number of shares to be issued in the future.

For options By adding the number of effectively 'free' shares to be issued when the options are exercised.

Use a table for full computation of the number of shares, as follows.

Date	Actual number of shares	Fraction of year	Rights issue bonus fraction	Total
1 January 20X4	8,280,000	9/12	1.80/1.70	6,575,294
1 October 20X4	9,936,000 (W1)	3/12		2,484,000
Number of shares to be used in EPS calculation				9,059,294

This is the basic weighted average table with an additional column
– you must learn this too! (again dates and numbers given for illustration).

Q 9. What are the required disclosures?

The disclosures are required are:
- Basic and diluted EPS are presented on the face of the P&L account
- The numerators for each calculation should be disclosed and reconciled to each other
- The denominators should be disclosed and reconciled to each other
- Any alternative measures of EPS (other than basic or diluted) must only be disclosed in the notes to the financial statements.

IAS 36 – Impairment of assets

Assets must not be carried on the balance sheet* at more than their recoverable amount.

Q 1. What do we mean by 'recoverable amount'?

A company can recover the amount it has invested in its assets in one of two ways:

- it can opt to sell the asset to someone else, generating a net selling price; or
- it can trade with the asset, making stuff, selling stuff, providing some form of service and generating cash flow. If we predict cash will be generated from the asset, the asset has what we call a 'value in use'. Value in use is the present value of the future cash flow.

Q 2. When do we perform an 'impairment test'?

Non-current assets and goodwill should be reviewed for possible impairment where there are indications that the asset could be impaired. These indications would include both internal and external factors to the business (e.g. damage of asset, future plans, new competitors, etc).

Goodwill and intangibles with indefinite lives should be tested annually for impairment.

Where possible the review should be carried out on individual assets. However, if this is impractical, a group of assets should be considered. The group of assets should be the smallest group on which cash flows can be identified and is called a cash-generating unit (CGU).

You mean there's more?

* Balance Sheet = Statement of financial position (see page 18)

IAS 36 – Impairment of assets

You mean there's more?

Q **3. Can you set out the impairment test?**

Impairment test

Carrying amount	x
Recoverable amount(W1)	x
Impairment loss	xx

Q **4. Can you calculate recoverable amount?**

(W1)
Recoverable amount is the greater of

Net Selling Price

Value in use
(present value of
the future cash flow)

Which ever is greater becomes the
RECOVERABLE AMOUNT

Q **5. How is an impairment loss accounted?**

It is like additional depreciation:
Dr Income statement
Cr Asset account

If an asset has been impaired the asset should be written down to its recoverable amount.
If a group of assets is impaired they should be written down to recoverable amount but charging the impairment in the order:

1st   Goodwill allocated to the group
2nd   Other assets pro-rated according to their carrying value (or on some more reasonable basis).

IAS 39 – Financial instruments: recognition and measurement

Q 1. How does IAS 39 classify financial liabilities?

IAS 39 recognises two classes of financial liabilities:
- Financial liabilities at fair value through profit or loss.
- Other financial liabilities measured at amortised cost using the effective interest method.

Q 2. What is amortised cost – can you draw up the 'amortised cost table'?

Period	Amount borrowed	Interest (at 9.5%) for income statement	Cash repayment 4% (200,000)	Rolled up interest	Bal c/fwd – Liability for balance sheet*
	$	$	$	$	$
1	157,763	14,988	(8,000)	6,988	164,751
2	164,551	15,651	(8,000)	7,651	172,402
3	172,402	16,378	(8,000)	8,378	180,780
4	180,780	17,174	(8,000)	9,174	189,954
5	189,954	18,046	(8,000)	10,046	200,000

Classification of financial assets
Remember for every company that raises finance, somebody must be providing it. These companies are purchasing 'investments'. IAS 39 applies to financial assets as well as financial liabilities.

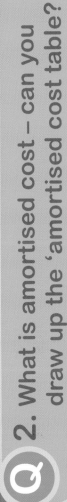

* Balance Sheet = Statement of financial position (see page 18)

Numbers shown for illustration purposes

You mean there's more?

IAS 39 – Financial instruments: recognition and measurement

Q 3. What are the four classes of financial assets?

- Financial assets at fair value through profit or loss.
- Held-to-maturity investments.
- Loans or receivables.
- Available-for-sale financial assets.

Q 4. How are financial assets and liabilities initially recognised?

Financial assets and liabilities should be recognised when the company becomes party to the contractual provisions of the instrument. The asset or liability is measured at fair value – the actual transaction price on the reporting date.

Q 5. How are financial assets and liabilities subsequently measured?

The following table summarises how financial assets and liabilities are measured and how changes in value are recognised:

Item	Measurement on balance sheet*	Gains/losses
Assets/at FV through profit or loss	FV	Income statement
Available for sale	FV	Equity until derecognition of the asset, then recycled to income statement
Held-to-maturity	Amortised cost	n/a
Loans and receivables	Amortised cost	n/a

*Balance Sheet = Statement of financial position (see page 18)

IAS 40 – Investment property

What is an investment property?

A property that is owner occupied may not be treated under IAS 40 as IAS 16 applies

Property held to earn rentals or for capital appreciation – held for its investment potential

You mean there's more?

Q 2. How is an investment property accounted for?

How is an investment property accounted for?

Initially at cost

Subsequently- choice

Revalued to fair value at each balance sheet* date (fair value model). No depreciation.

Using the benchmark method in IAS 16 (cost). The properties are depreciated like any other asset.

* Balance Sheet = Statement of financial position (see page 18)

IFRS 5 – Discontinued operations and presentation of assets held for sale

Q 1. When is a non-current asset classified as 'held for sale'?

Under IFRS 5, a non-current asset should be classified as 'held for sale' if its carrying amounts will be recovered principally through a sale transaction rather than its continuing use. The criteria which have to be met are:

- Management committed to a plan
- Actively trying to find a buyer and marketing assets
- Assets available for immediate sale
- Sale is highly probable
- Sale expected to complete within one year of classification.

Q 2. How are 'held for sale' assets accounted for?

Non-current assets held for sale should not be depreciated.

The assets should be measured at the lower of carrying amount and fair value less costs to sell.

You mean there's more?

You mean there's more?

IFRS 5 – Discontinued operations and presentation of assets held for sale

Q 3. When is an activity discontinued?

When
is an
activity
discontinued?

When
it has been
disposed of or is
classified as held for sale

When the
operations and
cash flows have been, or
will be, eliminated from the
on-going operations

When
you have no
significant continuing
involvement

IAS 27 – Consolidated and separate financial statements

Q 1. What is a subsidiary? — An entity that is controlled by another entity.

Q 2. What do we mean by control? — Control is the power to govern the financial and operating policies of an entity so as to obtain benefits from its activities.

Q 3. When does control exist?

Note: five examples when you have a parent/ subsidiary undertaking.

1. Majority votes (51%) (the standard one!!)

2. Right to exercise dominant influence

3. Controls voting rights (could be in agreement with other investors)

4. Managed on a unified basis

5. Appoint/ remove directors (assuming control of the entity is by that board)

Parent undertaking

Group accounts

IAS 27 – Consolidated and separate financial statements

Think of your own parents – are they?

- Dominant
- Controlling
- Always having the majority vote
- Managing
- Making key decisions (appointing/removing!!)

Q 4. Who has to prepare consolidated accounts?

A parent shall present consolidated accounts subject to some limited exemptions mainly for unlisted parents that are themselves wholly owned subsidiaries.

IFRS 3 – Business combinations

Q **1. What are the five core workings for consolidation of a statement of financial position (balance sheet*)?**

(W1) Group structure

This indicates that H owns 80% of the ordinary shares of S and when they were acquired.

H
|
| 80%
S

Date of acq

(W2) Net assets of subsidiary

	At date of acquisition	At the balance sheet* (B/S) date
	$	$
Share capital	×	×
Reserves:		
Retained earnings	×	×
	×	×

(W3) Goodwill on acquisition

		$
Cost of shares acquired		×
Less: Share of net assets at acquisition (see W2)		(×)
		×
Less: Impairments to date		(×)
		×

(W4) Minority interests

	$
Share of net assets at balance sheet* date (see W2)	×

(W5) Group retained earnings

	$
H reserve (100%)	×
S – group share of post-acquisition reserves	×
Less: Goodwill impairments to date	(×)
	×

* Balance Sheet = Statement of financial position (see page 18)

Group accounts

IFRS 3 – Business combinations

Q 2. What is the key concept that you are applying when you consolidate accounts and what does it mean?

> The single entity concept – it means you need to cancel all intra-group transactions.

Q 3. Give three examples of intra-group transactions that need to be cancelled?

- Intra-group sales (deduct from turnover and from cost of sales (purchases).
- Intra-group loan (exclude the investment line in the company providing the finance and the loan line in the company receiving the finance).
- Intra-group assets transferred at a profit (exclude the profit element from the asset and from the reserves).

Q 4. Do we use the book values of the subsidiary's net assets or the fair values?

> The fair values.

Q 1. What is an associate?

An associate is an entity, including an unincorporated entity such as a partnership, over which the investor has significant influence and that is neither a subsidiary nor an interest in a joint venture.

Q 2. What do we mean by significant influence?

Significant influence is the power to participate in the financial and operating policy decisions of the investee but is not control or joint control over those policies.

IAS 28 – Investments in associates

Q **3. What method of accounting do we use for associates?**

If a parent company has significant influence, it must use the equity method of accounting for its interest in the associate, in the consolidated accounts unless the investment is held exclusively for resale.

Q **4. what do we mean by equity accounting?**

Equity method

One line entry – our share of net assets of associate

Calculate goodwill on associate and add it in

This can also be calculated by adding together the cost of the investment and any post-acquisition profits

IAS 31 – Interests in joint ventures

Q 1. What is a joint venture?

A joint venture is a contractual arrangement whereby two or more parties undertake an economic activity that is subject to joint control.

Q 2. How do you account for a jointly controlled entity?

Benchmark (preferred) Proportionate consolidation
Allowed alternative Equity accounting

What is a joint venture ?

A jointly controlled activity

Equity method

Proportional consolidation

IAS 31 – Interests in joint ventures

Q 3. What is proportional consolidation?

When we add our share (percentage) into the accounts on a 'line-by-line' basis

Revenues

Costs

Assets

Liabilities

Q 4. Equity accounting – for what other type of entity do we use equity accounting?

Equity method is the same as we use for an associate.

Q 5. What is equity accounting?

One line entry – our share of net assets of associate

Equity method

Calculate goodwill on associate and add it in

IAS 19 – Employee benefits

Q 1. What are the two types of pension scheme and how are they accounted for?

Defined contribution schemes

Defined benefit schemes

Fixed contribution – variable benefit

Variable contribution – fixed benefit

Recognise a cost in the income statement equal to the contributions payable to the scheme for the period. A debit in the income statement and a credit to cash with an accrual if anything is outstanding at the end of the reporting period

The scheme assets are valued at fair value (usually market value). The scheme liabilities are measured at present value

Seriously advanced!!

IAS 19 - Employee benefits

Q **2. What goes in the statement of financial position (balance sheet*) on a defined benefit scheme?**

The **Statement of financial position (balance sheet*)** recognises the total of:

Market value of scheme assets	x
Less the present value of the obligations of the fund	(x)
Balance sheet* asset (liability), i.e. only the surplus/deficit	x(x)

Q **3. Can you draw the T accounts for the movement in the assets and liabilities?**

Pension fund assets

Bal b/fwd	x	Benefits paid out	x
Expected return on the assets	x		
Contributions	x		
Actuarial gain on assets	**x**	Bal c/fwd	x
	XX		XX
Bal b/fwd	X		

Pension fund liability

Benefits paid out	x	Bal b/fwd	x
Actuarial gain on liabilities	**x**	Current service cost	x
Bal c/fwd	x	Interest cost (1000 × 10%)	x
	XX		X
		Bal b/fwd	x

Note it could be actuarial losses not gains

* Balance sheet = Statement of financial position (see page 18)

Seriously advanced!!

IAS 21 – The effects of changes in foreign exchange rates

Q 1. Have you learnt the rules for translation of individual company transactions/balances?

Translation of individual company transactions into functional currency

Translation rules	Exchange difference treatment
(1) All transactions in the period should be translated at the rate in force on the date of the transaction (actual rate).	(1) All exchange differences are to be recognised in the income statement.
(2) At the year-end closing balances should be translated: • monetary items at closing rate • non-monetary items at historic rate.	
3) It is not acceptable to use forward contract rates.	

Note Actual rate can also be referred to as a 'spot rate'

Note Monetary items
– Cash   – Payables
– Bank   – Loans
– Receivables

Note Non-monetary items
- Property, plant and equipment
- Inventory
- Investments

IAS 21 – The effects of changes in foreign exchange rates

Q 2. What about for foreign subsidiaries?

Foreign operations

The following rules apply to foreign operations with a different functional and presentation currency.

Translation rules	Exchange difference treatment
(1) All net assets should be translated at the closing rate.	(1) Arise on the restatement of opening net assets from opening to closing rate, and retained profit from average rate to closing rate.
(2) Goodwill and fair value adjustments must be made in the local currency.	(2) The parent's percentage of the total exchange difference is shown as a movement in a separate item in equity (exchange difference reserve).
(3) The income statement must be translated at average rate.	

Note The closing rate is the rate of exchange as at the balance sheet* date

* Balance sheet = Statement of financial position (see page 18)

Q 1. Who are related parties?

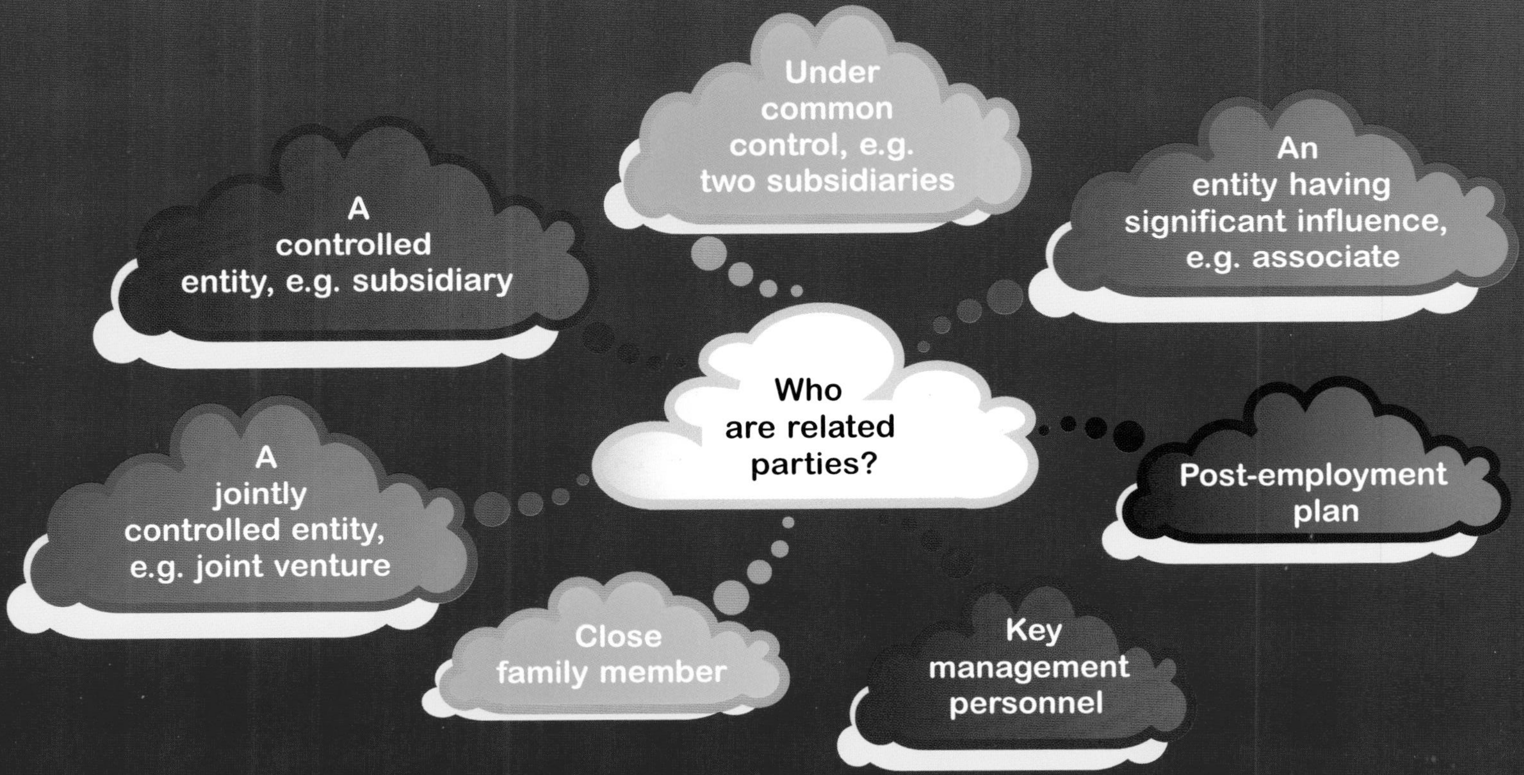

IAS 24 – Related party disclosures

Q **2. What are the disclosures?**

If a related party transaction has been entered into the following disclosures should be made:

- a description of the relationship
- a description of the transactions
- the amounts involved
- other elements of the transactions necessary for an understanding of the financial statements
- balances with related parties at the balance sheet* date (and any provision for doubtful debts from related parties)
- amounts written off in the period on debts due to or from related parties.

No disclosure is required of the name of the related party.

No disclosure of related party transaction is required in 100% owned subsidiary company individual company accounts.

Q **1. What constitutes hyperinflation?**

There is no prescriptive definition in the standard about what constitutes hyperinflation, but typical characteristics are:

(a) the general population prefers to keep its wealth in non-monetary assets

(b) the general population regards monetary amounts in terms of a relatively stable foreign currency

(c) sales and purchases on credit are at prices compensating for inflation

(d) interest rates, wages and prices are linked to a price index

(e) the cumulative inflation rate over three years is approaching or exceeds 100%.

IAS 29 – Financial reporting in hyperinflationary economies

Q **2. How do we prepare the financial statements in a hyperinflationery economy?**

- The financial statements of companies in hyperinflationary economies should be stated in terms of the measuring unit current at the at the end of the reporting period. The comparative amounts should also be restated to the measuring unit current at the balance sheet* date.

- The gain or loss on the net monetary position should be included in net income and separately disclosed.

- The restatement should be done using a general price index.

- The above rules apply to both individual company financial statements and consolidated financial statements.

* Balance sheet = Statement of financial position (see page 18)

IAS 34 – Interim financial reporting

Q **1. What is an interim financial report?**

An Interim financial report is a financial report containing either a complete set of financial statements or a set of condensed financial statements for an interim period.

Q **2. What is an interim period?**

An Interim period is a financial reporting period shorter than a full financial year.

IAS 34 – Interim financial reporting

Q **3. What are the contents of an interim report?**

(1) The minimum contents prescribed by the standard are:

- Condensed statement of financial position (balance sheet*)
- condensed income statement
- condensed cash flow statement
- condensed statement of changes in equity or STRGL equivalent
- selected explanatory notes.

The condensed information must at least have the same headings and subtotals as were in the latest annual financial statements published.

(2) Basic and diluted EPS should be presented in the interim report.

IAS 41 – Agriculture

Q **1. When does an entity recognise a biological asset?**

An enterprise should recognise a biological asset or agricultural produce when, and only when:

- the enterprise controls the asset as a result of past events
- it is probable that future economic benefits will flow to the enterprise
- the fair value or cost of the asset can be measured reliably.

Biological assets should be measured initially and at each balance sheet* at fair value less estimated point of sale.

Harvested produce should also be measured at fair value less point of sale costs at the point it is harvested.

Q **2. How are biological assets accounted for?**

Any gains or losses generated by measuring at fair value should be recognised in the income statement immediately.

Biological assets should be separately presented on the face of the balance sheet*.

* Balance sheet = Statement of financial position (see page 18)

Seriously advanced!!

IAS 41 – Agriculture

Q 3. What disclosures are required?

Physical change

Measure at fair value but split

Biological assets

Price change

IFRS 1 – First-time adoption of International Financial Reporting Standards

Q 1. When must an entity prepare an opening IFRS statement of financial position (balance sheet*)?

> An entity must prepare an opening balance sheet* at its transition date to IFRS as a basis for preparing the current and comparative financial statements.

Q 2. What exemptions exist from fully retrospective application?

The exemptions from fully retrospective application are:

Property, plant and equipment	A 'frozen' revaluation in previous GAAP is allowed as a deemed cost on transition to IFRS.
Business combinations	The rules in IFRS 3 can be applied from any previous business combination as long as all since that date follow the rules. Without any retrospective application, positive goodwill is frozen and subject to annual impairment review, and negative goodwill must be written back to retained earnings.
Employee benefits	On transition any actuarial gains and losses can be recognised within the pension asset or liability even if a spreading policy is adopted for those that arise after the transition date.
Exchange difference reserve	It is not required to recognise exchange differences arising before transition as a separate reserve if they were not recognised separately under previous GAAP. The exchange differences would not be recycled on disposal of the foreign subsidiary.
Financial instruments	Very complex rules, but the main issue is that IASs 32 and 39 do not need to be followed in the comparative periods for first-time adopters in 2005.

Any estimates made under previous GAAP should be brought forward into the first IFRS financial statements without adjustment unless they are so incorrect as to make the accounts not show a fair presentation.

---

* Balance sheet = Statement of financial position (see page 18)

Seriously advanced!

IFRS 1– First-time adoption of International Financial Reporting Standards

Q 3. What disclosures are required?

In the first IFRS financial statements the following extra disclosures are required:

- full balance sheet* reconciliations from previous GAAP to IFRS for the beginning of the first reporting period and at the date of transition to IFRS
- full income statement reconciliation for the comparative period income statement
- full explanations of the adjustments made in the above reconciliations.

* Balance sheet = Statement of financial position (see page 18)

IFRS 2 – Share-based payments

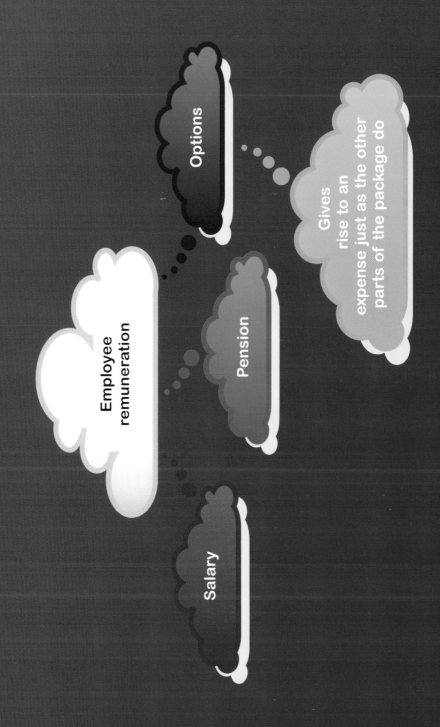

Employee remuneration

Salary

Pension

Options

Gives rise to an expense just as the other parts of the package do

Seriously advanced!!

Seriously advanced!!

Q 1. How do we calculate the expense?

For employee service it is the fair value of the equity instruments issued at their grant date.

The fair value of options at the grant date will usually be measured by using a pricing model (such as Black-Scholes), and must take into account:

- exercise price of the option
- life of the option
- current price of the underlying shares
- expected volatility of the share price
- dividends expected on the shares; and
- risk-free interest rate.

Q 2. What are the accounting entries?

The debit is to the income statement.
The credit entry is recognised as a separate item of equity.

IFRS 4 – Insurance contracts

Check this is examinable!!

Q 1. What is an insurance contract?

An insurance contract is a contract under which one party (the insurer) accepts significant insurance risk from another party (the policyholder) by agreeing to compensate the policyholder if a specified uncertain future event (the insured event) adversely affects the policyholder.

IFRS 4 – Insurance contracts

Q 2. To whom does the standard apply?

- The IFRS applies to:
  - insurance contracts; and
  - financial instruments with a discretionary participation feature.
- The IFRS applies to embedded derivatives in insurance contracts with the exception of a policyholder's option to surrender an insurance contract early.
- Some insurance contracts contain an insurance and a deposit element. If the contract does include these separate parts it is acceptable to separate the parts and account for them separately provided the information is available to split.

Q 3. What are the disclosures?

An insurer should disclose information about the following:

- information that identifies and explains the amounts in its financial statements arising from insurance contracts
- the amount, timing and uncertainty of cash flows that arise under insurance contracts.

IFRS 6 – Exploration for and evaluation of mineral assets

Check this is examinable!!

Q 1. What does this cover?

Exploration for and evaluation of mineral resources.

The search for mineral resources, including minerals, oils, natural gas and similar non-regenerative resources after the entity has obtained legal rights to explore in a specific area, as well as the determination of the technical feasibility and commercial viability of extracting the mineral resource.

The standard permits a company to continue with its existing accounting policies for mineral resources, and exempts them therefore from the normal requirements for setting accounting policies of IAS 8.

Impairment tests must be performed on exploration and evaluation assets if circumstances suggest the asset may have been impaired.

Seriously advanced!!

Q 2. What are the disclosures?

Disclosures are required that identify and explain the amounts recognised in the financial statements, including:

- accounting policies; and
- the amounts of assets, liabilities, income, expenditure and cash flows.

IFRS 8 – Operating segments

Q 1. What reconciliations does IFRS 8 require?

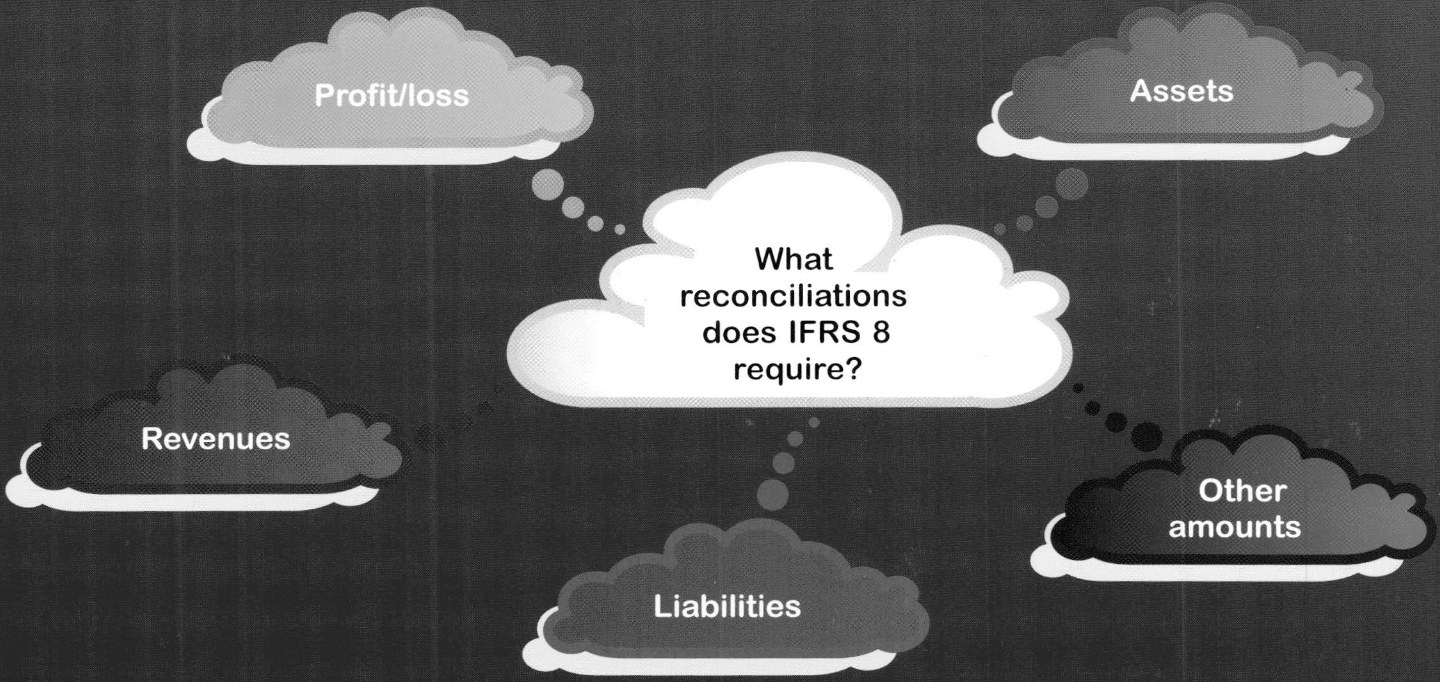

Seriously advanced!!

Seriously advanced!!

Q 2. What operating segment disclosures does IFRS 8 require?

What operating segment disclosures does IFRS 8 require?

Reconciliations

By product or service by countries in which it earns revenues

Descriptive information about the way operating segments were determined

Explanations